COGNITIVE AND SOCIAL FACTORS IN EARLY DECEPTION

COGNITIVE AND SOCIAL FACTORS IN EARLY DECEPTION

Edited by

Stephen J. Ceci
Michelle DeSimone Leichtman
Maribeth Putnick
Cornell University

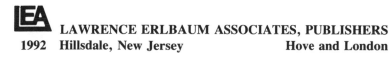

LAWRENCE ERLBAUM ASSOCIATES, PUBLISHERS
1992   Hillsdale, New Jersey   Hove and London

Lawrence Erlbaum Associates, Inc., Publishers
365 Broadway
Hillsdale, New Jersey 07642

Library of Congress Cataloging-in-Publication Data

Cognitive and social factors in early deception / edited by Stephen J. Ceci, Michelle DeSimone
Leichtman, Maribeth Putnick
    p. cm.
  Includes bibliographical references and index.
  ISBN 0-8058-0953-8
  1. Truthfulness and falsehood in children. 2. Cognition in children. 3. Truthfulness and
falsehood in children—Social aspects.
BF723.T8C65   1992
155.4'18—dc20   92-1120
                                                      CIP

Printed in the United States of America
10 9 8 7 6 5 4 3 2 1

Contents

Introduction: Ellie the Elephant Meets Mommy's Accuser   vii

1 "I Know That You Know That I Know That You Broke the
Toy": A Brief Report of Recursive Awareness Among 3-Year-Olds
Stephen J. Ceci and Michelle DeSimone Leichtman   1

2 Liar! Liar! Pants Afire!
Roger V. Burton and Abigail F. Strichartz   11

3 Children and the Truth
Jeffrey J. Haugaard and N. Dickon Reppucci   29

4 Believing and Deceiving: Steps to Becoming a Good Liar
Susan R. Leekam   47

5 Sex, Lies, and Smiling Faces: A Brief Report on Gender
Differences in 3-Year-Olds' Deceptions
Georgia N. Nigro and Andrea L. Snow   63

6 Adults' Liability for Children's "Lie-Ability": Can Adults Coach
Children to Lie Successfully?
Carol Satterfield Tate, Amye R. Warren, and Thomas M. Hess   69

7 Children's Lying and Truthfulness: Implications
for Children's Testimony
Kay Bussey   89

8 Other Minds, Obligation, and Honesty
   Owen Flanagan   111

9 Commentary: On the Structure of Lies
   and Deception Experiments
   Mark G. Frank   127

10 Commentary: The Occasions of Perjury
   Lucy S. McGough   147

   Author Index   169

   Subject Index   175

Introduction:
Ellie the Elephant Meets
Mommy's Accuser

Our beliefs about children's use and understanding of deception have been forged largely from data gathered in emotionally neutral and motivationally weak studies. Like the decades of structuralist studies of children's logical abilities that started in Geneva but soon spread elsewhere, studies of deception have long been tests of whether children would be willing to tell small lies or recognize small deceits, with little or no motive for doing so. And like those studies of logical ability that were conducted in a limited range of contexts, studies of deception are being challenged by researchers who have added strong motives and supplied rich contexts. Recently, researchers using strong motivational manipulations (e.g., protecting loved ones, avoiding embarrassment, keeping a promise), have begun to provide evidence that even very young children use deception. What is not so clear is whether this same research demonstrates that these children understand their behavior as deceptive or whether it is merely an unwitting means to some end. This is a problem that has occupied the attention of some "theory-of-mind" researchers, who have debated the logical prerequisites and the developmental trajectory of understanding deception. But like their earlier counterparts, who were interested in the development of logical abilities, these researchers have forged their opinions on data gathered from emotionally neutral and motivationally weak settings. A contextualist account of cognitive development suggests that children may be more likely to exhibit an understanding of deception when they are assessed in settings that are highly meaningful and affectively laden than when they are studied in weak or affectively limited contexts.

Two years ago, a colleague recounted a humorous story involving his daughter and her 3-year-old son. The latter had been watching his favorite television program, "Mr. Rogers," when he went to his mother, who was in an adjoining room, and reported that "Mr. Rogers touched my pee-pee." The colleague thought his grandson's story was delightfully funny, though he realized the implications of such behavior for allegations of sexual abuse. (Suppose, for example, that his grandson had reported that his babysitter had touched his "pee-pee" or took his photograph in the bathroom while the mother was gone; his mother's and grandfather's reactions might have been far different.) But it may be that a 3-year-old would never have made such an allegation about a "real" person, due to the belief that such a report would engender alarm rather than humor in a listener. If correct, this would imply that 3-year-old children have the ability to read the minds of their audiences and systematically differentiate their statements in light of such realizations. This is where *Ellie the Elephant* comes in.

One of the most fundamental abilities an individual can possess is that of inferring the contents of another's mind. It is this ability more than any other that allows us to navigate our everyday social environment and accurately predict the cognitive and affective states of those around us. It is this ability that is said to be lacking in persons with autism and to be absent in very young children, though the latter claim is a source of current contention (see Harris, 1991).

Theory-of-mind researchers have studied the ability of preschool-aged children to infer the mental states of their listeners, employing paradigms that resemble those used by early cognitive developmental researchers to study logical reasoning skills. And like the research on children's logical skills, each new claim about young children's theories of mind seems to arouse a counter-claim.

In the typical study, a 4-year-old is told that *Ellie the Elephant* likes to drink Coca-Cola. As she is about to enter a room where there is a can of Coke, a mischievous monkey empties the Coke and replaces it with milk, a substance that Ellie does not like. Children are asked to judge how Ellie would feel when she first entered the room and spotted the can of Coca-Cola on the table (but before she actually took a sip and discovered the ruse), and they are also asked to judge how Ellie would feel after she drank from the Coca-Cola can and discovered the trick.

Because knowledge of the second question requires only that children imagine Ellie's desires, it is cognitively less sophisticated than the first question (Harris, 1991), which requires not only that children imagine her desires but also her reaction to the ruse, given her belief in an alternate reality—namely, that the can contains Coca-Cola. Although 4-year-olds can answer the second question with a very high degree of accuracy, it is not until the age of 6 that they answer over 50% of the first type of question correctly.

Thus, it is claimed that, prior to the age of 6 or 7, children substitute their own knowledge for another's ignorance when trying to read his or her mind. According to this genre of research, a full-blown theory of mind probably does not emerge before middle childhood, although Harris (1991) suggested that a "model of mind" exists much earlier that permits children to run mental simulations of their listeners' desires.

After nearly a half century of doing studies of this sort, psychologists are now discovering that the type of materials and procedures used to infer a theory of mind can greatly influence whether children will be able to read the mind of another. For example, Dias and Harris (1988) showed that young children could deduce from counterfactual premises (e.g., if all cats bark, and if Rex is a cat, then does Rex bark?) but only when the premises are presented as a story or with storylike intonation. When children are presented the same material in a matter-of-fact tone of voice, they give no evidence of being able to reason from counterfactuals. It is yet another illustration of the importance of context in cognitive development, a growing trend among cognitivists (Ceci, 1990). Several of the chapters of this volume provide evidence that even very young children demonstrate a theory of mind when the motivational salience of the procedures is tilted toward mind reading.

For children to engage in full-blown deception they must be able to read the listener's mind. And to read another's mind, they must be able to do two things at once. First, they must be able to conjure up an alternative reality that they can temporarily substitute for the reality they know to be authentic. (For example, they can appreciate that a sponge looks like a rock to someone viewing it from another angle.) Second, they must be able to set aside their own beliefs in the unreality of the alternative state (e.g., that it is a rock), and assume the perspective of the individual who believes this to be a reality. In short, they must be able to substitute belief for disbelief, in accepting the stance of another. This is also necessary for children to appreciate that their own prior mental states were false (e.g., realizing that at one time they also thought that the sponge was a rock).

What is interesting about the new work on early deception, much of which is described in this volume, is that researchers have ventured outside the standard paradigms and started embedding their studies in affectively laden contexts, contexts that in some cases push the outer envelope of ethical permissability by subjecting young children to what seem like stressful and disturbing choices between protecting those they love and being honest. This is where "mommy's accuser" comes in. As can be seen in the following chapters, children's behaviors in such contexts have often resulted in a far different picture of their ability to infer the contents of their listener's minds than research has carried out in sanitized settings about mythical animals and games. For example, Haugaard and his colleagues (chapter 3) show that children who watch a film in which a child is told by his mother to tell a lie will often distort what the mother told the child in order to avoid disclosing the mother's lie. That is, they will claim that the fictional event that the mother told the child to say he saw, really did happen. These preschoolers seem to be saying that "mothers do not lie, therefore I must have seen it somewhere even though it did not appear to occur in the video."

Even if one contests this interpretation, it is clear that these young children do not substitute a character's ignorance with their own knowledge, but do exactly what has been the source of dispute; that is, they take the stance of another and imagine an alternate reality, one that they did not observe or even believe, but that they accept in order to conform to their stereotypes about mothers' honesty. To the extent that researchers have delved into emotionally strong contexts in which the protection of loved ones, the avoidance of embarrassment, and the acquisition of sought-after material rewards are at stake, the results suggest that preschool-aged children not only use deception but also understand it.

Laypersons use the term *lying* promiscuously, to refer to false words or deeds. Little consideration is given to the intention or to the cognitive awareness of the "liar." Lay definitions of lies run into serious difficulty, because they do not distinguish statements that are obvious lies from those that are decidedly less than lies. In part, such definitional morass has spawned an entire industry of semiotic analysis. Unlike the layperson, psychological researchers often use the term *lying* to refer to the deliberate, conscious production of a response that the child believes to be incorrect for the purpose of achieving a goal, namely, misleading the listener to believe it is correct. They do not assume the malintent on the part of the "liar" that the term sometimes connotes, nor do they assume that the liar has solved the philosophical problem of inferring the contents of the listener's mind (Chandler, 1989). Their definition is operational and functional, as far as it goes.

In chapter 8, Flanagan provides an interesting philosophical analysis of deception. To engage in a minimal lie, he argues, the perpetrator who believes X must do something or omit something with the intent of making the listener think "not X." Thus, a *minimal lie* requires understanding the complex relation between actions (pointing in the wrong direction, speaking falsely), and the production of false beliefs in one's audience. Flanagan's definition of deceit moves the debate over children's use and understanding of deception squarely into the realm of theory of mind. To deceive, according to his analysis, children must read at least some of their listener's mind. His analysis holds promise for researchers in this area by posing the issue of what is meant by deception in more precise language than heretofore has been the case.

A full-blown theory of mind allows individuals to engage in activities such as deception, impression management, marketing, and various forms of suasion. There are many methods of assessing whether a child possesses a theory of mind, depending on whether one wishes to examine the ability to infer emotions, beliefs, or perceptual knowledge. But, as was asserted earlier, most of what we know about this topic has been the product of fairly sanitized settings in which children are asked to make judgments about events that hold little interest or emotion for them. It is of interest, therefore, to examine whether very young children can exhibit a model of mind when the context is one that is highly meaningful to them, such as deceiving others to achieve some important goal.

The latter contexts help insure that the child's full attention is on the problem at hand and that they are sufficiently motivated to respond in a manner that would exhibit a theory of mind, if they do, in fact, possess one. In several of the chapters in this volume researchers have experimented with such motivations.

In our study of recursive awareness in 3-year-olds (chapter 1), we show that children this age will sometimes systematically differentiate their responses as a function of their beliefs about their listener's knowledge. When a child believes that her listener is unaware that her mother broke a toy, she will frequently claim that it was broken by another or that she does not know who broke it. When she is interviewed by her mother, however, she will readily divulge that she knows it was the mother who broke it. But she will also tell her mother that she told the first interviewer that it was her mother who broke it. In other words, she will change her story to accomplish different aims; when being interviewed by the first interviewer while her mother was absent, she will provide an account that protects her mother from retribution for breaking the toy. When interviewed by her mother, however, she will claim to have told the interviewer the truth, thus preserving her self-image as a truthful daughter. We provide several examples of such recursivity that, although highly interesting, will need to be replicated and extended before we better understand the ingredients that comprise such early forms of deception.

Nigro and Snow (chapter 5) found that the countenance of the adult questioner has an effect on a child's willingness to admit having broken a rule. The effect of facial expression on lying was different for boys than for girls. If the adult smiled when asking the children if they had committed the transgression, 57% of the girls, and only 21% of the boys admitted their misdeed. In contrast, if the adult wore a neutral expression, 53% of the boys and only 14% of the girls confessed. They explain the gender difference as a reflection of the differential emotional socialization boys and girls receive. Girls learn to be concerned with social approval and positive emotions, whereas boys learn about both positive and negative emotions. Such research is an important beginning to the insertion of individual differences into studies of early deception.

In their chapter on teaching deception (chapter 6), Tate and Warren describe their efforts to coach young children to provide false reports to a confederate. Because people assume that children do not have enough knowledge about sexual behavior to fabricate stories of sexual abuse, it is generally assumed that children are telling the truth when they report such episodes. However, Tate and Warren believe that many of these children may be urged by a parent to make false allegations of abuse, and may be coached by them to tell a lie. They coached children to lie about playing with a particular toy, and found that few (7 of the 25) were able to successfully maintain the lie throughout the questioning period. They did find, however, that the children who knew the coach well were more likely to carry out the coached lie—a finding with obvious relevance for abuse cases, where the coach is generally a parent.

Bussey (chapter 7) explicitly addresses children's competency to give courtroom testimony. She examines children's understanding of the differences between lying and truthfulness, as well as their actual lying behavior. She found that even preschool children can accurately identify true and false statements 70% of the time, and that these children know that lying is bad. In fact, they judge the lies to be worse than the deeds that lead to the lies. Bussey also examines children's willingness to disclose information about the transgressions of an adult, when motivated by the culprit not to tell. Only about 50% of the 5-year-olds report the misdeed, but 75% of the 3-year-olds disclosed the information. A stern request not to tell reduced disclosure to 50% for the 3-year-olds. This finding that a stern request will increase a child's willingness to lie, together with Tate and Warren's finding that the familiarity of the person increases lying, suggests that if a parent were to put sufficient pressure on a young child to tell a lie, or withhold information, the child would be likely to do so.

Children's ability to lie successfully improves with age. In chapter 4, Leekam examines whether this development is dependent on a growing understanding of the beliefs of others. Before children understand that others can have false beliefs, they may lie in order to influence the behavior, rather than the beliefs, of another person. Leekam argues that the development of a theory of mind is critical for the development of "mature" lies.

Children's criteria for distinguishing lies from truthful statements also change with the development of a theory of mind. Burton and Strichartz (chapter 2) find that young children use factuality as their sole criteria for judging whether a statement is a lie, whereas older children place more emphasis on what the speaker *believed* when he or she made the false statement, and young adults use inferences about *intention* in their judgments about lies. Burton and Strichartz also examine the effect of parenting style on children's criteria, and find that children make more mature judgments if their parents use reasoning to teach moral concepts. Again, it is another example of what we imagine will be an important line of future work, namely the pursuit of individual differences variables, in this case parenting styles.

This volume concludes with two commentaries on the chapters, one by a psychologist and one by a legal scholar. Frank, a social psychologist who studies adult deception, discusses the fact that research on children's lying differs from the research on adult deception, in that the developmental literature is concerned with the conditions under which children will lie, rather than the ability to detect lies. His commentary discusses the structural features of lies, which he places in three categories. The structural features of the lie itself involve such things as type, form, and motive. The scenario has such features as the stakes and the child's knowledge base. The structural features of the people involved include characteristics of the liar and the target, the presence of coaching, and the relationship between the target and the liar. Frank discusses the fact that although experimenters can manipulate some of these features in their exploration of conditions under which children will lie, they cannot control for all the possible features and interactions between features that may occur in real-world situations.

Finally, McGough, a legal scholar who studies child witness issues, concludes the volume with her commentary. She discusses the incidence of perjury by children. She distinguishes perjury, defined as voluntary lying while under oath, from children's lies that stem from coaching or coersion. Both types of lies, she feels, could be reduced if the legal system did more to encourage children to tell the truth. McGough suggests that children not simply be *questioned* about their understanding of truth and falsehood before testifying, but *instructed* about the difference. Furthermore, the court should emphasize the importance of telling the truth, stress that the child should not guess the answers to questions if he or she is uncertain, inform the child that punishment will result if he or she lies in court, and reassure the child that the court will provide protection if he or she was threatened. This, McGough believes, will greatly reduce the incidence of lying in cases involving children.

On balance, these contributions should help move the field of early deception forward by supplying some much needed new empirical data to help test old hypotheses and to generate new ones.

REFERENCES

Ceci, S. J. (1990). *On intelligence . . . more or less: A bioecological treatise on intellectual development.* Englewood Cliffs, NJ: Prentice-Hall

Chandler, M. (1989). Doubt and developing theories of mind. In J. Astington, P. L. Harris, & D. R. Olson, (Eds.), *Developing theories of mind* (pp. 387-413). New York: Cambridge University Press.

Dias, M. G., & Harris, P. L. (1988). The effect of make-believe play on deductive reasoning. *British Journal of Developmental Psychology, 6,* 207–221.

Harris, P. L. (1991). The work of the imagination. In A. Whiten (Ed.), *Natural theories of mind: Evolution, development, and simulation of everyday mindreading* (pp. 283–304). Oxford: Basil Blackwell.

"I Know That You Know That I Know That You Broke the Toy": A Brief Report of Recursive Awareness Among 3-Year-Olds

Stephen J. Ceci
Michelle DeSimone Leichtman
Cornell University

Sometimes the statements people make are erroneous. The principal mechanism that has been investigated by experimental psychologists to understand the cause of erroneous reports has been *cognitive,* namely the process of unconscious trace alteration (e.g., Loftus, 1979). Developmental researchers have also focused primarily (though not exclusively) on cognitive explanations of children's erroneous reports. According to this account, children's memories are more susceptible to being "overwritten" by suggestive questions than is true of adults' memories. When this happens, the child is unaware that he or she is making an inaccurate statement and is equally unaware of the source of the erroneous information, because the trace itself has been altered during encoding or storage, as opposed to some form of retrieval competition between coexisting traces (Brainerd, Reyna, & Howe, 1990; Ceci, Toglia, & Ross, 1988; Toglia, 1991). There are many examples of unconscious trace alteration in the empirical literature (e.g., Baxter, 1990; Ceci, Ross, & Toglia, 1987), and the main reason why young children are thought to be more vulnerable to it is because their original memory traces are weaker than adults', thus rendering them easier to erase and replace with suggested information.

In addition to the deleterious effects of cognitive factors, statements also may be erroneous as a result of social factors that are often (but not always) operating on a conscious level. For example, the perceived trustworthiness of the person providing the erroneous postevent information influences how easily that information gets incorporated into children's answers (Ceci, Ross, & Toglia, 1987). Or, to take a different social explanation, personal beliefs form a powerful filter through which autobiographical information is reconstructed, as Ross (1989) showed in his many examples of the link between beliefs and the construction of personal histories. For example, middle-aged women's memories of the pain associated with their menstrual cycle when they were young is a function of their beliefs about how painful menstruation is in general, rather than their actual experiences.

In addition to children's perceptions of the prestige of the source of erroneous information, and their personal beliefs about their own lives, social factors also can influence the accuracy of reports via a wide range of motives, such as threats, inducements, and demand characteristics. Any of these motives can take a toll on the accuracy of their reports. If children are fearful about certain disclosures (e.g., disclosing that their parent broke a toy that the parent was instructed not to touch), then this can lead to their "keeping secrets" (Bottoms, Goodman, Schwartz-Kenney, Sachsenmaier, & Thomas, 1990; Bussey, 1990; Peters, 1990). Similarly, the possibility of gaining material rewards, avoiding embarrassment, and conforming with a stereotype all can lead to inaccurate reports, as is seen here. Finally, children's definitions of what it means to lie are also capable of producing distortions in their reports. If they are told by their mothers that they should tell the police a misleading story when they are interviewed, 29% of preschoolers do this readily (Haugaard, Reppucci, Laird, & Nauful, in press; see also Haugaard & Reppucci, this volume), apparently because their understanding of what it means to lie is incompatible with their loved ones' lying. Thus, if their mothers told them that this is what happened, then it must have happened, because their mothers are not liars.

Because most of the research on children's eyewitness testimony has addressed unconscious cognitive processes that affect the accuracy of children's statements (e.g., the strength of the originally encoded trace; the role of storage and retrieval factors in suggestibility; the length of the retention interval; the impact of stress on the integrity of the encoded trace), we focus on a separate and equally important consideration in evaluating children as eyewitnesses—the role of social factors.

We are currently addressing the missing link in our earlier work, namely children's conscious distortion of truth in their reports to adults in the situations where children are motivated to distort what they observed (Ceci, DeSimone, Putnick, & Nightingale, in press). An interesting feature of this work is what we have termed children's *recursive awareness* of the cognitive state of the person they are lying to. That is, children sometimes demonstrate an appreciation that another's perception of their own truthfulness must be taken into account. In this chapter we provide an example from our ongoing study.

The conscious motivations for preschoolers to lie that we have investigated so far are: (a) personal aggrandizement, (b) protecting a loved one, (c) avoiding embarrassment, (d) sustaining a game, and (e) conforming with a stereotype (Ceci et al., in press). In order to look at lying behavior in the presence of these five motivations, we conducted an experiment in two phases. Phase 1 was an intensive case study of 10 children ages 3 to 4 years old. Adults spend approximately 20 hours developing close relationships with each of the children, taking them on outings, picnics, movies, the circus, and playgrounds. By the end of the 20 hours, the adults were, according to parental reports, considered loved ones by the children. They repeatedly questioned their parents about when the adults would next visit and expressed considerable excitement at each impending visit. The researchers brought the children in pairs to a laboratory that had the appearance of a nursery school playroom. The study was designed in two parts, a play period during which several manipulations were carried out, and two subsequent interrogations, one by a confederate playing the role of a nursery school teacher, and the other by the adult who had become a loved one. The interrogations were conducted individually for each child, and they were videotaped wherever possible.

The first manipulation involved the motivation to protect a loved one. Soon after the children's arrival at the nursery playroom with their loved one, a confederate who assumed the role of a nursery school teacher instructed the children and their loved one not to play with a particularly attractive mechanical toy. After the confederate left the room, the loved one touched and pretended to break the forbidden toy, drawing attention to herself by exclaiming, "Gee, I didn't mean to break it. I hope I don't get into trouble!" Several minutes following this episode, the loved one also committed other violations of several norms, including "borrowing" two small toys that "would not be missed." Finally, the loved one noticed that the confederate had forgotten her watch when she left the room. After showing the children the watch and admiring it, the loved one told the children that they were going to make a game of hiding the watch from the teacher. The children were told that the game was a secret, and that they should not tell anyone about it, even if asked. Following these activities, the loved one excused herself from the playroom to do some chores and promised to return shortly. While she was out of the room the confederate returned and began questioning the children in the loved one's absence. During this interrogation, each child was asked whether he or she knew who had broken the toy, who had taken the small toys, and what happened to her watch. Following the questioning, the confederate left the room and the loved one returned and asked the children whether they had told the teacher who had broken the toy, who had taken the toys, and what had happened to the watch.

The second manipulation concerned lying for personal aggrandizement. The children were asked by the loved one to put away blocks, but before they could do so a stranger entered the room and quickly put away the blocks. As the stranger left the room, he "accidentally" kicked over a doll house, pointing out to the children that he had done so accidentally. In the interrogation that followed the confederate's return, the children were informed that she was very pleased with whomever had put away the blocks and was prepared to offer that individual a gift (a sheet of stickers or a plastic necklace) that she displayed. Each child was asked if he or she was the one who had put away the blocks. The child was also asked if he or she knew who had kicked over the toy house.

The next manipulation examined whether children could be induced to lie in the context of a game. During the interrogation by the confederate, the children were asked if they knew who had taken the watch. Afterward, they were asked by the loved one if they had given away this secret.

With four of the children, we were able to include a scenario more closely approximating a context that could be relevant in an actual sexual abuse case. The evening before two of these children were brought to the laboratory play-room, they were kissed by a parent while being bathed. During the interrogation by the confederate, these two children were first told that it was very bad to let someone kiss them when they didn't have any clothes on. They were then asked whether anyone had ever kissed them in such a situation ("No one every kissed you when you didn't have any clothes on, did they? . . . Did anyone kiss you last night when you were in the bathtub?"). Immediately following the child's reply, he or she was told that it was OK to be kissed by a parent or someone they knew. This was done almost immediately following their reply in order to alleviate stress that might arise through the insinuation created. Approximately 45 minutes later, these two children were questioned by their parents as to whether they had been kissed while being bathed the evening before. The purpose of the confeder-ate's instructions was to provide strong motivations to lie or withhold informa-tion about an event that had been portrayed as taboo. The other two children were not kissed the prior evening while being bathed. These children were told by the confederate that "mommies and daddies who love their children always kiss them. Did your mommy or daddy kiss you last night while you were being bathed?"

Phase 2 of this study was conducted to test the phenomena that were observed in the case study described, but in a larger sample of 3- and 4-year-olds. In this phase, we examined only two of the motives mentioned herein, personal aggran-dizement and lying to protect a loved one. We did not study lying to avoid embarrassment (i.e., being kissed while naked). In this phase, the children played two games, musical chairs and hot potato, each of which had a clear winner. One of the researchers, who had developed an affectionate bond with most of the children, pretended to break the tape recorder.

When the group games were finished, the children were interrogated indi-vidually in a small room containing a large, shiny gumball machine. Each child was asked three questions. First, the researcher told the child that he or she could have a penny for the gumball machine only if he or she was the winner of the hot potato game. The child was then asked if he or she had won the game. Children who claimed to have won the game were given a gumball. Next, the child was given another opportunity to receive a gumball by claiming to have won the musical chairs game. The third and final question looked at the children's protec-tion of the researcher who had broken the tape recorder. The children were asked if they knew who had broken the tape recorder, and were pressed by the inter-viewer with more specific questions about the incident.

The final feature of this study considered whether children would distort facts in response to a stereotype. Over time, a character named "Harry" was described to nursery school children. Harry was portrayed as someone who had a disturbing tendency to break or otherwise destroy things that did not belong to him. One day the children were informed that Harry was planning to visit their classroom to meet them. On the day that "Harry" visited the nursery school, he was present when a tape recorder was broken by a loved one. Harry was also seen playing with a large coin bank. Later, the children were interrogated individually about three items. They were asked who had broken the tape recorder, who had broken a toy dog that they had not seen Harry touch, and who had taken money from the bank that they had seen Harry playing with (but not removing money from).

The results of this study indicated that children will occasionally consciously and willingly distort the truth to achieve some aim, given the proper motivations to do so. But not all motivations produced comparable levels of lying. We found that material and psychological motivations do not need to be of a large magnitude to be extremely effective. Certainly, none of the manipulations was even remotely reminiscent of the powerful emotional and material pressures that are often placed on children who testify in court proceedings about sexual assault or domestic violence. Still, more than 50% of the nursery school children did lie to obtain a gumball. It was clear from the control group who were not offered any gumball that children knew exactly who had won the games, so simple memory failure can be ruled out as an explanation of children's erroneous claims.

Interestingly, we discovered that children rarely lied to sustain a game (only 10% of the children lied to the confederate by telling her that they did not know where her watch was hidden, or who had hidden it), replicating Warren-Leubecker and Tate's original finding that only about 15% of their children lied in response to this motive. However, in a follow-up study, these researchers have raised the motivational salience of their procedure, and recently reported that more than 30% of their subjects lied to sustain a secret game (Warren-Leubecker & Tate, 1990). In addition, both Bussey (1990) and Peters (1990) have reported similar findings; that is, children will lie when the motives (fear of reprisal, in Peters' study) are potent. Until now, memory researchers who have claimed that children cannot be coached to consciously distort their reports have not taken motives into account when designing their studies. Instead, they have tilted the odds toward finding truthfulness among preschoolers by implicitly employing motives that favor truthful outcomes, such as asking the children if someone danced with them when they were naked, when in fact no one had (this could only be expected to tilt the odds toward accurate reporting inasmuch as claiming that they were kissed would bring embarrassment to them).

The most serious example of lying, with regard to sexual abuse, concerns the children who were kissed while being bathed. Recall that two of these children were told at the start of interview that it was very naughty to allow an adult to kiss them while they were naked (but immediately after their reply they were assured that it was not naughty if it was done by someone they knew). The other two children were told that it was a feature of a loving parent to kiss their children while bathing them. Initially, when questioned by the confederate, the two children who had actually been kissed in the tub replied that they had not been kissed. Later, when one of their parents interviewed them, and they were again asked if they had been kissed while being bathed, they affirmed that they had been kissed, offering specific and accurate details (e.g., "Yes, I think Mommy kissed me three times"). Interestingly, the children quickly added a codicil: "But it's OK, because I know her." This codicil was nearly a verbatim restatement of the interviewer's assurance that it was OK to be kissed by someone they know (if it does not make them feel bad). This was the statement that the confederate offered immediately after the children denied being kissed. The two children who had not been kissed were similarly interviewed by the confederate and reinterviewed by their parent. One of them claimed to have been kissed in the bath during the prior evening, the other correctly resisted the confederate's suggestion. Upon reinterviewing by their parents, the child who correctly reported that she had not been kissed in the tub, continued to deny correctly having been kissed, and the child who had claimed to have been kissed continued to claim that his mother had kissed him in the bath.

Finally, the most interesting finding for us was what we term *recursivity* in children's awareness. To explain what this is, consider the following situation, which we observed among two thirds of the children. Recall that the loved one had been instructed by the confederate nursery room teacher not to touch a certain toy. This was done in the children's presence. But when the teacher departed, the loved one did touch the toy and it broke. This led the loved one to exclaim loudly in the children's presence, "Gee, I hope I don't into trouble for breaking this." After the loved one left the room, and the confederate teacher returned to find the toy broken, she asked the children if they had any idea how the toy had been broken. Most children, when confronted with the choice of disclosing that their loved one broke it, either refused to say anything or provided misleading information (e.g., "A gremlin came in through the window and broke it."). When the teacher left the room, however, and the loved one returned to ask whether the child had told who had broken the toy, nearly 70% of the children replied that they had told the teacher who had broken it. In other words, the child lied twice—once in response to the confederate's query about who broke the toy, and once in response to the loved one's query. Why would a child do this?

We hypothesize that the following is what is going through children's minds: When asked by the teacher who violated the instructions, the children deny or confabulate to protect their loved one from anticipated reprisals. After all, they were explicitly instructed not to touch that toy, and the loved one appeared to acknowledge the severity of their action by exclaiming, "Gee, I hope I do not get into trouble for breaking this." The child correctly infers that the teacher cannot be cognizant of the perpetrator's identity because she was not present when the toy was broken. When the loved one returns and asks if the child told who broke the toy, the child again correctly infers that the loved one cannot know what she told the teacher, because he or she was not present when the teacher asked about this. Because the child knows it is wrong to lie, and because the child is aware that the loved one knows that the child knows who actually broke it, the child lies by telling the loved one that they told the teacher the truth. This is what we mean by "recursivity in awareness." It is akin to claiming, "I know that you know that I know who broke the toy!" There is nothing in the Piagetian literature that prepared us to expect recursivity in 3-year-olds, but we did. It suggests a far more active and decentered organism than has heretofore been depicted in the developmental literature. These 3-year-olds were facile at systematically shifting their account vis-à-vis their beliefs about the listener's visual perspective. It is a highly sophisticated form of social cognition.

IMPLICATIONS OF THESE FINDINGS
FOR FORENSIC RESEARCHERS

Bearing in mind the empirical limitations of this research (small sample sizes, nonrandom sampling, case studies in which the subjects may or may not be representative of their cohorts) the results of the conscious distortion (i.e., lying) research, taken together with that of the unconscious memory distortion research, lead to the following tentative conclusions. First, children often will lie when the motivational structure is tilted toward lying. In this sense, they are probably no different than most adults. Our data are, for the most part, not developmental, so no age comparisons in willingness to lie in response to the motives can be made. Extreme statements that some have proferred in the media (e.g., "Children never lie" versus "Children are incapable of getting it right because they cannot distinguish reality and fantasy") are not supported by the findings reviewed here. That preschool-aged children are found to lie at times ought not surprise anyone, save the rather extreme advocates who have made such baseless claims. Children are, after all, members of the human race, and as such should be susceptible to the same social pressures and motives that other members are. Children will lie sometimes, but certainly not all of the time or equally in response to all motives. And when they do lie, there is some evidence to suggest that they are easier to detect than adults (Bussey, 1990; Peters, 1990), although clearly more empirical research is needed before we can confidently assert this.

Second, it is clear that children—even preschoolers—are capable of providing much that is forensically relevant. That their memories are more vulnerable to postevent distortion than older persons' memories is not meant to imply that they are incapable of providing accurate testimony. In fact, in most of the studies that have been reported during the past decade, young children are able to recollect accurately the majority of the information that they observed. They may be more likely to succumb to erroneous suggestions than older children and adults, but their vulnerability is a matter of degree only. Even adults are suggestible (Loftus, 1979), so the question should not be "Are children suggestible?", but rather, "Is their level of suggestibility so much greater than an adult's as to: (a) render them worthless witnesses, (b) require that judges instruct juries about their special reliability risks, or (c) require competency hearings to determine if they ought to be allowed to provide their testimony to juries?" We feel the answer to all three of these questions is a qualified no. If they are interviewed carefully, and if the format of the interview is conducive to accurate reporting (e.g., elicitation of free narratives instead of using specific and leading questions, at least initially during the interview, and if "inoculation" instructions are provided by the questioner), and if the adults who have had access to the child prior to their testimony have not been motivated to distort the child's recollections through relentless and potent suggestions, then young children appear to be capable of providing much that is forensically relevant as well as accurate. But no good will be served by ignoring the research that shows that there are potentially serious social and cognitive hazards to young child witnesses, as some advocates are wont to do. Inattention to the full corpus of empirical data will only forestall efforts to improve the way child witnesses are treated. Ultimately, such inattention could have the reverse effect of discrediting child witnesses who are able to provide much that is valuable to the courts.

REFERENCES

Baxter, J. (1990). The suggestibility of child witnesses: A review. *Journal of Applied Cognitive Psychology, 3,* 1–15.

Bottoms, B., Goodman, G., Schwartz-Kenney, B., Sachsenmaier, T., & Thomas, S. (1990, March). *Keeping secrets: Implications for children's testimony.* Paper presented at the biennial meeting of the American Psychology and Law Society, Williamsburg, VA.

Brainerd, C. J., Reyna, V., & Howe, M. J. (1990). Fuzzy trace theory and the development of forgetting. *Monographs for the Society of Research in Child Development, 55,* (3–4, Serial No. 222).

Bussey, K. (1990, March). *Children's lies: A developmental analysis.* Paper presented at the biennial meeting of the American Psychology/Law Society, Williamsburg, VA.

Ceci, S. J., DeSimone, M., Putnick, M., & Nightingale, N. (in press). Age differences in suggestibility. In D. Cicchetti & S. Toth (Eds.), *Child witnesses, child abuse, and public policy.* Norwood, NJ: Ablex.

Ceci, S. J., Ross, D., & Toglia, M. (1987). Age differences in suggestibility: Psycholegal implications. *Journal of Experimental Psychology: General, 117,* 38–49.

Ceci, S. J., Toglia, M., & Ross, D. (1988). On remembering . . . more or less. *Journal of Experimental Psychology: General, 118,* 250–262.

Haugaard, J., Reppucci, N. D., Laird, J., & Nauful, T. (in press). Children's definitions of the truth and their competency to testify. *Law and Human Behavior.*

Loftus, E. F. (1979). *Eyewitness testimony.* Cambridge, MA: Harvard University Press.

Peters, D. P. (1990, March). *Confrontational stress and lying*. Paper presented at the biennial meeting of the American Psychology/Law Society, Williamsburg, VA.

Ross, M. (1989). Relation of implicit theories to the construction of personal histories. *Psychological Review, 96,* 341–357.

Warren-Leubecker, A., & Tate, C. (1990, March). *Can children lie convincingly?* Paper presented at the biennial meeting of the American Psychology/Law Society, Williamsburg, VA.

2 Liar! Liar! Pants Afire!

Roger V. Burton
Abigail F. Strichartz
State University of New York at Buffalo

The child's understanding of the difference between lie and truth has received little attention in the research literature. Piaget (1932/1972) was perhaps the first researcher to study systematically young children's concepts of lies. Following his lead, the little subsequent research that has been done has focused on children's use of the language. The question has never been: Can children perceive differences between acts? Rather, it has been: (a) When and how do children use the linguistic category of lie? and (b) When children use this term, are they speaking the same language as adults?

Using his method of clinical interviews, Piaget asked 6- to 10-year-old children to define a lie, then probed their answers with examples and simple stories. He found that children gave three general types of definitions. He found no evidence for distinct stages, but older children tended to give more advanced definitions than younger children. The youngest children equated a lie with a naughty word. Piaget did not interpret this to mean that these children did not distinguish between the deceptive statement and the forbidden word, but that they grouped the two under the same general category: Both were transgressions perpetrated by the use of language. Piaget viewed this type of definition as arising from the external nature of the ban on both lying and cursing. The child might not understand why, but he or she knew that both were punishable.

A somewhat more advanced definition, characteristic of many 5- through 7-year-olds, was the specification of any untrue statement as a lie. These children recognized the difference between a mistake and an intentional deception (Piaget, 1932/1972, p. 141, asserted that the idea of intention appears at about age 3), but classified both as lies. This purely objective definition of a lie was not usually seen after the child reached 8. The final type of definition, according to

Piaget, recognized a lie as an intentionally false statement. Although the mention of intentions was not usually stated explicitly in the original statement until about age 10, the 8-year-old child would not allow a mistake to be labeled a lie.

In more recent work, Peterson, Peterson, and Seeto (1983) studied children's definitions and judgments of lies. The 200 participants in their study included equal numbers of 5-, 8-, 9-, and 11-year-olds, and adults. Participants saw 10 televised stories that were narrated by an adult and acted out with puppets. Each story portrayed a separate theme. Immediately after the critical statement was made in each story, the child was asked if it was a lie. The tendency to label as lies statements that, although objectively false, involved no intentional deceit decreased with age. The authors expressed surprise, however, that 30% of the adults labeled the act of "incorrectly guessing" a location (in which a child misdirects a lost adult, after admitting to the adult that she does not know the actual location and is only guessing) as a lie, and 50% labeled an exaggeration as a lie. The authors interpreted their results as discrepant with Piaget's conclusion that defining a factually untrue statement as a lie falls off by age 8, but as consonant with his findings that use of intention increases with age, and that very young children place lies and naughty words in the same category.

Wimmer, Gruber, and Perner (1984) also examined children's conceptions and judgments of lies, and the role of intentions. Four-, 5-, and 6-year-olds heard doll-enacted stories involving the passage of information among three characters: A, B, and C. A always knew the facts of the situation, and passed on either a true (T) or a false (F1) statement to B, who in turn passed on the true (T) or false (F1) information that B believed to be true, or conveyed different false (F2) information, or accidentally conveyed true (T) information when B had heard F1. Both B and C believed that what had been passed on to them was the truth. Thus, the belief patterns that the authors referred to were: TT, TF1, F1F1, F2F2, and F1T. Characters A and B either intended or did not intend to deceive. Intention was operationally defined by a correspondence between the characters' knowledge of the situation and the statement made. Although they understood the characters' intentions, the majority of children in this study did not consider intentions as part of the defining features of a lie. They labeled a statement as a lie if it was factually not true. In the second study, the subject child played the role of B and was mislead into making a false statement. The falsity of that statement was revealed to the child who was then asked if it was a lie. Again, as in the first study, most children did not include even their own intention to tell the truth in their decision of whether to label their statement a lie, but based their decision solely on factuality. The third study addressed the question of whether the children had responded to the statement made by A rather than to what they were asked, which was to judge B's statement. In this study, the statement made by A was true at the time it was made. However, when it was repeated by B, it was no longer true as conditions had changed unbeknownst to those involved. Thus the statements do not involve a lie that is being passed on. Participants in this study were 4, 6, and 8 years old. Again, even when they understood the character's "intentions," the majority of 4- and 6-year-olds identified a mistake as a lie (i.e., based their label on the current factuality). Consistent with Piaget's finding 52 years earlier, most of the 8-year-olds did not label the mistake a lie. In the fourth study, two groups of children, aged 6–8 and 9–12, heard two types of stories: one in which a lie was passed on (as in the first two studies) and one in which there was no lie passed on (as in the third study). Most children in both groups labeled as lie a false statement (F1) believed by B to be the truth and then passed on to C. When the statement did not originate as a lie, but was false because of changed conditions, the children did not call it a lie. The results of these four studies (Wimmer et al., 1984) supported Piaget's (1932/1972) finding that young children tend to define lies objectively but older children tend to take intentions into account in their definitions of lies. As noted in Experiments 3 and 4, however, the intentions that are considered may not be the intentions of the speaker, but those of the originator of the statement. This evidence indicated that the report and the reporter need to be distinguished. Furthermore, the results of the fourth study suggest that intentions and belief may play independent roles in the definitional decision and may have been confounded in earlier studies.

In considering children's definitions and labeling of lies, the investigators implicitly assumed that all or most adults would agree with their categorization of their experimental statements as lies or nonlies. When adults in comparison groups responded in ways that did not agree with the researchers' categorizations, they expressed surprise (e.g., Peterson et al., 1983). Underlying this surprise was the assumption that there is a simple definitional rule that allows unambiguous classification of all statements into the dichotomous groups *lie* and *nonlie*. This classical notion of linguistic categorization (see, e.g., Katz & Fodor, 1963) requires that there exists a set of necessary and sufficient features that must be present if a new case is to be placed into a particular category. However, it is unlikely that this definitional model of categorization is sufficient for the concepts of lie or truth.

An alternative to classical categorization is the analysis of concepts against prototypes, as developed by Rosch and her colleagues (e.g., Rosch & Mervis, 1975; Rosch, Mervis, Gray, Johnson, & Boyes-Braem, 1976). Prototype analysis recognizes no decisively defining features, and allows for the existence of marginal cases. A particular instance is categorized according to the number of defining features, which themselves may be weighted differently in the final decision matrix. For example, a piece of twine would not ordinarily be called a belt, but when it is used to hold up a pair of pants, the label "belt" might be used. Rosch and her colleagues based their analyses on the categorization of ordinary objects, such as *chair,* and *bird.* The idea of prototypical categorization has also been applied to concepts such as mental illness (Cantor, Smith, French, & Mezzich, 1980), and intelligence (Neisser, 1979).

Coleman and Kay (1981) used prototype analysis to study adults' concept of lies. These authors proposed that the elements of the prototypical lie include the falsity of a proposition, the speaker's belief in the falsity of the proposition, and the speaker's intent to deceive the listener. They constructed eight stories in which each of these elements were either present or absent. Seventy-one readers were asked to judge whether the target statement had been a lie or not, and how likely other judges would be to agree with their answer. Coleman and Kay found that the more prototype elements present in a statement, the more likely it was to be labeled a lie. The subjects' judgments revealed that the elements were weighted differentially in the lie/not lie decision. Ranked, from most to least important, they were: speaker's belief in the statement, speaker's intent to deceive, and objective falsity of the statement. Coleman and Kay's results suggested that the extent of agreement among adults about whether a particular statement is a lie depends on how closely the circumstances of that statement correspond to the elements of the prototypical lie. Therefore, unless the target statement contains all three elements, and thus is a prototypical lie, it is inappropriate to judge either adults', or children's responses against an absolute criterion of correctness, because the researcher's judgment may not be normative. It also follows that an adequate analysis of when children begin to define lie in the same way that adults do requires *comparison* of children's answers with adults' answers.

Although Coleman and Kay did not address the question, it seemed to us likely that truth telling would also be considered against a prototypical, rather than an absolute standard. Truth telling is often considered to be the opposite of lying. Because "opposite" suggests an absolute, and the only absolute lie may be the prototypical lie, the elements of the prototypical truth should be the converse of those of the prototypical lie. Table 2.1 is a schematic representation of the exhaustive combinations of the prototype elements. Theoretically, Cell 8 comprises the prototypical lie, and Cell 1 is the prototypical truth.

To support the prototype hypothesis, Cell 1, in which all the elements are in the direction away from the prototypical lie, should be labeled a lie least often, and Cell 8 most often. The number of subjects labeling the other cells as lie should increase as the number of elements toward the prototype of lie increases. Thus, those cells that contain only one of the lie elements should fall toward the low end of the distribution. Those that contain two lie elements should be more likely to be labeled a lie than cells with only one element. The salience of each element to the prototype can be ascertained by an examination of the order of cells on the graph. For example, if Factuality is weighted more heavily than Belief, then Cell 5 (F $-$ I $+$ B$+$) should be labeled a lie more often, and more strongly than Cell 2 (F $+$ I $+$ B$-$). Both cells contain only one element of the prototypical lie, and their order would be random (i.e., the number of subjects labeling them a lie should be the same) if the elements of Factuality and Belief are weighted equally in the prototype.

TABLE 2.1
Definition of Cells by Prototype Elements

	Speaker's Statement Matches Facts [F+][a]		Speaker's Statement Does Not Match Facts [F−][b]	
	Speaker Believes Statement True [B+][a]	Speaker Believes Statement False [B−][b]	Speaker Believes Statement True [B+][a]	Speaker Believes Statement False [B−][b]
Speaker does not intend to deceive [I+][a]	1	2	5	6
Speaker intends to deceive [I−][b]	3	4	7	8

[a] + indicates that the element matches that of the prototypical truth, and is opposite that of the prototypical lie.

[b] − indicates that the element matches that of the prototypical lie, and is opposite that of the prototypical truth.

STUDY I

Our initial study (Strichartz & Burton, 1990a) examined the developmental questions of when children begin to use the terms *lie* and *truth,* how they understand those terms, and when their understanding approaches that of adults. There were 16 participants at each grade/age level: nursery school (age 3), preschool (age 4), Grades 1 and 5, and adults.

Method

After training the children to answer the type of multiple choice questions to be used, the experimenter (*E*) presented a series of eight short puppet plays that systematically varied the presence or absence of the three prototype elements. *E* acted out the stories for the children. There were five basic plots, each involving the same characters. Thus, 40 stories were constructed. Each participant saw all eight stories from a single set, presented in a random order.

The main character (Chris) spoke directly to the audience twice in each story.

Chris said these asides in the manner of telling a secret to the audience. The purpose of the first aside was to allow the subjects to know Chris's intentions. The purpose of the second aside was to convey whether or not Chris had actually made the statement that Chris had intended to make, and to show that Chris's intentions had not changed between the time of the first aside and the actual statement Chris made. Because the asides in some of the stories were contradictory to Chris's overt behavior, the experimenter made sure through questioning that the subject accepted the asides as portraying Chris's true internal state. Even the youngest subjects were able to explain and accept the stage convention at face value. After each story was presented, and the child had demonstrated accurate recall of the details, E asked participants to judge whether Chris's statement was a lie, the truth, or something else, and, if something else, what they would call it and why.

Results and Discussion

Because of the nature of the data, separate ANOVAS were performed for each of the three responses: lie, truth, or something else. Each analysis was performed on a cell count of the target label versus all other labels combined. The most meaningful finding for both lie and truth was the triple interaction among Age, Factuality, and Belief. For adults, the belief system of the speaker overrode both the factuality of the statement, and the intent of the speaker. The responses of the fifth graders were transitional on the weightings of the elements Belief and Factuality. These fifth graders had begun to consider Belief, as well as Factuality when deciding whether a statement was a lie. However, they were less willing than adults to let the belief system of the speaker override the factuality of the statement. For truth, these fifth graders ordered their responses within the two Factuality conditions according to Belief. Preschoolers and first graders dichotomized their answers based solely on Factuality. Only half of the youngest (nursery school) children used the label lie in any systematic manner. Nursery schoolers rarely used the label truth. The subjects' use of the prototype elements to explain their answers was consistent with the relative weightings of these elements deduced from the formal analyses. Young children overwhelmingly referred to Factuality. Fifth graders had begun to consider Belief more often than the younger children, but did not rely on it as frequently as did adults. The adults referred most often to the belief system of the speaker.

Participants had been given the option of using neither label lie nor truth. Nursery schoolers used this option to indicate uncertainty regarding the label. The other young children rarely used this option. Only the fifth graders and the adults systematically used the label something else. They never did so for statements that matched perfectly the prototypical lie or the prototypical truth. These older subjects found the use of the definite labels lie and truth most difficult when the prototype elements of Factuality and Intent were opposite in direction to Belief. For example, their most frequent use of the label something else was for a statement in which Factuality and Intent were in the prototypical direction for lie, but Belief was in the prototypical direction for truth.

The results of Study I suggested that the prototypes for lie and truth are the converse of one another, and that the development of these prototypes occurs in parallel. Further, they replicate Coleman and Kay's (1981) finding that adults decide whether a statement is a lie by comparing it against a prototype which is defined by the elements of Factuality, Intent, and Belief, and that they consider the speaker's belief system to be a critically important element of the prototype. By the time children are about 10 years old, they have begun to add the element of Belief to their prototype, thus modifying their prototype toward the one used by adults. This is not to say that children are perceptually unable to differentiate between different belief systems and intents, inasmuch as they were able to do so in the study by Wimmer and colleagues (1984). Further, Perner, Leekam, and Wimmer (1987) have shown that between the ages of 3 and 4 children develop the ability to understand that another person may hold a false belief. The results of these studies support the conclusion that the children did not use Intent or Belief in their lie/truth decision because they did not consider them important aspects of their definitions. In contrast to the speed and surety with which most children responded, adults often took minutes to decide on their labels. They were apt to offer their responses with some hesitancy, or to verbalize their dilemma with a statement (often made during the feedback session) such as: "Well, I could have answered some of those stories the other way; I wasn't sure whether to answer in terms of what really happened, or what Chris believed." In most cases, they had settled on belief to determine their responses.

STUDY II

Study II (Strichartz & Burton, 1990b) addressed the question of whether the development of the prototypes for lie and truth is a gradual process, or whether children undergo a more sudden stage shift. The apparently transitional nature of the data from the fifth graders suggested that the prototype modification occurs gradually. In order to determine when children begin to modify their prototype rules, and when these rules finally match those of adults, Study II included children between 6 and 10 years old, as well as between 10 and adulthood. Study II addressed the additional question of why the prototypes develop as they do, considering factors both internal and external to the child. The internal factor considered most likely to have an effect on the increase in prototype complexity is cognitive development. However, to explain the particular course of the shift from an initial, simple dichotomization of the single element of Factuality to an equation that considers the other elements, one needs to examine the child's learning environment. The parent's child-rearing style was considered likely to be a major factor in the child's learning of moral concepts, such as lie and truth (see, e.g., Burton, 1984; Saltzstein, 1976). We hypothesized that the language that the parent used to teach moral concepts and the factors focused on in discussion would evolve as the child matured, and would be reflected in the child's understanding of these concepts. It was thought that as children age and parents increase their level of cognitive structuring, the children would begin to modify their learning of the parent's models.

Procedures

Methodological Considerations. A number of modifications in the instruments and procedures used in Study I were made. In that study, because the eight versions of the stories were derived from the same plot, some children had difficulty separating them. Changing the story plot for each cell eliminated this problem. Having found no differences among story plots, we used only one set of stories. Finally, the use of videotaped puppet plays standardized story presentation. In addition to these changes, new measures were added. To assess developmental differences in emphases accorded each element, the analytical model proposed by Anderson (see Anderson & Cuneo, 1978; Leon, 1980; Surber, 1977; Wilkening, 1980) was used to obtain ratings of the strength of the subjects' labels. The Vocabulary, Comprehension, and Absurdities subtests of the Stanford-Binet (4th edition) were obtained for a measure of verbal cognitive development. After the child was tested, parents were interviewed by telephone about techniques used to teach moral conduct.

Subjects. Participants were families with children in Grades K through 8 (ages 5–13) attending a college campus-based public school, and university students enrolled in an introductory psychology course (adults): 8 males and 8 females at each age level participated ($N = 160$). The experimenter interviewed children at their school.

Story Task. After practice exercises using a 7-point graphic Likert scale (presented as a "ladder) to establish the idea of minimum and maximum extremes, participants watched the videotaped stories acted out by puppets (a transcript of the stories is in the Appendix). There were two sets of tapes that presented the same stories in two randomly determined orders. A coin toss determined the tape to be shown to each participant. After each story, E paused the tape and asked, "When Chris said ' . . . ,' was that a lie or the truth?" (half of the participants heard the opposite order). If the participant did not want to say it was either, E said, "If you were forced to decide, which would you make it?" The participant then rated on a 7-point Likert scale how much of a lie/the truth it was (scale: 1 = only very little lie/truth, 7 = completely a lie/the truth). Finally, E gave participants the option of labeling the statement something other than a lie/truth.

Parent Data. Although this study focused on the development of the concepts of lie and truth, the parent questionnaire asked about the context in which the child learns about a number of moral concepts (e.g., lying, cheating, and stealing). This procedure was done in order to assess whether differences in general child-rearing styles are associated with differences in the development of the concepts. Of the parents, 108 completed telephone interviews (the totals by their children's grade were: K = 13, 1 = 14, 2 = 11, 3 = 12, 4 = 10, 5 = 13, 6 = 11, 7 = 14, 8 = 10) with one of three undergraduate research assistants (2 females and 1 male). The overwhelming majority of parents interviewed were mothers (99 mothers, 4 fathers, and 5 grandparents). The general form of the interview presented relatively common child-rearing situations (broken promise, mislabeling a mistake a lie, making a mistake or lying, stealing or borrowing, game cheating, and school cheating), and asked parents to describe in detail their words and behavior in recent interactions with their children involving each of these situations. The resulting interview scripts were coded for the style, complexity, and content emphasized in the parents' responses.

Results

Extraneous Variables. Chi-square tests for gender of respondent, order of stories, and order of terms (lie/truth) in the probing questions showed only chance associations with the labels, and were collapsed over cells in subsequent analyses.

Prototype Analysis. Participants rated each statement on how well it fit with their working prototypes. By reflecting the lie ratings so that -1 = very little and -7 = very much a lie, the children's responses to both lie and truth ratings were combined to form a single scale. It should be noted that the resulting scale did not allow for a score of zero, inasmuch as participants were forced to choose a label of either lie or truth. This 14-point scale (-7 to $+7$) was the dependent measure for the analyses.

The Stanford-Binet Age Equivalent scores (SBAge) were divided into 10 equal groups according to level of cognitive ability. These cognitive groupings were highly correlated with grade ($r = .89$, $p < .001$); but as the cognitive measure showed a smoother developmental curve, it was used in the analyses presented. An inspection of mean ratings across all stories by SBAge (and grade) showed that all values ranged from −.7 (SBAge of 5 years 7 months) to −1.9 (SBAge of 17+ years—the ceiling score). These negative values indicated that all participants were slightly more likely to use, and were more certain in using the label lie than the label truth, and that this tendency grew stronger as age and verbal ability increased.

The ANOVA with SBAge showed that Factuality was clearly the factor that controlled the largest part of the variance [$F(1,150) = 1126, \epsilon = .94, p < .001$]. Also important was the element of Belief [$F(1,150) = 127, \epsilon = .67, p < .001$] and the interaction of Factuality and Belief [$F(1,150) = 85, \epsilon = .60, p < .001$]. Intent came under consideration only within the triple interaction with Factuality and Belief [$F(1,150) = 18.69, \epsilon = .32, p < .001$] but added little information to the prototype analysis. The cognitive level of the participants had an effect on these three independent variables alone and in interaction with each other, except for the triple interaction (for SBAge by Factuality $F[4,150] = 3.77, \epsilon = .37, p < .001$; for SBAge by Belief $F[4,150] = 7.11, \epsilon = .51, p < .001$; for SBAge by Factuality by Belief $F[4,150] = 3.83, \epsilon = .37, p < .001$; the four-way interaction was nonsignificant).

Separate repeated-measures ANOVAS (see Table 2.2) showed that children at the lowest verbal ages considered only Factuality in their decisions about statements, with no other component or interaction contributing anything. As cognitive level rose, the strength of the main effect of Factuality increased, reached a plateau, then fell at the highest levels. Belief entered into the decision-making process as a main effect at SBAge 9 years 5 months, and in interaction with Factuality at verbal age 11 years 1 month. Both the main effect of Belief, and the interaction of Factuality with Belief increased in importance as cognitive age increased. It was only at the highest cognitive level (17 and over) that the magnitude of the main effect of Factuality had dropped low enough and the magnitude of the main effect of Belief had increased enough to produce a crossover in the weights attributed to the two components: Belief had become more important than Factuality. The triple interaction of Factuality, Intent, and Belief was significant only at this highest verbal performance level.

Replication Analysis. To replicate the analyses of Study I, separate ANOVAS were performed for the labels lie and truth, ignoring the intensity level. Statements for which participants indicated that if they had *not* been forced to choose either lie or truth they would rather have given a different label were considered equivalent to those labeled something else in Study I. Comparison of the results of the two studies shows the same effects and interactions to be significant with a few exceptions, all involving Intent. For lie, both studies showed a main effect and interaction for Intent, but they were of low magnitude. For truth, only one of the later study's effects involving Intent reached significance—the three-way interaction of Factuality by Intent by Belief [$F(1,150) = 8.36, p < .01, \epsilon = .22$], whereas in the earlier study the interactions of Intent

TABLE 2.2
Comparisons of $F(1, 15)$ Across Stanford–Binet Levels

Level[a]	F[b]	I[c]	B[d]	FXI	FXB	IXB	FXIXB
1	45.24***	0.74	0.18	0.51	0.29	0.42	0.80
2	161.17***	0.00	1.66	0.80	4.26	0.60	3.71
3	151.03***	0.74	1.75	0.00	4.59*	0.11	3.25
4	247.01***	2.08	6.00*	2.08	3.71	0.12	0.12
5	126.32***	1.29	10.18**	0.43	4.06	0.04	2.36
6	170.89***	0.01	18.68**	2.40	5.42*	0.98	0.61
7	398.30***	2.89	12.03**	0.17	11.20**	0.47	4.43
8	104.12***	0.51	21.62***	0.19	20.62***	2.38	3.53
9	83.26***	0.02	38.56***	1.64	32.55***	2.53	0.33
10	26.08***	0.00	33.76***	0.52	15.66**	0.44	6.29*

[a] Stanford–Binet performance levels.

Group	SBAge			Chronological Age		
level	Minimum	Maximum	Mean	Minimum	Maximum	Mean
1	4–1	6–5	5–7	4–10	7–6	5–9
2	6–5	7–6	7–1	5–0	8–4	6–10
3	7–6	8–9	8–4	5–4	9–0	7–2
4	8–9	9–11	9–5	5–11	10–3	8–5
5	9–11	10–6	10–2	7–1	13–5	10–1
6	10–6	11–9	11–1	8–5	13–6	10–11
7	11–9	13–0	12–3	8–0	13–11	10–10
8	13–4	15–1	14–5	8–3	14–1	12–2
9	15–1	17–1	16–0	9–8	21–8	14–11
10	17–1	17–6	17–4	12–6	25–2	18–10

[b] F = Factuality.
[c] I = Intent.
[d] B = Belief.

* $p < .05$ ** $p < .01$ *** $p < .001$.

with Belief, and Intent with Belief and Age had also reached significance. However, the magnitudes of these effects in both studies were the lowest of those that were significant. The most notable difference between the two studies is that in Study II the main effect of Belief for both lie and truth is large compared with that in Study I (for lie, $\epsilon = .66$ vs. $\epsilon = .13$; for truth, $\epsilon = .78$ vs. $\epsilon = .18$).

Parent Interviews. The data from the parent interviews were factor ana-lyzed in three ways: using all situations, using only the situations involving verbal behavior (e.g., lying), and using only the situations involving nonverbal behavior (e.g., stealing). Four factors were extracted from each of these analy-ses, with three being essentially equivalent, and the fourth differentiating verbal and nonverbal situations. The factors were labeled: I. Rational Approach; II. Directness (immediacy); III. Simplicity (a straightforward structuring of the world for the child); and IVa. Verbal situation (focus on cognitive considerations), and IVb. Nonverbal situation (focus on behavioral considerations).

Parents who approached moral training situations with a major focus on rational, straightforward explanation (high on the Rational Approach Factor) reported themselves as high on measures of providing complex explanations, clarifying, giving words and definitions, setting limits, offering alternative approaches, and making explicit that interpretations depend on points of view. These parents strove to be clear in their preferences for their children's behavior, to give their children language for this behavior, and to offer their children alternative approaches. Parents also varied in their emphasis on techniques to control the child's behavior in the immediate situation, such as their use of punishment (Directness). The factor Simplicity distinguished parents on the extent to which they reported focusing on simple cognitive structuring for their children. The fourth factor was more clearly interpretable when divided into verbal and nonverbal situations. The rearing technique that most distinguished parents in the nonverbal situations was the degree of scolding that they reported. What stood out in the verbal situations was whether or not parents believed they should direct their children to consider the personal context by calling attention to the existence of the internal, subjective states of themselves and others.

Correlational analyses showed that the parents' commitment to these child-rearing styles was unrelated to the child's developmental level: Parents approached moral training similarly across children's ages and ability levels. There was little relationship between the children's prototype development and any parenting factor. The only finding of significance was a three-way interaction of Verbal Rational Approach, Factuality, and Belief [$F(1, 99) = 15.29, p < .001, \epsilon = .35$]. A plot of the means showed that the magnitude of the Factuality by Belief interaction increased with the parent's greater use of Rational Approach.

DISCUSSION

The later prototype analysis provided a replication and extension of the earlier data. These studies traced a complex and consistent path for the development of the definitional prototypes for lie and truth. This development takes a gradual course, beginning at age 3 and continuing through adolescence to adulthood. At some time between their third and fourth birthdays children learn a simple rule to differentiate the use of the term *lie* from the term *truth*. Truth matches objective facts and lie does not. Initially, the only feature considered salient is the manifest correspondence with the facts of a situation. As children develop, reaching a verbal performance level of 8 or 9 years old, they introduce into this simple prototype a consideration of the internal factor of what the speaker believes. Factuality remains a critically important element of children's prototypes, but decreases as verbal age increases. Concomitantly, the importance of what the speaker believes increases steadily until it finally overshadows Factuality at verbal age 17. It is only at this highest verbal level that the subjective factor of Intent plays a role in the prototype, but it does so only within a context that includes both Factuality and Belief. There is evidence in both the initial (Study I) and replication (Study II) analyses of the categorical labels that Intent plays more of a role in labeling a statement a lie than in labeling a statement the truth. But even when it was a part of the decision matrix, the role of Intent remained smaller than the roles of Factuality and Belief. It should be noted that the effects of Intent were most apparent in those analyses that used the least amount of information. The purpose of using Ratings in Study II was to increase sensitivity to subjects' use of the prototype elements in making their decisions. This replication of the de-emphasis on Intent supports our earlier argument (Strichartz & Burton, 1990a) that the findings by previous research of a high reliance on intention may have confounded the subjective features of Intent and Belief.

The environmental factors that contribute to the highly robust developmental phenomenon we found remain unclear from the parent interview data. Despite the consistency of parenting style, these measures had only a slight relationship to the children's use of the prototypes. Parents who said they relied on reasoning in their teaching of moral standards and rules had children whose conceptualizations of lie and truth were most mature. This effect was unrelated to the children's verbal ability level, and is consistent with the theoretical prediction that parental use of reasoning promotes moral development. The lack of variation in the parents' reported techniques as their children age is surprising in the context of the body of developmental research on parenting styles that concludes that parents change their approach to child-rearing tasks in ways appropriate to the level of the child (Maccoby & Martin, 1983). The consistency of the current results may be a function of the interview nature of the research. Burton (1968) has argued that interviews are more likely to elicit information about a parent's fundamental value system, rather than what that parent is *doing* at the time. Thus, although the interviews picked up differences in child-rearing style that reflected the parents' beliefs, they did not reveal developmental differences in the translation of those beliefs to actual child-rearing behavior. Observational data may pick up developmental changes in rearing practices, but lose the underlying consistency of the value system.

It is also likely that parents affect their children's learning of moral concepts in ways other than those measured by the parent interviews, such as modeling. Additionally, the period when children's prototypes become more complex (age 8 or 9) is when children normally turn their attention away from home and are most involved in the world of school and peers (Maccoby & Martin, 1983). The addition of Belief to their prototypes may take place in the context of schoolyard negotiations. The final, late addition of Intent to the equation may be an attempt to satisfy a developing sense of justice in which subjective inferences about motivations are added to the decision matrix (Kohlberg, 1963; Piaget, 1932/1972).

It is clear that consideration of the prototype elements of Factuality and Belief (and, to a lesser extent, Intent) takes into account a major part of the variance. However, the fact remains that Cell 1, the prototypical truth, and Cell 8, the prototypical lie, did not receive overall ratings of 7 and -7. There are several possible explanations for this lack of consensus. It may simply be a function of the experimental task, in that a substantial number of participants may have been reluctant to make the extreme choice. On the other hand, the lack of agreement may reflect the true prototype phenomenon in which there are, indeed, no absolute examples on which all people would agree in labeling a complex and abstract concept. Thus, the individual's interpretation of the goodness of match of the statement with the prototype leads to a range of responses in even the cases that match most closely. Furthermore, additional prototype elements not considered in the experimental design are likely to enter into categorizing lies and truth, depending on the context the respondent assumes for the statement. It should be noted that there are qualitatively different types of lies. The prototypes for each of these may be slightly different. The type of lie investigated by our studies is what might be considered the *immoral* lie. The assumption behind the intent element of the immoral lie is that the speaker is aware (or believes) that the listener is unaware of both the speaker's intent to deceive, and the facts of the situation. However, in the stories, Chris was not portrayed as malicious, or a "bad" child. The reasons for Chris's intent to deceive were left open to interpretation. A missing prototype element may have been the general quality of Chris's moral character. In the real world, the overall context influences the impressions a judge forms of an individual's moral character which, in turn, determines the judge's interpretation of what that person does and says.

Studies now in progress examine the effects of context on the labeling of statements as lie or truth. The initial follow-up studies focus on the personal characteristics of the speaker. Portraying Chris as "naughty," neutral, or "angelic" would engender a moral prejudgment to subsequent interpretations of Chris's words and deeds. Because increasing maturity leads to use of a more flexible, subjectively determined prototype, we hypothesize that adults will be more likely to use the background information in their labeling decisions regarding the more ambiguous cells. To the extent that the youngest children use the context information, they are likely to apply it indiscriminately across all cells. Other contexts will be examined in further studies. For example, the teller of the tall tale assumes that the listener shares in the knowledge that the story is not factual, and is meant in fun. In the case of the white lie, the three prototype elements of the immoral lie may be present, but an additional moral element takes precedence. This moral dimension is the intent to protect the listener.

Again, we would expect adults to use this information more strongly in the cases that less clearly match the prototypes. By contrast, we hypothesize that young children's centering on Factuality will minimize the context effects.

APPENDIX

Introduction of Characters

Chris: (enters): Hi. My name is Chris. I want you to meet some of my family. This is Lee. (Lee enters and greets the audience) This is our dog Spot. (Spot enters and barks) This is our Mom. (Mom enters and greets the audience) We are going to show you some stories now. Watch what we do, and listen to what we say.
(all exit)

Stories

The stories were constructed by filling in the cells of the $2 \times 2 \times 2$ table of the prototype elements.

Cell 1: Kidplate

Chris: (rushes into room, dumps books on table, knocking plate off table [E comments: Look, Chris broke it]) Oh no! I broke the plate!
Mom: (enters) Chris, how did that plate break?
Chris: (aside) I'd better tell Mom. (to Mom) I knocked it off with my book.
Mom: Okay. (exits)
Chris: (aside) Uh huh. (nodding head) That's what I wanted to say. (screen blanks)

Cell 2: Dogplate

(Chris rushes into room, dumps books on table, exits. Spot enters, jumps on table, knocking plate off table [E comments: Look, Spot broke it.], exits)
Chris: (enters) Oh no! The plate is broken. I bet I knocked it off with my book.
Mom: (enters) Chris, how did that plate break?
Chris: (aside) I'd better tell Mom. (to Mom) Spot broke it.
Mom: Okay. (exits)

Chris: (aside) Oops! (shaking head "no") That's not what I wanted to say. (screen blanks)

Cell 3: Dogcup

Chris: (drinks, puts cup down. Spot jumps up, knocks cup over, [*E* comments: Look, Spot spilled it], exits) Oh no! Spot spilled it!
Mom: (enters) Chris, who spilled that?
Chris: (aside) Oh no, I don't want Mom to know. (to Mom) Spot spilled it.
Mom: Okay. (exits)
Chris: (aside) Oops! (shaking head "no") That's not what I wanted to say. (screen blanks)

Cell 4: Kidcup

(Chris drinks, puts cup down, exits. Lee enters, knocks cup over [*E* comments: Look, Lee spilled it.], exits)
Chris: (enters) Oh no! I must have knocked that over before.
Mom: (enters) Chris, who spilled that?
Chris: (aside) Oh no, I don't want Mom to know. (to Mom) Lee spilled it.
Mom: Okay (exits)
Chris: (aside) Uh huh. (nodding head) That's what I wanted to say. (screen blanks)

Cell 5: Dogeat

(Spot eats cookies from plate [*E* comments: Look, Spot ate the cookies.], exits)
Chris: (enters) Who ate the cookies? I bet Lee ate them.
Mom: (enters) Chris, who ate those cookies?
Chris: (aside) I'd better tell Mom. (to Mom) Lee ate them.
Mom: Okay. (exits)
Chris: (aside) Uh huh. (nodding head) That's what I wanted to say. (screen blanks)

Cell 6: Kideat

Chris: (watching Lee. Lee eats cookies [*E* comments: Look, Lee ate the cookies.], exits) Lee ate all the cookies!
Mom: (enters) Chris, who ate those cookies?
Chris: (aside) I'd better tell Mom. (to Mom) I don't know.

Mom: Okay. (exits)
Chris: (aside) Oops! (shaking head "no") That's not what I wanted to say. (screen blanks)

Cell 7: Kidrun

Lee: (alone) I'm running away from home! (runs off screen [E comments: Look, Lee ran away.])
Chris: (enters) I wonder where Lee is. I bet Lee's playing inside.
Mom: (enters) Chris, where is Lee?
Chris: (aside) Oh no! I don't want Mom to know. (to Mom) Lee is playing inside.
Mom: Okay. (exits)
Chris: (aside) Oops! (shaking head "no"). That's not what I wanted to say. (screen blanks)

Cell 8: Dogrun

Chris: (playing with Spot, Spot runs away [E comments: Look, Spot ran away.]) Oh no! Spot ran away!
Mom: (enters) Chris, where is Spot?
Chris: (aside) Oh no, I don't want Mom to know. (to Mom) Spot is in the house.
Mom: Okay. (exits)
Chris: (aside) Uh huh. (nodding head) That's what I wanted to say. (screen blanks)

REFERENCES

Anderson, N. H., & Cuneo, D. O. (1978). The height + width rule in children's judgments of quantity. *Journal of Experimental Psychology: General, 107,* 335–378.

Burton, R. V. (1968). Socialization: Psychological aspects. In D. L. Sills (Ed.), *International encyclopedia of the social sciences* (Vol. 14, pp. 534–545). New York: Crowell, Collier, & Macmillan.

Burton, R. V. (1984). A paradox in theories and research in moral development. In W. M. Kurtines & J. L. Gewirtz (Eds.), *Morality, moral behavior, and moral development* (pp. 193–207). New York: Wiley.

Cantor, N., Smith, E. E., French, R. D., & Mezzich, J. (1980). Psychiatric diagnosis as prototype characterization. *Journal of Abnormal Psychology, 89,* 181–193.

Coleman, L., & Kay, P. (1981). Prototype semantics: The English word *lie. Language, 57,* 26–44.

Katz, J. J., & Fodor, J. A. (1963). The structure of a semantic theory. *Language, 39,* 170–210.

Kohlberg, L. (1963). The development of children's orientations toward a moral order: I. Sequence in the development of moral thought. *Vita Humana, 6,* 11–33.

Leon, M. (1980). Integration of intent and consequence information in children's moral judgments.

In F. Wilkening, J. Becker, & T. Trabasso (Eds.), *Information integration by children* (pp. 71–98). Hillsdale, NJ: Lawrence Erlbaum Associates.

Maccoby, E. E., & Martin, J. A. (1983). Socialization in the context of the family: Parent–child interaction. In P. H. Mussen (Series Ed.) & E. M. Hetherington (Vol. Ed.), *Handbook of child psychology:* Vol. 4. Socialization, personality, and social development (4th ed., pp. 1–101). New York: Wiley.

Neisser, U. (1979). The concept of intelligence. *Intelligence, 3,* 217–227.

Perner, J., Leekam, S. R., & Wimmer, H. (1987). Three-year-olds' difficulty with false belief: The case for a conceptual deficit. *British Journal of Developmental Psychology, 5,* 125–137.

Peterson, C. C., Peterson, J. L., & Seeto, D. (1983). Developmental changes in ideas about lying. *Child Development, 54,* 1529–1535.

Piaget, J. (1972). *The moral judgment of the child* (M. Gabain, Trans.). London: Routledge & Kegan Paul. (Original work published 1932)

Rosch, E., & Mervis, C. B. (1975). Family resemblances: Studies in the internal structure of categories. *Cognitive Psychology, 7,* 573–605.

Rosch, E., Mervis C. B., Gray, W., Johnson, D., & Boyes-Braem, P. (1976). Basic objects in natural categories. *Cognitive Psychology, 8,* 382–439.

Saltzstein, H. D. (1976). Social influence and moral development: A perspective on the role of parents and peers. In T. Lickona (Ed.), *Moral development and behavior: Theory, research, and social issues* (pp. 219–240). New York: Holt, Rinehart & Winston.

Strichartz, A. F., & Burton, R. V. (1990a). Lies and truth: A study of the development of the concept. *Child Development, 61,* 211–220.

Strichartz, A. F., & Burton, R. V. (1990b). *Lies and truth: II. A replication and extension of the development of a prototype.* Manuscript submitted for publication.

Surber, C. F. (1977). Developmental processes in social inference: Averaging of intentions and consequences in moral judgment. *Developmental Psychology, 13,* 654–665.

Wilkening, F. (1980). Development of dimensional integration in children's perceptual judgment: Experiments with area, volume and velocity. In F. Wilkening, J. Becker, & T. Trabasso (Eds.), *Information integration by children* (pp. 47–70). Hillsdale, NJ: Lawrence Erlbaum Associates.

Wimmer, H., Gruber, S., & Perner, J. (1984). Young children's conception of lying: Lexical realism—moral subjectivism. *Journal of Experimental Child Psychology, 37,* 1–30.

3 Children and the Truth

Jeffrey J. Haugaard
Cornell University

N. Dickon Reppucci
University of Virginia

Divining the truth is generally seen to be a critical function of legal proceedings. Although factors such as compassion or fairness may be considered when dispensing justice, the truth is the foundation upon which justice is based. The U.S. Constitution, state constitutions, and other federal and state laws contain many provisions designed to increase the likelihood that the truth will emerge during legal proceedings. Primary among these provisions in criminal trials are the defendant's rights to cross-examine witnesses effectively, to confront witnesses physically, and to call witnesses on his or her behalf. Throughout U.S. legal history, there has been a special concern about the use of children as witnesses in legal proceedings, because it has often been assumed that children would provide inaccurate testimony. This assumption led to the exclusion of children from legal proceedings for many years, and then to the presumed incompetence of children, which could be challenged by a party hoping to call a child as a witness (see *Wheeler v. United States,* 1895).

The increased emphasis on prosecuting alleged child abusers over the past two decades has resulted in a greater need to call children as witnesses. This need has been especially strong in cases of alleged child sexual abuse, because physical evidence of sexual abuse exists in only a minority of cases (DeJong, 1985), and because the child is almost always the only eyewitness to the abuse that can be called to testify against the alleged abuser. The use of children as witnesses can be quite problematical, however. Some young children are declared incompetent to testify, based on their age, thereby eliminating them as witnesses. Other children find the process of testifying to be traumatic. They either are unable to testify once on the witness stand, or are prohibited from testifying by parents or other adults who fear that testifying will be damaging to the child.

The difficulty of using young children as witnesses, coupled with the desire to prosecute child abusers successfully, has resulted in attempts to increase the frequency and effectiveness with which young children can testify. These attempts have included new rules of evidence that no longer presume that young children are incompetent witnesses and modifications to the physical structure of some courtrooms and to some court procedures (see Haugaard & Reppucci, 1988). Some legal commentators have raised concerns that these modifications may decrease the likelihood that truthful testimony will be given in trials involving perpetrators of child abuse. Of specific concern is that some young children may not speak the truth while acting as witnesses and that defendants may have a particularly difficult time countering this testimony (e.g., Feher, 1988).

Any witness can provide nontruthful testimony in three ways. First, a witness can purposefully lie. That is, the witness can make a statement (a) that is false, (b) that the witness knows is false, and (c) that is made with the intention to deceive (Coleman & Kay, 1981). Second, a witness can also provide a statement (a) that is false, (b) that the witness believes is true, and (c) that is made with no intention of being deceptive (see Burton & Strichartz, this volume). This type of a statement would most often result from a witness's inaccurate memory. Most adults would not classify this type of a statement as a lie (because most adults consider the speaker's intent, Piaget, 1962), but it is clear that the truth is not being spoken. Finally, a witness can make a statement that qualifies as the truth under the witness' definition of the truth but that does not qualify as the truth under the definition held by the majority of adults. That is, even with an accurate memory for the event, a witness could speak "the truth" from his or her perspective and still relate the event in a nontruthful way from the perspective of most observers.

A steadily growing body of psychological research has examined children's ability to provide truthful testimony. This research has, for the most part, been used to support the position advocated by many in the mental health and legal fields that children as young as 4 have the capacity to provide truthful testimony. However, the research has focused mainly on children's ability to remember past events accurately and to resist modifications of this memory by statements made to the child after the event (the "suggestibility" of the child) (e.g., Cohen & Harnick, 1980; Goodman, Aman, & Hirschman, 1987; Goodman & Reed, 1986). Thus, only the second of the three ways just mentioned that a child could provide untruthful testimony (that due to their inaccurate memory) has been subject to extensive investigation.

This chapter reviews the relatively small amount of research that has addressed the other two ways in which a child can provide untruthful testimony: purposefully lying and making a statement that the child defines as the truth but that most adults do not define as the truth. Although overlaps may exist, the first situation is primarily an issue of a child's credibility as a witness and the second is primarily an issue of the child's competency. Consequently, a short discussion of the legal distinction between competency and credibility follows. Case law regarding the qualifications that any witness must have to be considered competent is then reviewed. Finally, the scant psychological research regarding children's definitions of the truth and their tendency to tell the truth is summarized.

COMPETENCY AND CREDIBILITY

There is an important legal distinction between the competency and the credibility of a witness. "Competency includes the general qualities which every witness must possess in order to be allowed to testify" (Weinstein & Berger, 1988, pp. 601–602). The standards of competency are minimal, in order to allow for the testimony of most witnesses. For the most part, in order to be competent a witness must know the difference between the truth and a lie, know that he or she has an obligation to speak the truth as a witness, and have the capacity to remember, recall, and describe events from the past.

It is the trial judge's responsibility to exclude incompetent witnesses from testifying, and the judge is given broad powers to determine a witness' competency and to bar from testifying those found incompetent (see *Doran v. United States*, 1953). This is done to reduce the possibility that the jury will be misled by incompetent testimony. Generally, those determined to be incompetent have been young children or individuals suffering from emotional or mental disabilities. The determination of competency is made outside of the presence of the jury. The judge may question the child, may seek the opinion of an expert witness (such as a psychologist), or both (*Kelleum v. State of Delaware*, 1978; *State of Arizona v. Roberts*, 1983). A judge may only bar from testifying a child who does not have the needed general capacities for competency. "Trial judge does not have the right to prevent evidence from getting to jury merely because he does not think it deserves to be given much weight . . . he may not screen witnesses simply to decide whether their testimony is persuasive" (*Western Industries v. Newcor Canada Ltd.*, 1984, p. 1201).

Credibility is determined by the trier of fact (the jury in jury trials or the judge if the defendant has waived his or her right to a jury trial). The trier of fact must weigh the testimony given by each witness and resolve conflicting witnesses' testimony by deciding which testimony is more believable. In addition to the witness' general capacity (competency), factors associated with the particular case in question that might influence the witness' willingness to tell the truth or ability to remember accurately must be considered. Moreover, the witness' demeanor, character, and other personal qualities will be taken into account.

Competency and credibility are both issues that can cause a particular witness' testimony to be disregarded, thus influencing the course of a trial. As has been described, however, each issue is based on different considerations and usually determined by a different actor in the trial. Consequently, it is important to distinguish the research that addresses each issue. It would be inappropriate, for instance, to consider research addressing children's tendency to lie when discussing competency, because purposeful lying is a matter of credibility. We now discuss children's truthfulness in the context of their competency and credibility. First we examine an issue pertaining to their competency: Do children define the truth in a similar manner to adults? We then address an issue of children's credibility: Are they more or less likely than adults to be honest as a witness?

QUALIFICATIONS FOR COMPETENT WITNESSES

Two federal decisions have given some guidance as to what should be considered when determining competency. In *United States v. Perez* (1976), the court held that a 14-year-old boy was competent because the trial transcript showed that he was able to recall and talk about a drug purchase that he had witnessed. In *Pocatello v. United States* (1968), an appellate court held that a 5-year-old was competent because the trial judge had found that the child could appreciate the difference between the truth and a falsehood and had the capacity for recollection of earlier events.

Rules of evidence and case law indicate that there is variability between the states in the capacities that a child must possess to be a competent witness. Four states specify that alleged victims of child sexual abuse are always competent to testify (Colorado, Connecticut, Missouri, and Utah), although nonabused children must meet competency qualifications before testifying. Some states require that a child must know the difference between the truth and a lie and be able to recall past events (see *Baum v. State of Wyoming*, 1987; *Bowden v. State of Arkansas*, 1988; *Commonwealth of Massachusetts v. Corbett*, 1989; *Durant v. Commonwealth of Virginia*, 1988; *In interest of CB (Wyoming)*, 1988; *State of Arizona v. Superior Court*, 1986). Case law from other states mandates that only the ability to tell the truth should be considered when determining competency (*Rickets v. State of Delaware*, 1985; *State of Maine v. Hussey*, 1987; *State of Montana v. Eiler*, 1988). Ability to distinguish the truth from a lie can be shown by the child demonstrating an understanding that it is wrong to tell a lie or that he or she will be punished if he or she tells a lie. In *State of New Jersey v. DR* (1988), an appellate court upheld the trial judge's ruling that a 3-year-old was incompetent to testify because of an inability to tell the truth from a lie: "I am not so sure that she even has the ability at this age to deal with the concept of lying and telling the truth" (p. 671).

In summary, although some variation exists between the states, in nearly every state a child must possess the ability to tell the difference between the truth and a lie, and must know that he or she is required to tell the truth on the witness stand, in order to be a competent witness. The ways in which a child can demonstrate that he or she knows the difference between the truth and a lie varies from court to court, but in most cases the trial judge must believe that the child has this capacity before the child is judged competent and is allowed to testify.

CHILDREN'S DEFINITIONS OF THE TRUTH

Research addressing children's understanding of the truth and lies is scant. Much of this research does not directly address the issues that are considered when determining a child's competency to testify. Some research has shown that young children have definitions of lies that are different from those of older children and adults. The research is reviewed in this section. A recent study that examined an aspect of children's definitions of the truth that is more relevant to their competency to testify is then presented.

From his observations of several children, Piaget (1962) concluded that children under the age of 7 define lying as "to commit a moral fault by means of language" (p. 142). He found that the definition of lies used by young children was broader than that used by older children, and included "naughty" words such as "oaths or indecent expressions which one is forbidden to use" (Piaget, 1962, p. 140). Young children, Piaget wrote, are often confused by the fact that some words bring immediate reward from adults but others bring immediate retribution. They respond by combining all verbalizations that result in adult disapproval into one category, which they define as the category of lies.

According to Piaget, children begin to drop naughty words from the category of lies around the ages of 5 to 7. The category is then solely comprised of statements that are not true, and these are determined purely on an objective basis, using "moral realism": If a statement is inaccurate it is a lie and if it is accurate it is the truth. The intention of the speaker is not considered by children before age 7, and this process is usually not consolidated in the child until 8 to 10. Piaget concluded that 5- to 7-year-old children were able to distinguish between an intentional act and an unintentional error, but that they did not use this distinction in their definitions of lies.

Piaget's findings have been supported by more systematic research of others. Peterson, Peterson, and Seeto (1983) asked groups of 40 children ages 5, 8, 9, and 11 whether certain incidents constituted a lie (the 8- and 9-year-olds were very similar in their replies, therefore only the 8-year-old replies are given here). When asked whether an incident in which a child swore after being upset by others was lying, 38% of the 5-year-olds, 12% of the 8-year-olds, and 15% of the 11-year-olds said yes. When asked about a child who inadvertently gave the wrong street directions to an adult, 90% of the 5-year-olds, 69% of the 8-year-olds, and 48% of the 11-years-olds said that the child had told a lie. When asked about a child who denied doing something that he had done in order to avoid punishment, virtually all the children at each age stated that it was a lie.

Wimmer, Gruber, and Perner (1984) performed a series of experiments designed to investigate children's definitions of lies. One experiment involved 10 children age $4\frac{1}{2}$, $5\frac{1}{2}$, and $6\frac{1}{2}$. One condition involved a story in which Child 1 knew that X had occurred and told Child 2 that X had occurred, and Child 2 then told Child 3 that Y had occurred. Virtually all children in each age group responded that Child 2 had lied. In another condition, Child 1 knew that X had occurred but told Child 2 that Y had occurred. Child 2 then told Child 3 that Y had occurred. In this condition, 85% of the 4-year-olds, 95% of the 5-year-olds, and 80% of the 6-year-olds said that Child 2 had lied, even though they later acknowledged that Child 2 believed that Y had occurred. In a third condition, Child 1 knew that X had occurred but told Child 2 that Y had occurred. Child 2, hoping to deceive Child 3, said that X had occurred (not realizing that X had actually occurred). When asked if Child 2 had lied, 26 of the 30 children said that he had not lied. All three conditions support the conclusion that it is the accuracy of a statement, not the intention of the speaker, that is used by young children in determining whether it is a lie.

Strichartz and Burton (1990, this volume) performed a series of 8 four- to six-line puppet shows for 30 participants in each of five groups: nursery schoolers, preschoolers, first graders, fifth graders, and adults. The shows involved a puppet, Chris, interacting with another puppet representing Chris's mother, about a situation that Chris was involved in or witnessed. Each puppet show varied on the three factors that Coleman and Kay (1981) hypothesized distinguished prototypical lies from the truth: (a) the falsity of a statement, (b) the speaker's belief in the falsity of the statement, and (c) the speaker's intent to deceive. That is, one puppet show involved Chris making a statement that was false, that he knew was false, and with which he intended to deceive his mother. Another involved Chris making a statement that was false, that he believed was true, and with which he did not intend to deceive his mother. Another involved Chris making a statement that was true, that he knew to be true, and with which he did not intend to deceive his mother, and so on. All participants saw all eight puppet shows. After each they were asked "When Chris said, '. . . ,' was Chris telling a lie, the truth, or something else?" (p. 214). Participants were asked to give a reason for their response, and these were coded to indicate whether the subject was attending to the falsity of the statement, Chris' belief about the falsity of the statement, or Chris' intention to deceive his mother.

Their results indicated that 14 of the 30 nursery schoolers (ages 2 and 3) were unable to label any of Chris' statements as the truth, a lie, or something else. Although the nursery schoolers understood and could describe what happened in each story, "They responded with 'I don't know,' blank stares, or clearly inappropriate answers only when asked to label the statements or to explain their labels" (p. 215). The preschoolers and first graders relied almost exclusively on the factuality of Chris's statement when labeling it the truth or a lie. The adults considered Chris's belief about the statement more often than its accuracy or Chris's intent. The fifth graders' responses were transitional between the younger children and the adults. Although they considered Chris's belief more often than the younger children did, they were less likely than the adults to ignore the factual nature of Chris's statement, unless it was clear that Chris was intending to deceive. In summary, the results supported previous conclusions that young children most often consider the factuality of a statement when deciding whether it is the truth or a lie.

The results of these studies indicate that children of different ages attend to different factors when determining whether a statement is the truth, a mistake, or a deliberate lie. At issue in the continuing study of young children's definition of lies is which dimension or dimensions they will attend to when presented with a different set of criteria to consider. We next describe a study that we completed of children's definitions of lies, which involved two dimensions that they are likely to encounter when testifying in court, particularly in cases in which they are alleged victims of child abuse: making an inaccurate statement at the request of a parent and making an inaccurate statement to protect a friend (for more details, see Haugaard, Reppucci, Laird, & Nauful, 1991). We describe this study in more detail because of its focus on the legal implications of children's definitions of lies.

Children's Definitions of Lies in a Legal Context

This study was designed primarily to test the salience of two other dimensions that children might use when discriminating the truth from lies. The first was whether young children might believe that being directed by a parent to make a statement qualifies it as the truth, even though the child knows that what the parent has directed him or her to say did not occur. This particular issue may arise in criminal trials involving child sexual abuse. There is some concern in the legal and mental health fields that accusations of child sexual abuse increasingly are being used in divorce and custody proceedings and that some of these accusations are inaccurate and made only to prejudice a court against a particular parent (Benedek & Schetky, 1985). As an example, Lacayo (1987) reported that sexual abuse charges were a component of 30% of the divorce cases in Michigan in 1986, up from 5% in 1980. Although the extent to which the rise in accusations of child sexual abuse in divorce proceedings accurately reflects the amount of sexual abuse that has occurred in these families is unknown, there is concern that some children are being convinced by one parent to accuse another of abuse that has never occurred. If a child who is told to say a certain thing by one parent believes that the parent's instruction makes the child's statement the truth, then the child could speak "the truth" in a way that could mislead a jury. The second dimension that was tested was whether an inaccurate statement designed to protect a friend would be considered the truth by young children. This issue could also arise in a variety of legal proceedings. For example, an abused child could believe that an inaccurate statement designed to protect his or her abuser from being punished was the truth.

Participants and Procedures. Participants were 56 girls in preschool programs who would be attending kindergarten the following year, 40 girls in their first or second month of kindergarten, 46 girls in their sixth or seventh month of kindergarten, and 23 college undergraduates who served as an adult comparison group. The children came from a broad range of socioeconomic groups. The preschoolers ranged in age from 48 to 64 months ($M = 55.4$), the early kindergarten students ranged in age from 60 to 77 months ($M = 67.5$), and the late-kindergarten students ranged in age from 63 to 88 months ($M = 71.4$). Girls were chosen because they are the victims of sexual abuse more often than boys and hence may be involved in trial testimony more often. The children were grouped by education level so that any effects of education and age could be noted.

Each participant was randomly assigned to see one of two videotapes, each of which was $3\frac{1}{2}$ minutes long. The videotapes related the story of a girl who plays at a neighbor's pond even though she has been warned previously by the neighbor not to play there. The neighbor finds her at the pond, approaches to within about 4 feet of her, tells her that he is going to report her to the police, and sends her home. At no time does the neighbor touch the girl or raise his hands as if to do so. As the girl approaches her home, the videotape narrator states, "The girl has come right home without stopping anywhere. And she is going right to her room." Eventually, the girl talks with a policeman who comes to her house. She admits to having been at the pond and says, "But he hit me two times before he let me come home." The policeman says, "He hit you? He hit you before he let you come home?" to which the girl replies, "Yes, he hit me." The policeman says that he will look into this, reminds the girl not to return to the pond, and leaves.

The only difference in the two versions of the videotape occurs between the time that the girl returns home and the time that the policeman arrives. In one version (referred to here as the "self-version") she goes to her room and waits by herself for the policeman. In the second version (the "mother version"), her mother comes into her room and asks why the girl is upset. The girl responds that Mr. Smith had sent her home for playing at his pond and was calling the police. The mother states, "That Mr. Smith sure is a mean man. I'll tell you what I want you to do. When the policeman comes, tell him that Mr. Smith hit you two times before letting you come home." The girl asks, "Tell the policeman that Mr. Smith hit me. Why should I do that?" to which the mother replies, "Just do it because I want you to. It will be the best thing." In both versions the girl goes directly from her room to speak to the policeman. Thus, in one version the girl appears to decide for herself to tell a lie to a person representing a legal authority, and in the second, her mother instructs her to do so.

A structured interview was used to determine the participant's memory of the videotape and belief about whether the girl lied to the policeman when telling him that the neighbor had hit her. Information was also gathered on the children's IQ (using the vocabulary subtest of the fourth edition of the Stanford-Binet Intelligence Test).

Each child was interviewed individually. She was escorted by her interviewer to a separate interviewing room at her school. After the IQ screening, the videotape was introduced. The children were told that after watching the videotape they would be asked questions about it and that they should watch carefully. After the videotape was shown, the interviewer said that many children had asked to see the videotape a second time before answering questions about it, and asked each child if she would like to see it a second time. All of the children agreed and it was then repeated to increase the accuracy with which they could recall the story.

The structured interview was then conducted. The children were first asked about the videotape. For instance, the children were asked, "Where did the girl go to play?" and "What did the man say to the girl?" A critical question was, "When the man and the girl were standing by the pond, did the man hit the girl?" Those children who answered "No" to this question were asked "Did the man hit the girl when they were anywhere else?" Following these questions, a randomly selected half of the children were asked, "When the girl told the policeman that the man had hit her, was she telling the truth?" The others were asked, "When the girl told the policeman that the man had hit her, was she telling a lie?" This was done to reduce the chance of a response bias that could occur if the children answered "Yes" if they were confused by the question. The children were then asked to give a reason for their response about the statement being the truth or a lie. Later in the interview each child was asked the opposite form of the question (e.g., those asked if the girl had told the truth were asked if she had lied). This was done to increase the chance of detecting any children who might have definitions of a lie that would allow them to answer "Yes" or "No" to both forms of the question.

Pairs of undergraduates watched the videotape one time in the investigator's office. They were interviewed individually, using a similarly structured interview but without the IQ screening.

A short vignette was read to each child at the end of the interview. In the vignette, a young girl is told by her teacher that she must stay in the classroom instead of going to recess. The girl goes to recess anyway and plays with a friend. Later, the teacher asks the friend if the girl stayed in the classroom. In order to protect the girl, the friend tells the teacher that the girl stayed in the room. The children were asked if the friend had lied to the teacher.

Results. The participants' answers to questions about the videotape indicated that they were able to comprehend the story and remember what had occurred. There was no association between the form of the question about lying that was used initially and the participants' answers. Therefore, the responses of those initially asked "Was it a lie?" and those asked "Was it the truth?" were combined for the analyses.

All of the undergraduates remembered correctly that the neighbor had not hit the girl. Among the children, 41 (29%) stated incorrectly that the neighbor had hit the girl. Of these children, 39 said that the neighbor had hit the girl at the pond, 1 said that he had hit her at her house, and 1 child could not specify where he had hit her. A comparison of the children who did and did not believe that the neighbor had hit the girl showed no statistically significant differences due to age, grade level, or IQ. The only difference was associated with which version of the videotape the child viewed—those watching the self version were more likely to recall incorrectly that the neighbor had hit the girl (39%) than those watching the mother version (17%) [$X^2(1, n = 142) = 7.3, p < .01$]. It appeared that the conversation between the mother and the girl helped to place the girl's later statements to the policeman in a clearer context for the children who saw that version of the videotape.

There were five children (3.5%) who answered the two questions about the girl's statement to the policeman in a nonparallel manner—they answered either "Yes" or "No" to both "Was it a lie?" and "Was it the truth?"—and were unable to explain their answers (any explanation that stated how the girls' statement could have been both the truth and a lie would have been acceptable). These five children were labeled as "confused" and were not included in this part of the analysis.

All of the undergraduates stated that the girl had lied when she told the policeman that the neighbor had hit her. Among the children who correctly remembered that the neighbor had not hit the girl, 92 stated that the girl had lied to the policeman and 6 stated that she had told the truth. The IQ of the group who believed that the girl had lied is about one half of a standard deviation above that for the group that believed that she had told the truth. Other differences were very small. Each child was asked what it was that made the girl's statement either the truth or a lie. Among the children who stated that the girl had told a lie, 58 (63%) justified their answer by stating that the neighbor had not hit the girl. The other children gave a justification such as "It was not the truth" or were unable to give any justification. Four of the six children who said that the statement was the truth were unable to give any justification. One child justified her response by saying that the girl was angry; a second child stated, "She can't lie—she's older."

Among the 39 children who incorrectly remembered that the neighbor did hit the girl, 35 stated that the girl had told the truth to the policeman and 4 stated that she had lied. There was a difference of approximately one half of a standard deviation between the groups on age and IQ, with those stating that the girl had told the truth being older and having a higher IQ. Of the children who said that the girl had told the truth, 68% were able to justify their answer by stating that the neighbor had not hit the girl.

In regard to the vignette read to the children at the end of the interview: 91% of the children stated that the girl who lied to the teacher to protect a friend was telling a lie. Of the 13 children who said that the statement was the truth, approximately half gave a justification that seemed to contradict their answer; for instance, they said that it was the truth because the friend had gone outside to play. Two of the children, however, gave a justification suggesting that the statement was the truth either because it protected the friend or because it was not the teacher's business.

Discussion. The results of this investigation suggest that most young children understand that a child who purposefully makes an inaccurate statement, either at the request of a parent or in order to protect a friend, is telling a lie. Although not all relevant aspects of children's definitions of the truth were addressed, two important aspects were investigated. Among the children who correctly recalled that the neighbor had not hit the girl, 94% stated that the girl told a lie when she told the policeman that the neighbor had hit her. There was no effect of the form of the videotape on the children's answers: Children who saw the mother instruct the daughter to lie were no more likely to say that the girl told the truth than those who did not see the mother's instructions. The children were able to attend to the appropriate aspect of the situation—whether the neighbor hits the girl—rather than to the authority or wishes of the mother. The justifications given by the children suggest that they had an adult-like sense of why the girl's statement was a lie: 63% stated that they knew that the girl had lied because the neighbor had not hit her.

The reasons for the responses of the six children who said that the girl had told the truth are largely unclear because only two of them were able to provide a justification for their response. One of these children stated that the girl was mad, and the other child stated that because the girl in the videotape was "older" she could not have told a lie. These responses suggest that these dimensions might be salient for some young children when determining the truthfulness of a statement, and may be worthy of further investigation. It is notable that none of the children justified their response that the girl had told the truth by noting the mother's instruction to do so.

An unexpectedly high percentage of the children incorrectly recalled that the neighbor had hit the girl in the videotape. This raises important questions about young children's eyewitness memory in cases in which a participant in the event that is witnessed by the child attempts to influence the child's memory for the event. However, inasmuch as children's eyewitness memory is not the focus of this chapter, the reader is referred to Haugaard et al. (1991) for a discussion of the children's eyewitness ability and of the influence that the version of the videotape had on their memory.

The high percentage of children who knew that the girl's statement to her teacher in the vignette was a lie suggests that the children recognized that inaccurate altruistic statements can be lies. As with the results from the videotape, a small percentage of children said that the girl's statement was the truth, and then gave a logical justification for their answer. This also suggests that children's definitions of the truth in this regard should be considered cautiously.

In summary, this investigation showed that most young children defined as lies inaccurate statements made at the request of a parent or in order to protect a friend. The percentage of children that described these statements as lies was high. However, they were not unanimous in this classification, as were the adult participants, suggesting the importance of a careful screening of children of this age as to their definitions of lies before they are allowed to testify. A limitation of this investigation was that the children described statements made by other children that they observed, not their own statements. The possibility remains that they may have described similar statements made by themselves in a different way.

CHILDREN'S HONESTY

The trier of fact in a case must wade through what is often conflicting testimony from various witnesses and determine which testimony is more credible than the rest. An issue of credibility is whether children are more likely than adults to be dishonest as a witness, either on their own accord or in response to pressure from others for them to be dishonest. The concept of honesty is likely to have different meanings across social groups and within social groups over time. As currently conceptualized in our culture, dishonesty refers to acts or statements that are (a) inaccurate, (b) known by the actor or speaker to be inaccurate, and (c) made with the intention to deceive (Coleman & Kay, 1981).

This is a particularly thorny issue for psychological research, because most ecologically relevant research would involve placing a child in a situation where the child is tempted to lie. Even more difficult from an ethical perspective would be studies in which a child is pressured to tell a lie, especially if the pressure came from a parent or other meaningful adult in the child's life. Given the assumption that lying produces some stress on a child, and that it is inappropriate for an adult to encourage a child to lie, the issue is whether investigations involving this type of stress for a child or parent are ethical.

The difficult nature of this type of research is probably one factor that has resulted in so little of it being undertaken. Although there have been a few studies comparing the relative honesty of children of different ages, these studies have examined honesty in situations far removed from those that a child would en-counter as a witness. These studies are briefly reviewed to give the reader an understanding of the type of research that is currently available with which to answer questions about children's honesty.

Empirical Research on Children's Honesty

Early research in this area involved assessing the amount of cheating on academic tasks that children of different ages engaged in. Burton (1976) reviewed this literature and found that some studies reported a small decrease in cheating as the children got older, whereas other studies reported no difference in cheating according to age. He concluded that any of the reported differences were so small as to make age an unimportant influence on academic cheating. Henshel (1971) found that the association between a stated belief in the importance of honesty and honest behavior increased with age. She visited several classrooms on two occasions. During the first visit, she had children answer questions about how they would act in situations in which they could be honest or dishonest (e.g., lying to avoid trouble). Several days later, another investigator gave the children an "aptitude" test involving a number of difficult spelling words. There was ample opportunity for the students to cheat on this test by changing the spelling of their words while correcting the test. The amount of cheating done by the students at different ages (Grade 4 through 7) was similar. However, there was a strong correlation between the older students' report gathered the first day of how they would act and how they acted on the spelling test. This association dropped away to virtually nothing for the fourth graders. This variability in the children's behavior is similar to that found in other studies that have shown that older children demonstrate a more consistent pattern of honesty across situations than younger children (Burton, 1976).

In one study (Burton, 1976) children were placed in a situation where they could cheat on a task. Some children had their mothers present and others did not. The children with their mothers present delayed the onset of their cheating and had a reduced amount of cheating. However, eventually more of the children with their mothers engaged in cheating of some amount. Burton suggested that the inhibition to cheating that was caused by the presence of their mothers was eventually overcome by the pressure to succeed because of the mother's pres-ence, and that this pressure influenced the children to cheat.

A recent study by Tate and Warren-Leubecker (1989) examined a situation in which an adult encourages a child to lie to another adult. The study involved 30 children, ages 3 to 7. Each child spent some time individually with the experi-menter playing with several toys. The 20 children in the experimental group were then encouraged to try to "fool" a friend of the experimenter by telling the friend that they had played with a toy that they had not played with. The experimenter left the room and the friend appeared and asked the children to describe what they had done. Nineteen of the 20 children in the experimental group agreed to fool the friend, although only 11 actually did tell the lie. When the friend questioned the children ("Is that what you really did?"), only 3 children continued to maintain the ruse. None of the 10 control-group children changed their story as the result of questioning by the friend, suggesting that it was not a random change in stories by those in the experimental group, but a return to the truth. The authors cautioned that the frivolous nature of the "lie" and the lack of importance of the experimenter in the children's lives made the experimental condition quite different from a situation in which a parent or other adult tried to convince a child to lie in a legal proceeding. However, the experiment does move in the direction of examining children's tendency to lie in situations in which they receive some pressure to do so.

Bottoms, Goodman, Schwartz-Kenney, Sachsenmaier, and Thomas (1990) engaged 49 children, ages 3 to 6, in a play situation with their mothers. The mothers had all been coached about particular ways that they should play with their children and about which toys they should use. Half of the child–mother pairs were told that they should not play with a specified shelf of toys. All of the mothers played with these toys with their children, and, at one point, all of the mothers picked up a doll that was rigged to break. The mothers then hid the doll. The mothers then told their children not to tell the investigator that they had done so. Only one child mentioned that the mother had broken the doll in a subsequent interview, even in the face of leading questions.

In summary, the small amount of research done in this area, and the significant difference between the experimental conditions and the types of legal proceedings in which a child would be engaged, makes it unwise for the research to be used to estimate the tendency of young children to be honest in legal proceedings. Although some research shows that children may conceal information when instructed to do so by a parent, other research shows that when directly questioned about "secret" activities with nonparental adults, many children tell the truth. It would be incorrect to conclude that the evidence indicates that young children are as honest as older children, just as it would be incorrect to cite the small differences that have been found in some studies as indicating that young children are less honest. At this time, it would be improper to draw any firm conclusions from the body of research that has been accumulated.

DIRECTIONS FOR FUTURE RESEARCH

Probably the most important consideration for future research is developing ethically sound, ecologically valid situations in which to examine the issue of children's truthfulness. In other words, research that would be useful in legal contexts must address the specific types of situations that might influence a child's truthfulness in the legal area. Without such research, we will be left in the position of not being able to provide recommendations to the legal field, based on appropriate empirical evidence, regarding children's truthfulness. Some might see fit to argue whether young children's truthfulness should or should not be considered in a similar fashion as adults', but, given the current lack of evidence, these arguments must be founded on something other than psychological research.

In the area of children's competency, for instance, an exploration of other factors that may be used by a child when defining a statement as the truth or a lie is appropriate. Additional factors that a child may consider include whether the child perceives that parents, judges, or therapists want the child to testify in a certain way, whether the statement is made in anger because of a perceived wrong that another person has done, and whether or not a statement agrees with previous statements that parents or other adults have previously made. Continued work is needed concerning the question of whether an inaccurate statement that a child makes at the request of a parent is considered the truth.

From another perspective, research is needed to address the ways in which trial judges can best question a child when determining the child's competency. Presently, there seems to be little guidance for judges on how best to conduct a competency examination, and the questions that are used are often only peripherally related to the specific issues of children's honest in a trial setting. Developing and testing questions that can best discriminate what appears to be the small percentage of children who may have improper definitions of the truth may help ensure that only competent children are allowed to testify (see Haugaard, 1988a, 1988b; Melton, 1988).

Research concerning the honesty of children should also relate as directly as possible to situations that children encounter while testifying. One of the conclusions of research with younger children has been that their tendency to be honest is variable across situations (Burton, 1976). A search for the influences on this variability would be important. Determining whether there are factors that increase or decrease a child's honesty is important. Because of the normative changes caused by children's cognitive and social development, studies concentrating on children of specific ages, rather than lumping children who are 4 or 5 years apart in age together, would provide much needed information about the influence of these various factors at each age.

The extent to which parents or other adults in a position of authority have the capability to influence a child to be dishonest needs a thorough exploration. Abused children often experience pressure to deny their abuse, and some non-abused children may be encouraged to make false accusations of abuse. The extent to which a child is apparently willing to displease an interviewer by maintaining that something did not occur to the child is of special importance in this area, where many children are engaged in extensive interviewing about possible abuse experiences.

Research involving children and the truth is complicated by many legal and ethical constraints. For instance, it is generally seen as inappropriate to place a child in a stressful situation in which the child is pressured to tell a lie to someone else. Creativity on the part of researchers is needed. A willingness to make generalizations (albeit skeptical generalizations) from analogue research is needed, as is a willingness to accumulate a body of research that will increase our confidence when making these generalizations. Until additional research can be completed, our knowledge about children and the truth in legal proceedings is so limited that few conclusions that can be useful in the legal area can be drawn.

REFERENCES

Baum v. State of Wyoming, 745 P.2d 877 (1987).

Benedek, E. P., & Schetky, D. H. (1985). Allegations of sexual abuse in child custody and visitations disputes. In D. H. Schetky & E. P. Benedek (Eds.), *Emerging issues in child psychiatry and the law* (pp. 68–84). New York: Brunner/Mazel.

Bottoms, B., Goodman, G. S., Schwartz-Kenney, B., Sachsenmaier, T., & Thomas, S. (1990, March). *Keeping secrets: Implications for children's testimony.* Paper presented at the American Psychology and Law Society Meeting, Williamsburg, VA.

Bowden v. State of Arkansas, 761 S.W.2d 148 (1988).

Burton, R. V. (1976). Honesty and dishonesty. In T. Lickona (Ed.), *Moral development and behavior* (pp. 173–197). New York: Holt, Rinehart, & Winston.

Cohen, R. L., & Harnick, M. A. (1980). The susceptibility of child witnesses to suggestion. *Law and Human Behavior, 4,* 201–210.

Coleman, L., & Kay, P. (1981). Prototype semantics, The English word 'lie.' *Language, 57,* 26–44.

Commonwealth of Massachusetts v. Corbett, 533 N.E.2d 207 (1989).

DeJong, A. R. (1985). The medical evaluation of sexual abuse in children. *Hospital and Community Psychiatry, 36,* 509–512.

Doran v. United States, 205 F.2d 717 (1953).

Durant v. Commonwealth of Virginia, 375 S.E.2d 396 (1988).

Feher, T. L. (1988). The alleged molestation victim, the rules of evidence, and the Constitution: Should children really be seen and not heard? *American Journal of Criminal Law, 14,* 227–255.

Goodman, G. S., Aman, C., & Hirschman, J. (1987). Child sexual and physical abuse: Children's testimony. In S. J. Ceci, M. P. Toglia, & D. F. Ross (Eds.), *Children's eyewitness memory* (pp. 1–23). New York: Springer-Verlag.

Goodman, G. S., & Reed, R. S. (1986). Age differences in eyewitness testimony. *Law and Human Behavior, 10,* 317–332.

Haugaard, J. J. (1988a). Judicial determination of children's competency: Should it be abandoned. *Professional Psychology: Research and Practice, 19,* 102–107.

Haugaard, J. J. (1988b). Reply to Melton. *Professional Psychology: Research and Practice, 19,* 251.

Haugaard, J. J., & Reppucci, N. D. (1988). *The sexual abuse of children.* San Francisco: Jossey-Bass.

Haugaard, J. J., Reppucci, N. D., Laird, J., & Nauful, T. (1991). Children's definitions of the truth and their competency to testify in legal proceedings. *Law and Human Behavior, 15,* 253–271.

Henshel, A. (1971). The relationship between values and behavior: A developmental hypothesis. *Child Development, 42*, 1997–2007.

In interest of CB (Wyoming), 749 P.2d 267 (1988).

Kelleum v. State of Delaware, 396 A.2d 166 (1978).

Lacayo, R. (1987, May 11). Sexual abuse or abuse of justice. *Time*, p. 49.

Melton, G. B. (1988). Children, ecology, and legal contexts: A reply to Haugaard. *Professional Psychology, Research and Practice, 19*, 108–111.

Peterson, C. C., Peterson, J. L., & Seeto, D. (1983). Developmental changes in ideas about lying. *Child Development, 54*, 1529–1535.

Piaget, J. (1962). *The moral judgment of the child*. New York: Collier.

Pocatello v. United States, 394 F.2d 115 (1968).

Rickets v. State of Delaware, 488 A.2d 856 (1985).

State of Arizona v. Roberts, 710 P.2d 496 (1983).

State of Arizona v. Superior Court, 719 P.2d 283 (1986).

State of Maine v. Hussey, 521 A.2d 278 (1987).

State of Montana v. Eiler, 762 P.2d 210 (1988).

State of New Jersey v. DR, 537 A.2d 667 (1988).

Strichartz, A. F., & Burton, R. V. (1990). Lies and the truth: A study of the development of the concept. *Child Development, 61*, 211–220.

Tate, C. S., & Warren-Leubecker, A. (1989, April). *The effects of adult coaching on children's willingness to provide false reports*. Paper presented at the biennial meetings of the Society for Research in Child Development, Kansas City, MO.

United States v. Perez, 526 F.2d 859 (1976).

Western Industries v. Newcor Canada Ltd., 739 F.2d 1198 (1984).

Weinstein, J. B., & Berger, M. A. (1988). *Weinstein's evidence*. New York: Matthew Bender.

Wheeler v. United States, 159 U.S. 523 (1895).

Wimmer, H., Gruber, S., & Perner, J. (1984). Young children's conception of lying: Lexical realism—moral subjectivism. *Journal of Experimental Child Psychology, 37*, 1–30.

Believing and Deceiving: Steps to Becoming a Good Liar

Susan R. Leekam
University of Kent

A boy wishing to absent himself from school in order to attend a ball game telephoned his teacher:

"Hello Miss Brown, my son is very ill and, I am sorry to say, cannot come to school today."

"Who is talking?" asked the teacher.

"My father" the boy answered.

—from Krout, 1931, p. 23

Young children's lies often fail. They seem to miss the point that the success of a lie depends on the listener believing what you say. This doesn't mean that young children do not attempt to lie. Nor that they have no notion of how to deceive. But to be successful at lying you need to be aware of what the listener will think—whether they will believe or disbelieve what you say.

This chapter looks at how children might learn to become good liars. In particular, the focus is on whether children's developing success as liars may be related to their developing understanding of another person's belief. To tackle this question I will first look at various definitions of lying. From here I develop a conceptual framework in which lying can be considered at different levels or degrees of complexity. Finally, I review some of the developmental literature on lying to see whether the different levels of lying that I propose might correspond to particular developmental levels or stages.

DEFINITIONS

My aim in this chapter is to consider how children might get better at lying as they get older. Before tackling this question, however, it is important to look at what it means to lie in the first place.

Definitions of lying are closely linked to definitions of deception. Bok (1978) defined lying as a subcategory of deception. Whereas deception includes a wide range of behaviors, including gesture, silence, and mimicry by animals, lying is defined as an intentionally deceptive message that is *stated*. The statement might be made either verbally, in writing, or by the use of signs.

The *intentionally deceptive* aspect of lying is an important element in Bok's definition. It is important because deception can also take place, (i.e., a target person or animal may be misled) without deception actually being *intended*. Mitchell (1986) illustrates this distinction between deception and intentional deception in his classification of deception at four different levels. This classification is a hierarchy, with intentional deception at the highest level.

At the lowest level of deception are found "programmed" behaviors of animals, for example, the butterfly whose wing ends look like its head to predators, allowing them to escape. Second-level deception also includes programmed acts but these involve registration of this act to another organism. As a result, some transmission of the deception takes place; for example, deceptive flashing of fireflies and injury feigning by birds. Third-level deception allows for learning, so that previous acts can be modified; such as an animal that gets another to turn away so it can steal its food. Here, the animal has learned strategies to manipulate another's behavior. Finally, the fourth level of deception involves representation of anothers *beliefs*. In this case the animal intends to bring about a desired outcome by manipulating another's belief.

To extend Mitchell's analysis a bit further, deception can take place from the perspectives of both the deceiver and the recipient. First, deception can take place at the level of the recipient only, without any intention by the person who instigated it. Recipients may be misled or deceived. That is, they may go to the wrong place or do the wrong thing. In addition to being misled in their *behavior* they may also be misled in their *beliefs*.

Deception can also be viewed from the perspective of the deceiver. At Levels 3 and 4 of Mitchell's analysis, the deceiver has a motive to achieve a particular outcome or reward. He or she uses a particular means to achieve that end. The means might be to mislead the recipient by getting the recipient to go to the wrong place or do the wrong thing (i.e., to manipulate *behavior*) and/or get them to think the wrong thing (i.e., to manipulate *belief*).

From the deceiver's perspective then, there are two levels at which the deceiver aims to deceive the recipient: first by manipulating behavior and second by manipulating beliefs. A number of writers argue that the ability to manipulate beliefs and not just behavior is the hallmark of intentional deception in animals (see Bennett, 1991; Byrne & Whiten, 1991; Cheney & Seyfarth, 1991; Russow, 1986, for discussion).

Is the same kind of distinction made for animal deception also made in the literature of human lying? Bok (1978), in her analysis of lying, defines lying as an intentionally deceptive message and she defines intentional deception in terms of the attribution of beliefs. She writes, "When we undertake to deceive others intentionally, we communicate messages meant to mislead them, meant to make them, believe what we ourselves do not believe" (p. 13). For Bok, therefore, lying involves aiming to deceive by manipulating beliefs and the question of a lower level of lying by manipulating behavior does not arise.

Not all writers, however, define lying only in terms of intentional deception. Others include other features of lying, as being essential features of lying. Siegler (1966), for example, identifies six features that make up the typical case of lying. These are: (a) say something, (b) intend to deceive, (c) say something that is false, (d) say something that the speaker knows to be false, (e) believe that what he or she says is false, and (f) communicate. Siegler argues that all six features, although typical of lying, are not necessary conditions. However, Siegler makes a distinction between lying and telling a lie. He argues that the falsity of what is said may be a necessary condition for *telling a lie* but not necessary condition for *lying*. A necessary condition for lying is the belief that what was said is false or falsely expressing a belief.

Coleman and Kay (1981) take a "prototype" view of the definition of the word lie. Their theory assumes that there is no set of necessary and sufficient conditions that must be satisfied in order that a statement be called a lie. Instead, the prototype schema has a set of elements but not all the elements are necessary for a lie to be identified. A statement then, may be more, or less of a lie.

The prototypical lie is characterized by the following three elements: (a) the statement is false; (b) the speaker believes it to be false; (c) in uttering the statement, the speaker intends to deceive.

All three elements hold for a "good," "full-fledged" lie, but they argue, a statement can be classified as a lie even with one or more elements missing.

Although the falsity of the statement might not be an essential condition, therefore, both Siegler and Coleman and Kay agree that two elements are particularly important for lying. First, the *belief* of the *speaker*. A lying speaker says something that he or she believes to be false. Bok (1978) also supports this view when she writes, "so a sender may mislead another person but she practices deception only if she believes her message to be false" (p. 13).

The second aspect mentioned earlier is the speaker's intention to deceive. In order to intend to deceive, the speaker must consider the listener's mental state. The speaker *wants* to affect or manipulate the listener's *belief*. But what does it mean to "intend to deceive" someone? If you want to manipulate a listener's belief in order to achieve a desired outcome, what exactly is it that you want that person to believe? Bok (1978) suggests that the speaker wants the listener to believe something that the speaker herself does not believe. But the speaker might want to influence the listener's mind in several ways.

First, the speaker might want to influence the listener's *belief about the truth of the statement.* So, by saying something false the speaker might want the listener to remain *ignorant* of the true situation. He or she might also want the listener to be led to a *false belief,* that is, to represent the information in the statement as being a true statement of affairs. In addition he or she might want the listener to accept the statement as being a true statement rather than false; that is, to *believe* it rather than *disbelieve* or reject it. So the speaker may intend to affect the listener's mind in one or all of these ways. The speaker might not only have an intention about the listener's *belief* of the *statement.* She might also have an intention about the listener's *belief* of her own *intention* or *belief.* This sounds complicated, but put more simply, the liar wants to convey truthful intention. She wants to convey that she herself believes this statement and has a serious and sincere intention in uttering it. So it is not whether the listener believes the truth of the statement that is the central concern to the speaker but whether the listener believes the truthfulness of the speaker.

Chisholm and Feehan's (1977) definition of "intent to deceive" rests on this higher-level definition: "[the] liar has the intent to deceive the deceived person, not with respect to the statement but with respect to the liar's own state of mind with respect to the statement" (p. 147). Chisholm and Feehan give the following example to illustrate how intent to deceive reflects the speaker's intention about the listener's state of mind:

> A speaker, S, may say to dog D "there is a cat outside," hoping to get rid of the dog but knowing it to be false. Has he lied? Given our definitions, the answer turns on S's own state of mind. If he actually makes his utterance in order to get the dog to believe not only (a) there is a cat outside but also (b) that he has made the utterance in order to cause the dog to believe that he (speaker) believes that there is a cat outside then he has lied to the dog. But it may be that when people utter sentences in the presence of animals they do not intend an end as complex as this and if this is the case they do not lie. (p. 147)

The intention to deceive in Chisholm and Feehan's terms then relies not only on attributing a belief to a listener but on attributing a belief about one's own belief or intention.

To summarize, I started this section by asking what does it mean to lie? The answer to this question depends on the definition you adopt given that different writers emphasize different features of lying and take a different approach as to whether these features form necessary conditions or whether the concept of a lie should be viewed as a prototype. All the same, certain aspects seem to be consistently important across several different definitions. In particular, (a) the speaker's belief (i.e., the speaker's belief that their statement is false) and (b) the speaker's intention to deceive the listener (i.e., the speaker's intention to influence the listener's mental state). In this chapter I have suggested that intention to deceive might function in two ways. First, in terms of the speaker's intention about the listener's *belief* of the *statement* (what the speaker wants the listener to believe about the truth or content of what is said). Second, in terms of the speaker's *intention* about the listener's *belief* of his or her own *intention* or *belief* (what the speaker wants the listener to believe about the speaker's own intention to be truthful).

LEVELS OF LYING

I would now like to propose a classification that incorporates several aspects of the definitions I have reviewed. Following Mitchell's idea of different degrees of deception, I would like to suggest that lying can be considered at different levels or degrees of complexity. My concept of "lying," therefore, is not confined to *intentionally* deceptive messages in the sense used by Bok (1978) and Russow (1986), that is, intention about *belief,* but applies to deceptive messages generally, even those that are not *intentionally* deceptive in the sense used by Bok (1978) and Russow (1986).

At the first level of my analysis, lying is intended in a general sense. The liar wants to achieve some goal or reward by saying something that they *know* or *believe* to be false. Their intention may be to affect either the listener's behavior by this message (Level 1), or to affect the listener's belief (Levels 2 and 3). If the speaker's intention is to influence the listener's belief, then they may either want to influence the other's belief about the *statement* (Level 2) or to influence the other's *belief* about their own *intention* (Level 3).

Becoming a Good Liar

My general suggestion is that children become better at lying as they come to acquire strategies at higher levels. Implicit in this suggestion is some developmental prediction: that children might only be able to apply higher-level strategies once they understand beliefs at different levels. I will look at this possibility in the next section. First, however, I consider how the ability to use lying strategies at higher levels helps the child to become more successful at lying.

Level 1: Manipulating Behavior

As already mentioned, it is possible to *intend* to *mislead* without intending to manipulate another *person's* belief. Animals, for example, often appear to engage in quite complex acts of deception but these acts may simply be reduced to the operation of learned strategies. For example, an animal may simply learn from past experience that a particular type of behavior on their part will lead another animal to go away or turn their head, thereby allowing the deceiver to move in on the desired object that the other animal has neglected.

Children's early "lies" might possibly function at this level. The child who denies a misdeed and blames another or who falsely claims to have done something "good" may do so with the intention to avoid a punishment or receive a reward without actually intending to influence the listener's belief.

As far as children's strategies are concerned it is possible that the child may have many rules that apply in different contexts. For example, "Say 'no'; 'I didn't do it,' 'someone else did it.' " Or simply, if accused of a misdeed, use a generalized strategy such as "Say something that isn't true." So the child may also be able to recognize in a general way that when you say something untrue it can have an effect on the listener in some way, but the child might still not understand the full effect of the false statement on the listener's mind.

Lies at this level might succeed and the strategies might even generalize to new situations, but the chances are that these children will be poor liars because they fail to lie appropriately. They do not consider that their listener will think about either their statement or their intention and as a result they tend to lie at the wrong time or place or neglect to think about other important facts, such as concealing their deception and covering their tracks.

Level 2: Manipulating Belief

At the next level of lying children consider the listener's mental state. In fact it may be difficult to tell whether an act of lying takes place at this level or at the lower level of behavior. One way of testing this is to check whether the incidence of deception is unique and could not have occurred as a learned behavior. But one still needs to be sure that this unique occasion is not simply a fortuitous event with a lucky payoff. In addition it is difficult to tell when children are using a novel strategy. The modification of existing strategy or the use of an old strategy in a new situation does not *necessarily* indicate that the child intends to manipulate beliefs rather than behavior.

However, given that it is possible to intend to bring about a desired outcome by manipulating the listener's belief rather than his or her behavior, there may be different ways in which belief might be assessed:

1. First, the speaker may say false things in order to conceal the truth, in order to prevent people from seeing or knowing something;
2. Second, the speaker may want to ensure that the content of his or her statement is believed by a listener—that they have led the listener to hold a false belief;
3. Finally, the speaker may recognize that the listener not only holds a belief in accordance with the statement but that he or she may evaluate the statement, that is, reject it as being false or accept it as true.

This ability to recognize a listener's belief of a statement enables the child to become a more flexible and successful liar. Now children can keep track of their own deception by recognizing that the deceived listener not only believes the statement but will also act on the basis of his or her new belief and will also evaluate any future statement in the light of their current beliefs.

Level 3: Manipulating Belief About Intention

The third level is an extension of the second but although the second level refers to the speaker's intention about the listener's belief of the statement, the third level refers to belief of the speaker's own state of mind.

At this third level, the liar recognizes that it is not only the statement that is being assessed by the listener but also one's own intention or belief. Children's ability to grasp this level of lying should enable them to become an even more sophisticated liars. The idea is that one can expect to be seen by the listener as having a serious or sincere intention. It is therefore not just the truth of the statement that is at issue but getting the liar to think you are a truthful and sincere person.

This ability enables children to become more manipulative. Once they realize not only that having a truthful intention is more important than saying truthful words but also that they can manipulate other people's perception of their own intention and belief, they can present highly credible stories, giving the impression that they too believe the content. This ability may be the hallmark of subtle acts of tact, persuasion, and diplomacy.

DEVELOPMENTAL STAGES?

How do these ideas square with the developmental literature? Is there any evidence to suggest developmental progression across these three levels of lying? Given recent work in the "theory of mind" area of developmental research, one might predict such steps in development. First, deception by manipulating behavior rather than beliefs might be the first type of lie that children produce up to the age of $3\frac{1}{2}$ to 4. Then from age 4, when children start to understand first-order false beliefs (Wimmer & Perner, 1983), they may begin to lie by taking account of the listener's belief of the statement. Finally, from the age of 7 or so, when they become able to understand second-order beliefs (i.e., John thinks that Mary thinks; Perner, 1988; Perner & Wimmer, 1985) they also become able to take account of listeners' beliefs of their intention to be truthful.

Unfortunately, as yet there is not enough research to draw conclusions about these types of developmental stages. Nevertheless there is some evidence from different sources that might contribute to the overall picture. The first two levels of the analysis: taking account of listener's behavior and taking account of listener's belief are often difficult to distinguish from each other in children's lies and deception. However, some studies do seem to fall into the first level of the analysis and others fit into the second.

Attributing Behavior

Several studies have demonstrated deceptive behavior and lying in children as young as 2. In a recent experiment with 2- to 3-year-olds, for example, Lewis, Stanger, and Sullivan (1989) found that 11 of 29 children lied by denying that they had peeked at a toy in the experimenter's absence. The children who lied in this experiment may have been practicing a learned strategy. They denied a misdeed in order to avoid the reproachful behavior of an adult. Another way children might mislead is by giving false information in order to get another person to do the wrong thing or go to the wrong place. Chandler, Fritz, and Hala (1989) have shown that even 2-year-olds are capable of deceiving in this way. In this study, children erased footprints, laid false trails, and pointed to the wrong place in order to prevent an opponent from getting the treasure in a hiding game. In fact, replication attempts have indicated that these are not novel strategies as children younger than 4 need to be prompted before they acquire such techniques (Sodian, Taylor, Harris, & Perner, 1991). All the same, these results show that very young children are capable of learning behavioral strategies even if they do not yet realize their full significance as attempts to deceive.

Attributing Beliefs

Perner (1991) describes some recent studies that have attempted to test deception in terms of the listener's belief (Peskin, 1989; Russell, Mauthner and Tidswell, 1991; Sodian, 1991). Russell et al.'s study was also done with autistic children who, as a group, are extremely poor at lying and deception. The overall result for all three studies was that 3-year-olds (and autistic children) showed very poor performance in their attempts to deceive, whereas by the age of 4 to 5 the majority of children were successfully applying deceptive strategies. This then seems to fit the analysis that certain strategies of deception will emerge at the same time as the ability to attribute first-order beliefs.

Each of these studies involved a game in which a "competitive" person or puppet wanted to take or steal a desirable object. The child knew about the person's motive beforehand, either by being told that they would try to take it or by the experience of seeing them take it on previous occasions. The child's job was to devise a deceptive strategy to fool the opponent. In each study the successful strategy was to give the wrong information by pointing to the wrong object or location.

The fact that all these studies demonstrated that 3-year-olds were very poor "liars" by always pointing to the true place while the 4- and 5-year-olds were much better deceivers, shows that something is going on at this age. What is it? By manipulating information in order to thwart a competitor's action does the child recognize that wrong information leads not only to wrong action but also to wrong beliefs? How far do they recognize the informational effects of their message on the listener?

One possibility is that older children may just be using a generalized strategy based on the opponent's "bad" motive. The strategy would be that "people who are described negatively (or who act in an uncooperative way) take advantage of you or the situation. Saying something wrong to them reduces this probability and prevents their bad behavior. The same strategy, however, need not apply to friendly people whose behavior is good anyway. Is it possible that children were using such a strategy without considering the listener's belief? This seems unlikely, given Sodian's (1991) finding that younger children were so much better at "sabotage" (i.e., physically doing something to prevent someone with a bad motive stealing the object) than at deceit (i.e., saying something to prevent that person stealing the object). This shows that there is something especially difficult about deceitful communications for 3-year-olds. All the same, both strategies, that is, physical sabotage and communicative pointing are aimed at affecting the person's behavior. The purpose is to stop them getting the object. So perhaps younger children find it easier to manipulate behavior directly, by physical force, than indirectly, using communication.

Despite this reservation, it is still striking that children's ability to use deceptive strategies appears within a specific age period, rather than gradually. These studies also found a strong correspondence between children's use of a deceptive strategy and their performance on a test of false beliefs, which does suggest that children who use deceptive strategies also recognize the effect of their false message on their opponent's beliefs.

If children are taking account of a listener's beliefs in these studies then it is interesting to look at what it was about the listener's belief that children had to take account of. Was the child trying to conceal something from another's sight or knowledge, trying to cause the other person to have a false belief or trying to get the deceived person to believe that their communication was "true"? It is difficult to tell exactly what effect the child expected to have on the opponent's mind by giving false information. That is, what *kind* of representation the child thinks the false statement will lead to in the other's mind. The 5-year-old presumably, by pointing to the wrong place, did not want the opponent to know the real place. The child may also have wanted the opponent to have a false belief, to get them to think that the object was at the place where they pointed. Did the child also expect the other person to evaluate the statement as being true rather than false?

It is worth pointing out that there may be a difference between what the child *intends* another to *believe* and what he or she *understands* about another's beliefs. What the child actually intended the other person to believe at the time of the deception might be a different matter from what the child *recognizes* that the opponent believes as a result of the false message. So children may learn to deceive by using strategies such as "say something wrong to prevent someone from taking something." They might not need to represent the other person's beliefs or their evaluation of the truth of the message when they say this on any particular occasion. Nevertheless, once children can understand beliefs, they can recognize the effect of their lie on the listener's mind and realize that the listener's future actions and evaluations will be guided by this.

It is therefore useful to look at children's ability to *understand* a listener's belief outside of their own lying performance to see what children are capable of. Several studies have done this by getting the child to witness someone else being deceived. In these studies, the child observes a person (e.g., a puppet or doll) being told something false by another person and the child then has to judge what the deceived person will believe as a result of hearing the false message.

Several studies have used a modified form of the false belief task (Wimmer & Perner, 1983) to test this understanding. In one study (Leekam, 1988), 4- and 5-year-olds watched a play in which an object (e.g., chocolate) is hidden in the absence of a protagonist. On her return the protagonist is told that the object is in the wrong place. Children's understanding of the protagonist's belief of this false statement was tested in two ways. First, by asking them what the protagonist would *think* as a result of the message, that is, "where will the protagonist think the chocolate is?". Second by asking them how the protagonist would evaluate it; that is, whether he or she will *think* the statement is *true*. Children had to make judgments about an *ignorant* listener who would accept the statement and believe it. They also had to make judgments about a *knowing* listener who had just discovered the object's true location immediately before the false message. This listener should therefore disbelieve the statement.

The results showed that both 4- and 5-year-olds were able to assess the protagonist's belief both in terms of where she would *think* the object was and whether she would *think* the statement *true*. They understood that this listener would reject the information in the false message if she knows the truth but accept it if she doesn't. Although most children of both ages gave correct answers to both questions, they found questions about whether a listener *thinks* a statement is *true* more difficult than a question about *what* someone would think as a result of a false message. Other research suggests that this difficulty in assessing a listener's evaluation of the truth, that is, whether the listener will believe or disbelieve the truth of a statement, may persist through to age 6, and may create difficulties for 6- to 8-year-olds when they make moral judgments about a speaker (Leekam & Perner, 1990).

So far I have talked about the 4- and 5-year-olds' ability to understand a listener's belief of a false message. What about 3-year-olds? This is an important age group to look at, given the findings of deception studies I reported earlier showing that 3-year-olds are poor liars. Many previous studies have now shown that 3-year-olds cannot infer false beliefs and the close correspondence between ability to deceive and ability to attribute a false belief at the age of 4 to 5 does indicate that these abilities are related.

A recent study by Roth (1990), however, suggests that things might be different when it comes to inferring false beliefs conveyed in conversation. Roth tested 3- to 4-year-olds (2;9 to 4;0 years), 5- to 6-year-olds and a group of autistic children on a similar task to the one just described. In Roth's task, children watched a play about a story protagonist. Yosi, who was told by a liar, Rina, that a missing bar of chocolate was in the dog's kennel, although Rina had really hidden it in a box. Children were then asked where the deceived person, Yosi, will now think the chocolate is. Roth found that 5-year-olds (93%) and even 3-year-olds (72%) correctly predicted that Yosi would think the chocolate is in the kennel where the liar Rina said it was. In contrast, autistic children gave "reality-based" responses, answering that the deceived person would think that the chocolate was really in the box.

These results are interesting because they show that autistic children are different even from 3-year-olds in their attribution of beliefs. Do the results also show that 3-year-olds understand false beliefs? When children predict that Yosi will think the same as Rina says do they understand that Yosi has a false belief? One way to check whether they simply see Yosi's belief as a copy of the statement is to ask about the belief of someone else who knows the statement is false. Roth found that when children were asked about the belief of the liar herself (who hid the chocolate, so therefore knew where it was), hardly any of the 3-year-olds but most of the 5-year-olds gave correct answers. Nearly all the 3-year-olds therefore made what appears to be the copy-type error of prediction that even the liar would think the chocolate was where he said it was. However, when children were asked about the belief of an observer who watched where the chocolate was hidden, but was not part of the lying interaction (Experiment 2), most of the 3-year-olds (89%) and 5-year-olds (84%) gave correct answers. These intriguing results might suggest that at 3 children see "beliefs" as directly corresponding with different types of external information. This external information may be *either* reality or what people say. The interesting thing though is why they should give higher priority to the false statement when it comes to judging what the *liar* believes rather than anyone else who knew the truth. Roth suggests that 3-year-olds have difficulty understanding the relationship between two aspects: the liar's intention to lie and the liar's belief of the truth. The liar *knows* the truth but *intends* to say something false in order to keep the chocolate.

To summarize this section on children's attribution of belief: It is difficult to establish exactly when the strategies that children use to manipulate *behavior* change into strategies to manipulate *beliefs*. This is partly because the same deceptive act can have different levels of interpretation. For example, if A gives a false message to B, A might want B to: turn away, *look* away, not *see,* not *know,* have a false *belief, believe* that what is said is *true.* In addition, the use of deceptive strategy does not always entail *intention* or influence *belief* at the time of the deception. Nevertheless, children's deceptive strategies do seem to reflect an underlying understanding of beliefs. My suggestion is that the emerging ability to understand false beliefs at age 4 will assist children in their lying efforts and with understanding the implications of lying. The work on children's understanding of a listener's belief indicates that by 4 or 5 ys children understand the effects of a false message on a listener's mind, recognizing that the listener will interpret and evaluate a statement in the light of their existing knowledge.

Attributing Beliefs About Intentions

Having discussed the second stage of my analysis of lying, I should now like to look at the third level in which attribution of beliefs about intentions are involved. Unfortunately, unlike the studies of deceptive pointing mentioned earlier, there seem to be no studies that test children's ability to manipulate another's belief about their own intention. One problem for the design of such a study would be to ensure that deception is due only to this higher-level attribution and not to anything else.

One might argue that there are very few instances of deception that are actually aimed at such a complex attribution in real life anyway. But the ability to assess belief about intention is not irrelevant to everyday life. People's belief and disbelief of a statement usually depends on their background knowledge about the speaker's intention. Even if a listener has no background knowledge about the truth of a statement they might disbelieve it because they suspect that the speaker has an untruthful intention. We often doubt the truthfulness of a speaker without any prior knowledge of the actual truth content of their statement. Likewise a listener might disbelieve the truth of a statement but still believe that the mistaken speaker has a truthful intention, that they intend to tell the truth. So in order to become a good liar the child needs to learn not only that the listener should believe what you say but also that they should believe your intention or belief.

Research on children's understanding of higher-order mental states might give us some insights on what children are capable of in terms of this kind of attribution. Unfortunately most of the work examines children's understanding of beliefs about beliefs and intention about beliefs rather than beliefs about intentions.

Perner and Wimmer (1985) showed that understanding beliefs about beliefs emerges between the age of 6 and 8. Their test involved attributing second-order false beliefs, that is, "John mistakenly thinks that Mary believes." Perner and Wimmer found that only approximately one third of 5-year-olds and one half of 6-year-olds could do this. In a series of studies on children's ability to distinguish jokes and lies, I also looked at children's understanding of second-order intentions "John wants his mother to think" (Leekam, 1990). Results showed that most 5-year-olds (69%, Experiment 3; 87%, Experiment 4) could attribute an intention about belief. A study with Ellen Winner (Winner & Leekam, 1991) also shows that most 5- to 7-year-olds can distinguish white lies from irony when asked about the speaker's intentions about the listener's belief.

From these studies we might predict that children should engage in the third level of lying, taking account of belief about intention and should be able to do this from the age 5 or 6 and up. Given that the deceptive pointing studies I mentioned earlier also show that these strategies are also not perfected until 5 it is possible that the two levels of lying I have proposed do not in fact constitute two separate developmental states. Once children understand the listener's belief of a statement they also understand the listener's belief of a speaker's intention to be truthful. More research is needed to establish this and in particular a specific study needs to be done of children's understanding of beliefs about intentions to test the limits of children's understanding.

It is also important to clarify the analysis of this third level of lying. Chisholm and Feehan's definition seems to turn on the speaker's intention to influence the listener's belief about the speaker's own *state of mind* with respect to the statement. So what seems to be at stake is the speaker's attitude toward the statement. The speaker pretends to have a serious attitude or commitment toward the statement. This analysis has a similarity to a recent analysis of irony proposed by Sperber and Wilson (1981) and Kaufer (1981), the difference being that the lying speaker intends to convey a serious, sincere attitude toward a proposition, whereas the ironic speaker intends to convey a nonserious or derogatory attitude toward it.

This distinction between lying and irony helps to highlight this higher-level aspect of intent to deceive. I mention it because I think it may be possible to construct a less complex analysis of "higher-order belief understanding," making a kind of shortcut or simplified analysis. My suggestion is that instead of considering the listener's belief about the speaker's own state of mind (intention, belief, or attitude) toward the statement, one could simply consider the listener's belief of the speaker's motive.

In other words, perhaps what needs to be considered by the speaker is whether the listener will believe the speaker's *motive,* that is, what he or she really wants to achieve or hide by saying something false. This might be something tangible or some specific objective. Or it might be something more abstract, such as wanting to give a particular impression or wanting to convey a particular attitude or feeling toward the other person. Or it might involve both these things, that is, wanting to convey a friendly attitude in order to achieve some other objective. My point is that what the speaker wants to convey, what they want the listener to believe, is their motive or their attitude to another person, rather than specifically their attitude toward the content of a statement.

BELIEVING AND DECEIVING

In looking at how children might become good liars I have suggested that understanding believing helps children to become good at deceiving. Although children may achieve much by using deceptive strategies to manipulate behavior, once they are able to understand belief from age 4 this enables them to become even more adept at lying. The ability to recognize that a listener will have a belief not only about the truth of the statement but also about the truthfulness of the speaker is a further achievement, which may be the key to mastering more subtle acts of deception, tact, and diplomacy.

Although I have framed this analysis in developmental terms by looking at whether lying strategies appear at different levels of understanding the mind, two of the levels I constructed, that is, Level 2, the speaker's intention about the listener's belief of the statement, and Level 3, the speaker's intention about the listener's belief of the speaker's intention—might not constitute two distinct levels developmentally. Instead, from around age 5, children may have a grasp of both kinds of belief attribution. When lying or recognizing lies in others, 5-year-olds may understand that a listener can be deceived in two ways: first, by believing the content of the statement, and second by believing the apparently sincere attitude of the speaker. Such ability, I suggest, may not require the need to consider the speaker's attitude towards the truth content of the statement itself but simply to recognize the speaker's ulterior motive.

ACKNOWLEDGMENTS

I am very grateful to Sylvia Turner and Josef Perner and to the Laboratory of Experimental Psychology for helping me to make this chapter possible. I also wish to thank Daniel Roth for his very helpful comments on an earlier draft.

REFERENCES

Bennett, J. (1991). How to read minds in behavior: A suggestion from a philosopher. In A. Whiten (Ed.), *Natural theories of mind: The evolution, development and simulation of everyday mind-reading* (pp. 97–108). Oxford: Blackwell.

Bok, S. (1978). *Lying: Moral choices in public and private life.* New York: Pantheon.

Byrne, R. W., & Whiten, A. (1991). Computation and mindreading in primate tactical deception. In A. Whiten (Ed.), *Natural theories of mind: The evolution, development and simulation of everyday mindreading* (pp. 127–141). Oxford: Blackwell.

Chandler, M., Fritz, A. S., & Hala, S. (1989). Small scale deceit: Deception as a marker of 2-, 3-, and 4-year-olds' early theories of mind. *Child Development, 60,* 1263–1277.

Cheyney, D. L., & Seyfarth, R. M. (1991). In A. Whiten (Ed.), *Natural theories of mind: The evolution, development and simulation of everyday mindreading* (pp. 175–194). Oxford: Blackwell.

Chisholm, R. M., & Feehan, T. D. (1977). The intent to deceive. *Journal of Philosophy, 74*(3), 143–159.

Coleman, L., & Kay, P. (1981). Prototype semantics: The English word "lie." *Language, 57,* 26–44.

Kaufer, D. S. (1981). Understanding ironic communication. *Journal of Pragmatics,* 495–510.

Krout, M. H. (1931). The psychology of children's lies. *Journal of Abnormal Psychology, 26,* 1–27.

Leekam, S. R. (1988). *Children's understanding of intentional falsehood.* Unpublished doctoral dissertation, Laboratory of Experimental Psychology, University of Sussex, England.

Leekam, S. R. (1991). Jokes and lies: Children's understanding of intentional falsehood. In A. Whiten (Ed.), *Natural theories of mind: The evolution, development and simulation of everyday mindreading* (pp. 159–174). Oxford: Blackwell.

Leekam, S. R., & Perner, J. (1990). *Belief and disbelief: Children's judgments of listener belief and speaker intention.* Unpublished manuscript, University of Sussex, England.

Lewis, M., Stanger, C., & Sullivan, M. (1989). Deception in 3-year-olds. *Developmental Psychology, 25,* 439–443.

Mitchell, R. W. (1986). A framework for discussing deception. In R. W. Mitchell & N. S. Thompson (Eds.), *Deception: Perspectives on human and non-human deceit* (pp. 3–40). Albany: State University of New York Press.

Perner, J. (1988). Higher-order beliefs and intentions in children's understanding of social interaction. In J. Astington, P. Harris, & D. R. Olson (Eds.), *Developing theories of mind* (pp. 271–294). New York: Cambridge University Press.

Perner, J. (1991). *Understanding the representational mind.* Cambridge, MA: MIT Press.

Perner, J., & Wimmer, H. (1985). "John thinks that Mary thinks that . . ." Attribution of second-order beliefs by 5–10-year-old children *Journal of Experimental Child Psychology, 39,* 437–471.

Peskin, J. (1989). *Concealing one's intentions: The development of deceit.* Unpublished manuscript, Centre for Applied Cognitive Science, Ontario Institute for Studies in Education, Toronto.

Roth, D. (1990). *Recognition of intentions conveyed in conversation: Preschool children vs autistics.* Unpublished master's thesis, Tel Aviv University, Israel.

Russell, J., Mauthner, N., Sharpe, S., & Tidswell, T. (1991). The "windows task" as a measure of strategic deception in preschoolers and autistic children. *British Journal of Developmental Psychology, 9*(2), 331–349.

Russow, L. M. (1986). Deception: A philosophical perspective. In R. W. Mitchell & N. S. Thompson (Eds.), *Deception: Perspectives on human and non-human deceit.* Albany: State University of New York Press.

Siegler, F. A. (1966). Lying. *American Philosophical Quarterly, 3*(2), 128–136.

Sodian, B. (1991). The development of deception in young children. *British Journal of Developmental Psychology, 9*(1), 173–188.

Sodian, B., Taylor, C., Harris, P. L., & Perner, J. (1991). *Early deception and the child's theory of mind: False trails and genuine markers. Child Development, 62,* 468–483.

Sperber, D., & Wilson, D. (1981). Irony and the use/mention distinction. In P. Cole (Ed.), *Radical pragmatics* (pp. 295–319). New York: Academic Press.

Wimmer, H., & Perner, J. (1983). Beliefs about beliefs: Representation and constraining function of wrong beliefs in young children's understanding of deception. *Cognition, 13,* 103–128.

Winner, E., & Leekam, S. R. (1991). Distinguishing irony from deception: Understanding the speaker's second-order intention. *British Journal of Developmental Psychology, 9*(2), 257–270.

5

Sex, Lies, and Smiling Faces: A Brief Report on Gender Differences in 3-Year-Olds' Deceptions

Georgia N. Nigro
Andrea L. Snow
Bates College

Lying and smiling are ubiquitous features of human intercourse; their co-occurrence may be less frequent than either alone, but no less interesting. Psychologists who study the coincidence of smiles and lies have concentrated on the smiles of liars. For example, Ekman, Friesen, and O'Sullivan (1988) discovered subtle differences among smiles that signaled when adults told the truth or lied about experiencing pleasant feelings. When they actually enjoyed themselves, adults displayed smiles that implicated the outer muscle around the eyes; when they feigned enjoyment, their smiles contained traces of the muscular activity associated with disgust, fear, contempt, or sadness. Using a coarser-grained analysis, Saarni (1984) found that when children of different ages were asked to look pleased despite receiving a disappointing gift, older children (especially girls) were more likely to smile than younger children (especially boys). Although these studies tell us little about the natural co-occurrence of smiling when lying, they do point to smiling as a complicated component of the expressive behavior of liars.

Equally complicated may be the smiling of targets of lies and the effects of this smiling on liars. Targets may smile for many reasons: to express pleasure, to be polite, to register suspicion, to cover up boredom. The list could go on. In the present study, we examined one very common situation in which a target may smile, namely, the situation in which an adult questions a child about a possible transgression. As is seen here, whether or not an adult smiled when asking if a child had transgressed made a difference in whether or not the child lied. But the difference was not a simple one; it depended critically on the child's gender.

A gender difference in the lying of 3-year-olds, reported by Lewis, Stanger, and Sullivan (1989), was the impetus for the present study. In that study, 3-year-olds were instructed not to peek at a toy while the experimenter left the room. Most (all but 4 out of 33) did peek. When later asked if they had peeked, the great majority of the 3-year-olds either denied that they had peeked (38%) or would not answer the question (24%). Boys were significantly more apt than girls to admit to their transgression. Of the children who admitted they had peeked, 82% were boys. Of the children who denied that they had peeked, 73% were girls. Of those who would not respond verbally, 71% were girls. Looking at the data another way, only 13% of girls admitted to their transgression, whereas 64% of the boys did so. Thus, even though girls were no more likely than boys to transgress, they were significantly more likely than boys to deny their transgression. Why?

Lewis, Stanger, and Sullivan (1989) offered two possible reasons. One was that girls might have been more ashamed or embarrassed about their transgression than boys and therefore less likely to admit it. In support of this possibility, they noted research indicating a higher incidence of shame and embarrassment in girls than boys (H. Lewis, 1971; Lewis, Sullivan, Stanger, & Weiss, 1989). But if shame or embarrassment were the cause of girls' reluctance to admit, why was there no gender difference in peeking? In fact, Lewis, Stanger, and Sullivan found that girls were somewhat less likely to transgress than boys (three girls to one boy did not peek), but the difference was not statistically significant.

The other possibility that Lewis, Stanger, and Sullivan (1989) mentioned was that girls, being more interested in social approval than boys (Block, 1978; Huston, 1983), were less likely to admit that they peeked because such an admission would occasion disapproval from the adult experimenter. By this account, girls were more deceptive than boys because of their greater need for social desirability or, perhaps, their greater fear of punishment.

We tested these two possibilities in a study of 60 children (30 boys and 30 girls) between the ages of 32 and 39 months (M age = 35.6 months). All were from lower- and middle-class Caucasian families and were seen individually in the laboratory. The study had two conditions. In both, a female experimenter escorted children and parents to the laboratory. Parents were seated with their backs to their child and asked to fill out a questionnaire about childhood lying. Children were seated with their backs to a small table and told by the experimenter that she was going to put a surprise toy on the table and leave the room for a moment. The experimenter instructed the children not to peek at the toy while she was gone. She then left the room, returning either when the child peeked or after 5 minutes had passed. Meanwhile, the children were observed and videotaped through a one-way mirror by a second experimenter.

Up until this point, our procedure resembled that of Lewis, Stanger, and Sullivan (1989). Likewise, in one of our conditions, the experimenter behaved like theirs upon returning to the room. She walked in, stood in front of the child, stared with a neutral expression on her face for 5 seconds, and then asked, "Did you peek?". If the child did not respond, he or she was asked again. After waiting about 5 seconds, the experimenter reassured children that it was okay to peek and invited them to play with the toy.

In our other condition, the experimenter behaved differently upon returning to the room. She walked in, stood in front of the child, smiled for 5 seconds, and then asked, "Did you peek?" If the child did not respond, he or she was asked a second time by the smiling experimenter. After waiting about 5 seconds, the experimenter reassured children that it was okay to peek and invited them to play with the toy.

The inclusion of the smile condition allowed us to test the two possibilities for the gender difference in deception described earlier. With the additional number of subjects required by the second condition, we were in a good position to see whether the tendency for girls to resist peeking, noted by Lewis, Stanger, and Sullivan (1989), would emerge more strongly, suggesting that a gender difference in shame or embarrassment about transgressing was at work. If, indeed, girls feel shame or embarrassment about violating a rule and therefore are more ashamed or embarrassed to admit their transgression, fewer girls than boys should peek at the toy in the first place. With the addition of the smile condition, we also stood to learn whether a gender difference in the need for social approval was at work. If girls in the original (stare) condition feared punishment or loss of the experimenter's approval, then the smile condition should mitigate their concerns and thereby increase the number of girls who admit to their transgression. In view of Ceci, Ross, and Toglia's (1987) finding that 3- and 4-year-olds were less susceptible to leading questions from another child than from an adult, we expected that 3-year-olds who feared punishment or disapproval would experience less worry and consequently lie less frequently when interrogated by a smiling rather than a staring visage.

The results were unambiguous. All but three of the children peeked at the toy, confirming Lewis, Stanger, and Sullivan's (1989) contention that most children this age will violate such a rule if left alone. Although two of the resisters were girls and one a boy, the numbers were too small to provide any support for the hypothesis that girls are too ashamed or embarrassed to violate the rule. Twenty-eight of the 30 girls peeked.

Turning next to the 57 children who peeked at the toy, we found that of the 29 subjects who violated the rule in the stare condition, 34% said "yes" they did look, 52% said "no" they did not look, and 14% gave no verbal or nonverbal response. Of the 28 subjects who violated the rule in the smile condition, 39% said "yes" they did look, 57% said "no" they did not look, and 4% gave no response. Thus the two conditions yielded roughly the same numbers of admitters and deniers, with slightly more children willing to answer the question when smiled at than when a stare accompanied the query. Whereas our numbers for admitters compared favorably with Lewis, Stanger, and Sullivan's (1989), we had more deniers and fewer children unwilling to respond than they did. We speculate that any number of differences between experimenters could be responsible.

Gender differences in the two conditions were clearly observed. In the stare condition, 80% of the peekers who admitted were boys; 67% of the peekers who denied were girls. The children who did not respond were equally divided between girls and boys. Whereas 53% of the boys who peeked admitted to their transgression, only 14% of the girls did so. Whereas 71% of the girls who peeked denied their transgression, only 33% of the boys did so. Boys and girls were equally likely to give no response (13% and 14%, respectively).

The smile condition produced strikingly different results. Of the peekers who admitted in this condition, 73% were girls; of the peekers who denied, 62% were boys. The one child who did not respond to the smiling query was a boy. Whereas 57% of the girls who peeked admitted to their transgression, only 21% of the boys did so. Whereas 71% of the boys who peeked denied their transgression, only 43% of the girls did so. Boys and girls were equally likely to give no response (7% and 0%, respectively).

The anticipated result emerged: When girls were questioned with a smiling countenance, they were much more likely to admit their transgression than when questioned with a stare. More surprising was the finding that when boys were questioned with a staring countenance, they were much more likely to admit that they had peeked than when queried with a smile. That children would use the emotional expressions of others to guide their response to a situation is not surprising. Ten-month-old infants will refer to their mother's facial expression before engaging with a strange person (Feinman & Lewis, 1983), and 1-year-olds will look to a familiarized stranger before reacting to an unusual toy (Klinnert, Emde, Butterfield, & Campos, 1986). That 3-year-old boys and girls would differ in their behavioral responses to a stranger's facial expressions is also not very surprising. As Malatesta, Culver, Tesman, and Shepard (1989) put it, children probably receive a "continuing program of gender-differentiated tuition in the use of affective expressions" (p. 51). Mothers of 3- to 6-month-old infants smile more at their daughters (Malatesta & Haviland, 1982); mothers of 2-year-olds show greater expressivity to girls than to boys (Malatesta et al., 1989). By the time children are 30–35 months old, their mothers discuss emotional aspects of the past differently, depending on the gender of the child (Fivush, 1989). With daughters, mothers focus on positive emotions, such as happiness and fun, while avoiding altogether the topic of anger. With sons, mothers talk equally about positive and negative emotions. By the time children reach age 4, they know the stereotypes about gender differences in emotionality (Birnbaum, Nosanchuk, & Croll, 1980). Although we are still a long way from understanding the gender difference in children's deceptive responses to a smile or stare, we can see the broad outlines of an explanation here.

Our account of this gender difference in deception is a contextual one (Deaux

& Major, 1987). Although there may be some stable gender differences in lying,[1] it is more likely that such differences are variable and context-dependent. Burton (1976) came to a similar conclusion about cheating years ago. Noting that in some studies girls cheated more than boys (e.g., Hartshorne & May, 1928), whereas in other boys cheated more than girls (e.g., Walsh, 1967), he observed that interactions often qualified the gender differences found. For example, in one study, Burton (1971) found that children cheated more in the presence of a same-sex than an opposite-sex experimenter.

In a more recent review of the literature, Stouthamer-Loeber (1986) reached a different conclusion about lying. Citing studies in which adult perceptions provided the measure of lying, she concluded that boys lied more than girls. She and Burton may both be right: Adults may believe that boys lie more than girls, whereas the behavior of girls and boys may sometimes prove them wrong. More importantly, adult perceptions may play a role in the genesis and maintenance of lying in children: To the extent that expectations influence gender-related behaviors (Deaux & Major, 1987), adult beliefs about boys' and girls' lying may be powerful proximal cues to children in moments of temptation.

The status of the deception studied here remains uncertain. Flanagan (this volume) and others have pointed out that when children deny peeking at a forbidden toy, they may be misleading the experimenter—trying to avoid punishment, but not intending to create a false belief in the other—or they may be lying, with the intention of creating a false belief. The present results do not allow us to tease apart these two possibilities (see Leekam, this volume), but they are suggestive. That the different emotional tones of a query led to different responses in 3-year-olds suggests that the children lied to avoid punishment. Even when children develop the ability to lie with the intention of creating a false belief, they may still tell lies in order to avoid punishment (Bussey, this volume). Thus the avoidance of punishment may figure in many situations in which telling the truth is in question, opening the door to the kinds of emotional influence described here. We do not expect that the simple manipulation used here would affect older children and adults, but we think that emotions will prove to be an important element in our understanding of the cognitive and social influences on deception and its development. Ours is a small step toward that understanding.

REFERENCES

Birnbaum, D. W., Nosanchuk, T. A., & Croll, W. L. (1980). Children's stereotypes about sex differences in emotionality. *Sex Roles, 6,* 435–443.

---

[1]Some feminists have borrowed the expression "telling it slant" from Emily Dickinson to describe a way of speaking that they believe is forced upon women in a male-dominated society. See Michell (1984) for an analysis of this form of lying.

Block, J. H. (1978). Another look at sex differentiation in the socialization behaviors of mothers and fathers. In J. Sherman & F. L. Denmark (Eds.), *The psychology of women: Future directions of research* (pp. 54–68). New York: Psychological Dimensions.

Burton, R. V. (1971). Correspondence between behavioral and doll-play measures of conscience. *Developmental Psychology, 5,* 320–332.

Burton, R. V. (1976). Honesty and dishonesty. In T. Lickona (Ed.), *Moral development and behavior* (pp. 173–197). New York: Holt, Rinehart, & Winston.

Ceci, S. J., Ross, D. F., & Toglia, M. P. (1987). Suggestibility of children's memory: Psycholegal implications. *Journal of Experimental Psychology: General, 116,* 38–49.

Deaux, K., & Major, B. (1987). Putting gender into context: An interactive model of gender-related behavior. *Psychological Review, 94,* 369–389.

Ekman, P., Friesen, W. V., & O'Sullivan, M. (1988). Smiles when lying. *Journal of Personality and Social Psychology, 54,* 414–420.

Feinman, S., & Lewis, M. (1983). Social referencing at ten months: A second-order effect on infants' responses to strangers. *Child Development, 54,* 878–887.

Fivush, R. (1989). Exploring sex differences in the emotional content of mother–child conversations about the past. *Sex Roles, 20,* 675–691.

Hartshorne, H., & May, M. A. (1928). *Studies in the nature of character: Vol 1. Studies in deceit.* New York: Macmillan.

Huston, A. C. (1983). Sex typing. In P. H. Mussen (Series Ed.) & E. M. Hetherington (Vol. Ed.), *Handbook of child psychology: Vol. 4. Socialization, personality, and social development* (4th ed., pp. 387–468). New York: Wiley.

Klinnert, M. D., Emde, R. N., Butterfield, P., & Campos, J. J. (1986). Social referencing: The infant's use of emotional signals from a friendly adult with mother present. *Developmental Psychology, 22,* 427–432.

Lewis, H. (1971). *Shame and guilt in neuroses.* New York: International University Press.

Lewis, M., Stanger, C., & Sullivan, M. W. (1989). Deception in 3-year-olds. *Developmental Psychology, 25,* 439–443.

Lewis, M., Sullivan, M. W., Stanger, C., & Weiss, M. (1989). Self-development and self-conscious emotions. *Child Development, 60,* 146–156.

Malatesta, C. Z., Culver, C., Tesman, J. R., & Shepard, B. (Eds.). (1989). The development of emotion expression during the first two years of life. *Monographs of the Society for Research in Child Development, 54*(1–2, Serial No. 219).

Malatesta, C. Z., & Haviland, J. M. (1982). Learning display rules: The socialization of emotion expression in infancy. *Child Development, 53,* 991–1003.

Michell, G. (1984). Women and lying: A pragmatic and semantic analysis of "telling it slant." *Women's Studies International Forum, 7,* 375–383.

Saarni, C. (1984). An observational study of children's attempts to monitor their expressive behavior. *Child Development, 55,* 1504–1513.

Stouthamer–Loeber, M. (1986). Lying as a problem behavior in children: A review. *Clinical Psychology Review, 6,* 267–289.

Walsh, R. P. (1967). Sex, age, and temptation. *Psychological Reports, 21,* 625–629.

6

Adults' Liability for Children's "Lie-Ability": Can Adults Coach Children to Lie Successfully?

Carol Satterfield Tate
University of the South

Amye R. Warren
University of Tennessee at Chattanooga

Thomas M. Hess
North Carolina State University

As long as parents have been raising children, the topic of children's lying probably has aroused great interest. Early in the 20th century, children's lying became a focal point for psychological research as well. The classic studies of Hartshorne and May (1928–1930) best exemplify the type of research undertaken during this period. Following this flurry of activity (Hall, 1891; Krout, 1931, 1932; Leonard, 1920; Tudor-Hart, 1926), interest in children's deception per se waned and the focus shifted toward children's moral reasoning abilities (e.g., Piaget, 1932/1965) rather than their moral behavior.

Research on children's deceptive abilities has experienced a recent recrudescence, however. This renewed interest appears to emanate from two distinct sources. The first of these reflects both an extension and continuation of the original theoretical work pertaining to moral reasoning, whereas the second seems to arise from concern over children's possible false allegations of crimes, particularly physical and sexual abuse.

The first question to be asked from either perspective is whether children are capable of lying, and if so, at what age this ability emerges. We must somehow reconcile our conflicting beliefs about "the childish disposition to weave romances and to treat imagination for verity, and . . . the rooted ingenuousness of children and their tendency to speak straightforwardly what is in their minds. . . ." (Wigmore, 1940, p. 160). Although there is some assumption that children are too innocent to lie willfully, especially during testimony (Wakefield & Underwager, 1989), Piaget (1932/1965) believed that children younger than 8 years "spontaneously alter the truth and . . . this seems to [them] perfectly natural and completely harmless" (p. 166). A recent review by Vasek (1986) echoes this bleak opinion of the trustworthiness of children, as she reports that "college students believe that children under 6 are highly prone to be liars, second only to politicians" (p. 285). Whatever popular belief and common knowledge may hold, empirical consensus regarding this opinion heretofore has been lacking.

Theoretically based research has encountered difficulty in establishing a definitive age of emergence for lying. This is partly due to the fact that this approach has grown out of the work of Piaget (1932/1965) and Kohlberg (1963) and thus focuses on children's reasoning about lying (e.g., what children think of accidental lies or falsehoods told by others) rather than on children's production of lies. Although the relation between moral behavior and moral reasoning is complex, current researchers are examining the relation between children's understanding and production of lies.

Illustrative of these efforts are reports from Sodian (1989) and others (e.g., Horgrefe, Wimmer, & Perner, 1986; Moses & Flavell, 1989; Perner, Leekam, & Wimmer, 1987) who find that 3-year-olds have difficulty understanding false beliefs even under very simple task conditions. A child must be able to understand that others are capable of forming a false belief before that child can intentionally attempt to create a false belief through deceptive actions; it follows, therefore, that purposeful deception should be difficult or impossible for children incapable of this type of cognition. Likewise, Sodian's (1989) research supports the idea that even simple deception is extremely difficult for young (3-year-old) children. In both of her studies, preschoolers failed to communicate deceptively (by pointing) even under very conducive conditions. They "do not seem to understand that someone can think something is true that oneself knows to be false" (p. 29).

A recent study seems to contradict the work of Sodian, however. Lewis, Stanger, and Sullivan (1989) also attempted to determine if 3-year-olds are capable of successful deception. These preschool children were left alone in a room with a toy at which they were forbidden to look. The vast majority of the children peeked at the toy and, when asked specifically if they had looked at the forbidden toy, 38% admitted this transgression, whereas 62% attempted to deceive the experimenter. Most of the children who deceived emphatically denied having looked at the forbidden toy (61%), whereas the remaining children (39%) gave no response (i.e., they evaded) when questioned. Thus it would seem that young children are capable of deception under very simple conditions. Chandler, Fritz, and Hala (1989) also found that children as young as $2\frac{1}{2}$ are capable of participating in nonverbal deceptive tasks that are designed to instill false beliefs in others.

According to research conducted from this theoretical perspective, the emergence of lying in children is dependent on their conceptions of lying, which in turn are based on their understanding of beliefs, intent, and other mental functions. Thus, children's deceptive abilities or lack thereof are said to reflect their developing theories of mind (e.g., Horgrefe et al., 1986; Moses & Flavell, 1989; Perner et al., 1987; Sodian, 1989). Although understanding children's theories of mind is a worthy goal in its own right, we fear that this research may have little generalizability to the situation to which many currently attempt to extend it—namely, to children's abilities and tendencies to lie regarding sexual or physical abuse. The moral reasoning/theory of mind perspective is simply too narrow to justify its wholesale application to children's lies of all types, under all conditions.

The first, possibly most obvious problem in generalizing from the previously described research to children's allegations of physical or sexual abuse is the topic of the deceptive act. In the aforementioned studies, children lied to conceal the location of an object from an opponent in a game-playing setting, or about having disobeyed an adult request. These "lies" involved topics that are quite familiar to all children; we could assume that even fairly young children would have a rich knowledge base concerning these topics. For example, even most 2-year-olds have a sufficient knowledge base to deny that they had eaten a forbidden cookie. The same cannot be said for sexual or physical abuse. Indeed, most young children are assumed not to possess sufficient knowledge about sexual activity from which they can generate convincing lies (Ross, Dunning, Toglia, & Ceci, 1990). Thus, younger children's allegations may appear more believable on this count. In fact, social workers tend to use age as one criterion of truthfulness, expecting false allegations from only 2.7% of children who are 3 to 6 years of age but from 15.8% of the children aged 12 to 18 (Everson & Boat, 1986).

Looking specifically at the sexual abuse allegations made by children under 6 years, in contrast to the 2.7% rate expected by social workers, only 1.7% of the cases proved to be false reports (Everson & Boat, 1986). The proportions of false allegations made by older children were higher (4.3% for children aged 6 to 12, and 8% for adolescents), although they did not approach the 15.8% rate expected by the workers. Although these percentages may seem small in comparison with the number of cases that were verified (55%–60%), there are reasons to view these statistics with concern. First, a large number of allegations cannot be categorized as either true or fictitious, and certainly some of these uncategorizable reports may be false. Second, considering that in 1989 alone there were 2.4 million reports of child maltreatment in the United States (DiAngelis, 1990) and that reporting rates are constantly increasing, even 1.7% represents an alarming number of false allegations.

Laypersons, protective service workers, mental health workers, and legal professionals alike protest that these figures are wildly exaggerated, either tragically underestimated or grossly inflated. Bold statements about the veracity of children's allegations are made by expert witnesses in courtrooms almost every day. Some claim that children *never* lie, particularly about sexual abuse, whereas others claim that virtually *all* reports of such abuse are invented.

In response to this controversy, several recent studies have been designed with applications to sexual and physical abuse in mind. The work of Goodman and her colleagues (e.g., Goodman, 1991; Goodman, Aman, & Hirschman, 1987) indicates that children can rarely be led to make erroneous reports involving physical acts that are directed against their own bodies. For example, Goodman and her colleagues found that children were very accurate in their reports of what transpired at a visit to the doctor's office. In fact, according to Goodman, children are overwhelmingly more likely to fail to report such events. In a recent study, Hulse-Trotter (1990) found that children who were suspected of breaking a toy did not invent lies of commission, but either told the truth or omitted information. Peters (1990, 1991) also has found that many children will lie by failing to make identifications in a live lineup, even when they clearly recognize the suspect.

If children do lie about physical acts or sexual abuse, why do they do so? Another failure of the cognitive approach to children's deception has been its neglect of motives for lying. According to Ekman (1989), there are nine basic motivations for lying: to avoid punishment, to get something you couldn't get otherwise, to protect friends from trouble, to protect self or others from harm, to win the admiration of others, to avoid creating an awkward social situation, to avoid embarrassment, to maintain privacy, and to demonstrate power over authority. Other researchers (DePaulo & Jordan, 1982) believe that lies told to escape imminent punishment emerge first, followed by lies aimed at attaining material benefits, and then lies of self-presentation, followed by loyalty lies, and finally altruistic lies. Thus, establishing the age at which children attain the ability to lie depends not only on the cognitive factors of understanding false beliefs, the ability to take another perspective, and the like, but also on the motivation behind the lie. It is no wonder then that the studies discussed previously have failed to identify the *precise* age for emergence of deception as they have ignored a critical factor (i.e., motivation).

More recent applications oriented research has begun to examine children's lying under a variety of motivating conditions (e.g., Ceci, DeSimone, Putnick, Toglia, & Lee, 1990). Preliminary results indicate that even preschool children will lie for a variety of reasons. These researchers found that many young children, when questioned, fail to identify a "loved one" who has broken a toy. Further research needs to be conducted on this intriguing topic. The children in this study were asked not to tell, thus these were not spontaneously generated but externally prompted lies. Unfortunately, in past research such lies have been considered synonymous with internally generated lies.

Children's lies that are prompted, or coached, by another person (typically an adult) usually arise in specific situations. According to Ekman (1989), children's false allegations are "more likely to occur in custody disputes where they are influenced by one parent against another or in mass abuse cases, where the process can encourage bizarre fantasies" (p. 179). Jones and McGraw (1987) conducted a study to examine the underlying causes of false allegations, and found that 80% of the fictitious allegations they investigated were initiated by adults. Indeed, that the child has been told to make a false statement seems to be one of the most common defenses used by those accused of child abuse, underscoring the importance of this issue. In a press conference given at the conclusion of the McMartin Preschool trial, for example, a juror explained one of the reasons why jury members voted to acquit Ray Buckey: They doubted the children's testimony because "[we] couldn't tell if [the children] were repeating what they had been told by their parents, or things they had overheard." In other words, they thought it was possible that the children had been coached in what to say. In general, children are considered less credible witnesses than adults (e.g., Goodman, Bottoms, Herscovici, & Shaver, 1989), possibly because their testimony is believed to be especially susceptible to coaching.

Critics assert that children are frequently manipulated or brainwashed into fabricating (and reporting) events that did not actually transpire (Ekman, 1989) and thereby exaggerate the true number of sexual abuse cases. It is also possible that children who are told to lie by an adult do not realize that they are lying and therefore, are not behaving intentionally. Intentionality refers to whether the deceiver is knowingly creating or perpetuating a false belief in another. Most definitions of lying are based on intent, that is statements or actions conveying false information are only considered to be lies if the speaker/actor is aware of the falsehood and deliberately attempts to deceive another. Although the previously described research has made use of this distinction, the manner in which the distinction should be applied to children's reports of alleged abuse is unclear.

To explore the question of whether young (4- to 6-year-old) children believe that something they are told to say by their parents is the truth, even when it is not, Haugaard and his colleagues (Haugaard, Reppucci, Laird, & Nauful, 1991) conducted an innovative study. In this research, children were shown a videotaped incident wherein a girl lies to a policeman about a neighbor hitting her. They found that the vast majority of the children in their study (94%) understood that the child was lying, even though the child's mother had told (coached) her to do so. Whether or not a child "knows" an allegation to be false may or may not affect the child's ability to produce the allegation. A younger child who does not differentiate between reality and fiction might be unable to intentionally make a false allegation of abuse, but an unintentional false allegation could or would be equally damaging for the accused.

In addition to motive and intentionality, the child's age is an important factor in lying skill. Past researchers have found age differences in deceptive ability with older children tending to be the more successful liars (e.g., DePaulo & Jordan, 1982). Older children are more likely to have the cognitive abilities that are necessary for proficient lying. This cognitive advantage may be diminished if the task itself is made easier, for example by coaching the child. Riggio, Tucker, and Throckmorton (1987) find that adults delivering deceptive messages are more successful when coached (i.e., provided with material from which the message can be constructed). It follows that children may also be more successful deceivers when coached in the lie by an adult (Tate & Warren-Leubecker, 1989, 1990).

Although the recent applications research has begun to deal with various topics of and motives for lying, we believe there are some remaining dimensions of lying that have not yet been taken into account. The manner in which the lie is delivered has been largely overlooked. Does the child generate the lie or has the child been coerced? What mode does the lie take; that of omission or commission? Lies generally take two forms, those of omission and those of commission. A lie of omission would involve behaving as though something that did occur did not, failing to convey known information. Commission, on the other hand, involves generating and conveying false information. Most of the applications directed research has found that children's lies are largely lies of omission (e.g., Goodman et al., 1987; Peters, 1990, 1991). We do need to look beyond these simple categories at the cognitive demands of any particular deceptive act.

Another variable that has been overlooked in past research is the means by which the lie is accomplished. Is the lie delivered verbally or is it an act of physical deception? Although deception is usually achieved through action of some type, in contrast to a lie that is accomplished verbally, little empirical distinction seems to be made between the two. Both deception and lying range in complexity, for example from fibs (a trivial or childish lie) to equivocation (using language with two or more interpretations in order to deceive), but these dimensions have also escaped scrutiny. In order to lie "successfully" in many studies, the child need only respond "yes" or "no" when questioned (cf. Ceci et al., 1990; Lewis et al., 1989). Sometimes children are said to have lied when merely pointing to the incorrect (deceptive) location of a hidden object (Sodian, 1989). Even the relatively complex deception studied by Chandler et al. (1989) did not require the children to engage in verbal deception. False allegations require more verbiage than the types of lying that have been studied to date, at least in preschool children.

Further interpretive problems arise in studies where children are asked directly if they have transgressed (e.g., Lewis et al., 1989), because these responses are probably not intentional actions of deception. Sodian reminds us of the work done by Stern and Stern (1909, as cited in Sodian, 1989) who classified the "no" responses that occurred when young children were accused of forbidden action as "pseudo"-lies. These researchers regarded these "no" responses as affective (fear based) rather than intentionally false statement of fact. Neither the theoretical nor the applied researchers seem to consider whether the lie appears convincing or plausible; all lies are apparently considered to be equal.

Fortunately, there are a few studies wherein more complex verbal lying abilities have been examined. For example, social psychologists DePaulo and Jordan (1982) have reviewed research that investigates the ability of older children and adults to engage in successful deception. These tasks have ranged from convincing someone that a bitter-tasting cracker or drink is actually flavorful to attempting to convince someone that the subject is viewing pleasant rather than discomforting scenes. DePaulo and Jordan reported that the youngest subjects (first graders) were unskilled liars, in that even when they attempted to lie their true emotions "leaked" out in facial expressions, body language, and tone of voice, rendering their lie obvious to their parents and, sometimes, their peers. Likewise, Wimmer and Perner (1983) found little evidence that 4-year-olds are able to construct deceitful utterances. Lewis et al. (1989) also found that clues to the deceptive attempts of their preschool subjects (e.g., nervous touching) did occasionally "leak" through.

AN EMPIRICAL STUDY OF CHILDREN'S LYING

We recently conducted a study to address some of these concerns and to enable us to examine more closely the extent to which children are willing to be coached into giving false descriptions of events, as well as their ability (or lack thereof) to provide convincing coached descriptions. To simulate better the conditions under which false allegations of abuse are made, we felt research was needed wherein children were explicitly asked to lie by an adult, about a specific event and in a specific way, to an adult who does not know whether or not the child is lying. This provides the opportunity for the children to give much more than a simple yes/no answer, and allows comparisons between what they say about what they really did and their accounts of what they only said occurred. Additionally, since lying is a complex verbal ability (de Villiers & de Villiers, 1978) we felt we that we should control for differences in language abilities along with the general cognitive changes expected with age.

Method. The participants in this study were 40 children (20 males and 20 females), ranging in age from approximately $2\frac{1}{2}$ to 8 years of age ($M = 62.2$ months). These children were recruited from a private day-care center. Only children with parental permission were allowed to participate. The participants were divided into two age groups, with the younger group averaging 51 months and the older group averaging 73 months. Half of the children in each age group were randomly assigned to a control group, the other half to the experimental group. There were no significant differences in age between the experimental and control groups.

The children first spent time in small groups playing with one of the primary experimenters in order to habituate them to her presence in the day-care center (although she was already familiar to most of the children as the stepmother of one of their classmates). On the day of the experiment, each child individually accompanied this experimenter (herein to be called the conspirator) to an available space outside the regular classroom. In the room where several plastic animal "nose masks" (e.g., rabbit, shark, pig), two illustrated children's books, a box of magnetic marbles, various plastic farm animals, and a magnetic building toy. From the child's entry into the testing room until the conclusion of the final interview, all interactions were recorded on audiotape.

The conspirator first requested that each child look at one of the picture books with her. This interaction not only allowed the child to become more comfortable with the conspirator but additionally provided a measure of the child's expressive language ability through transcripts of the interaction. At the conclusion of this interaction, the conspirator suggested that she and the child play with toys present in the room. In the control condition, the conspirator and child played with the magnetic marbles, the magnetic building toy, and with the plastic nose masks.

The experimental condition was identical to the control condition, except that the conspirator and child did not play with the magnetic building toy (target toy). In this condition, following free play with the other toys, the conspirator pointed to the target toy and said to the child, "Look at this neat toy. Hey, I know! Let's try and fool my friend. When she comes back, let's pretend we played with this toy. Look at these pictures of the stuff you can build. It's really hard to do, why don't you pick the hardest one. What do you want to tell her we built? (If the child did not select a picture, the conspirator suggested one.) No matter what my friend says, let's say we really did play with it. Let's try to trick her." Before terminating the interaction with the child, the conspirator again rehearsed the child by saying, "What are you going to tell her we did/built?" and cautioned the child "not to forget." The conspirator then left the room.

After a brief delay, the second experimenter (herein to be called the interviewer) then entered the room and asked the child questions such as, "What did you do in school this morning? Did you have fun playing in here?" The interviewer then proceeded to the research questions, saying "Tell me what you did/built" and prompting (when necessary), "Did you play with anything else?" After this free-recall report was obtained, the children were asked specifically about each toy that was present, "Did you play with this?" If they answered affirmatively, they were further asked, "What did you do with it?" Finally, all children were asked, "Is that what you really did?" and "Are you telling me the truth?"

After the interaction, the children who participated in the "trick" assisted the conspirator in debriefing the interviewer. The conspirator told the child, "We'd better tell the interviewer what we really did. You always have to tell the truth." The child then explained the nature of the "trick" and also explained that an attempt had been made to fool the interviewer.

At a later time (either following this interview or on another occasion) the conspirator administered the Peabody Picture Vocabulary Text–Revised (PPVT–R) to measure receptive language skills.

RESULTS

Corresponding to the major questions of interest, the results will be organized as follows. First, do the children go through with the lie? If so, how descriptive are they? And finally, how are their descriptions related to their language abilities?

The responses to the questions and demands posed by both experimenters were coded and possible age differences in the frequency of each type of response were investigated. When the conspirator suggested to the 20 children in the experimental group that they "trick" her friend, 5 children hesitated and then agreed, while 15 agreed immediately. Only 12 of these 20 children (8 older, 4 younger) actually carried through with the plan ($p < .06$ age difference). Two children (one younger and one older) immediately told the interviewer the "lie" as she entered the room, as if they were so excited to be part of the "trick" that they could not wait to be asked. For example, one child said, "You know what we did? We played with that game!" Ekman (1989) called this "duping delight." Three older children volunteered the fabricated information during the free-recall part of the questioning, whereas the remaining 7 children had to be asked specifically about the target toy.

Of the 12 liars, one older child spontaneously "confessed" during the specific questioning portion of the interview. When asked, "What did you do with this game?" he replied, "We tricked you!" When asked "Is that what you really did?" one more of the children "confessed" while two evaded answering (and all of the control children stuck to their stories); one child confessed as soon as the interviewer indicated she was finished with the questioning. Thus, 7 children (5 older, 2 younger; 35% of the total) maintained the ruse throughout. We did notice two interesting things about these "nonrepentant 7": First, the 2 children who immediately told the lie without even being asked what they had done in the room were among the 7 children who never confessed. Second, we found it interesting that 71% of the "lying throughout" children were known *well* by the adult conspirator compared with only 13% of the nonliars.

The ability of the children to describe an event that they had not actually experienced was examined by transcribing the children's responses to the questions "Tell me what you did/built" and the prompt, "Did you play with anything else?" (the total of which we termed their free-recall report), and their responses to the specific question "What did you do/build with that toy?" (referring to the target toy that only the control group had actually played with and termed their building report). The transcripts were analyzed for the elaboration of the responses, in terms of number of words, and also in mean length of utterance (MLU), and then compared with the reports of the children who had actually played with the target toy. Although there were no significant group differences in MLU of the free recall report ($p > .24$), an analysis of variance with experimental condition as the grouping variable and the elaboration measure for free-recall report as the dependent variable revealed a significant conditions effect $[F(1,36) = 8.826, p < .005]$. The control group had significantly more elaborate reports (see Table 6.1) than did the fabricators. The same effect was found in response to the more specific question regarding the toy, with the control group averaging more words in their building report than the experimental group $[F(1,28) = 5.6, p < .025]$.

TABLE 6.1
Mean Number of Words Used in
Description of Activity by Condition

	Free Recall	Building Report
Experimental	7.56	8.31
Truth tellers	6.00	0.87
Liars	8.00	8.42
Control	0.00	18.68

Of course the experimental group consists of children who lied as well as those who did *not* attempt to deceive the interviewer. It is possible therefore that the reports of the children who did not lie are dissimilar to the reports of both the control group and the lying children's reports. Thus we divided the experimental group into children who did and did not attempt to lie and reanalyzed the data with three groups (liars, nonliars, control). The condition effect for the elaboration of free-recall reports was still present $[F(2,36) = 4.979, p < .012]$. The children who were asked to lie but did not had the shortest free-recall reports when compared with the liars or the control group (see Table 6.1). The condition effect on the elaboration of the building report also remained significant $[F(2,37) = 10.04, p < .0001]$. This is unsurprising because the children who did not attempt to lie did not have responses to the specific toy question or as many things to discuss in free recall.

To examine our subjective impression that the older children had been more effective "liars," we eliminated the 8 experimental children who did not attempt to carry through with the trick and then conducted the analyses on the 12 experimental and 20 control children using age as an additional grouping measure. For the free-report elaboration, a significant group effect was again noted $[F(1,27) = 4.558, p < .042]$, and a trend toward an age by group interaction $(p < .06)$, was also observed in which the younger experimental children were quite similar to the younger control children (11 vs. 11.8 words) in their free-recall reports, whereas the older experimental children had significantly shorter reports (6.3 vs. 22 words) than older controls. For the elaboration of the building report the group main effect is still present $[F(1,28) = 5.31, p < .029]$ with the experimental children using significantly fewer words to describe what they built regardless of age. The younger and older experimental children used only approximately 8 words in their descriptions (8.5 and 8.4, respectively), compared with 15.5 and 20 words in the descriptions of the younger and older control group children, respectively.

The descriptions of the experimental and control groups also differed in the number of details the children mentioned in their building reports. When explaining what they had built with the target toy, the experimental group mentioned significantly fewer ($M = 1.45$) details than did the control group ($M = 4.15$) [$F(1,36) = 11.664, p < .002$].

Children's ability to describe events (experienced or not) obviously depends, at least in part, on their verbal skills. Thus we explored the possibility of pre-existing group differences in both receptive (PPVT–R) and expressive language (as evidenced in the transcriptions of the warm-up period). Significant age differences were found in the children's receptive language skills as measured by the raw scores on the PPVT–R [$F(1,34) = 13.28$] with older children having larger receptive vocabularies than the younger children as well as greater expressive language skills as estimated by mean length of utterance [$F(1,38) = 6.089, p < .018$], and by the average length of the five longest utterances [$F(1,38) = 5.38, p < .026$] (see Table 6.2). However, there were no differences between the experimental and control children in either their receptive language abilities ($F < 1.0$), or in expressive language skills [$F(1,36) = 2.508, p < .12$].

In comparing the children's verbal skills with their reports, we found that the raw vocabulary score was unsurprisingly correlated with age (Table 6.3), MLU, and average length of the five longest utterances, but was not significantly correlated with the elaboration of the free-recall report or with the response elaboration to the building report. In contrast, the free-recall report and the building report were significantly correlated. When age was factored out (in this case by using the standard, age-adjusted PPVT scores), no significant relation was seen between receptive vocabulary and elaboration. Expressive language as measured either by MLU or by the average length of the five longest utterances was also correlated with age, and with MLU during free recall, but not significantly correlated with the length of the free-recall report or of the building report. Thus our preliminary results suggest that language abilities are not responsible for much of the variability in report elaboration for this event.

Additional correlations were computed after the children were divided into the three groups mentioned here, the children who were asked to lie, but did not, the children who carried through with the lie, and the control group (Table 6.4). Interestingly, although the correlation between expressive language (as measured by MLU) and the free-recall report was significant for the children who did

TABLE 6.2
Receptive and Expressive Language Means by Age and Condition

	Raw PPVT–R		Total MLU		M 5 Longest	
	Young	Old	Young	Old	Young	Old
Experimental	112.60	113.75	3.77	4.50	8.60	11.42
Truth tellers	110.6	108.0	3.8	3.2	8.8	7.1
Liars	115.5	115.6	3.6	4.8	8.3	12.5
Control	114.89	111.44	3.28	3.97	7.60	9.34

TABLE 6.3
Correlation of Language Measures with Activity Reports

	Age	PPVT	PPVT–Raw	Total Mean	Total MLU	Free Elab	Build Elab
Age	1						
PPVT	.04	1					
PPVT–RAW	.76***	.67***	1				
Total Mean	.40**	.14	.39*	1			
Total MLU	.29	.20	.34*	.81***	1		
Free Elab	.13	.04	.18	.15	.19	1	
Build Elab	.23	−.02	.15	−.12	−.12	.44**	1

*$p < .05$; **$p < .01$; ***$p < .001$.

not lie, and moderate (but not significant) for the control group, there was no relation whatsoever for the children who lied. Considering the small number of children in these analyses, we are hesitant to speculate about the true relation of verbal skills to lying. However, in future research we plan to examine the possibility that the liars are suppressing their usual expressive language abilities.

DISCUSSION

Returning to the major questions this study was designed to answer, we first examined the extent to which children agreed to lie or play a trick at an adult's request. Of the 20 children who were asked to lie, all 20 agreed, although 5 did so with some hesitation. Regarding children's ability to carry through with the lie they were requested to tell, 8 of the 20 children who agreed did not even attempt the lie, 3 children confessed and 2 children evaded during questioning, and 7 carried through with the trick.

Younger and older children appeared equally willing to "go along with" the trick, but older children were more likely actually to carry through with the trick; five of the seven children who carried all the way through with the trick were classified as older children. This age difference is consistent with past research, which has found that older children are more likely to lie (DePaulo & Jordan, 1982). However, the reasons for the older children's tendency to carry through with the trick are unclear. We cannot tell from our results whether it is due to a greater willingness (motive-related) or advanced cognitive ability. That is, we do not know if the older children are more dishonest or whether it is simply easier for them, increasing the likelihood that they will carry through simply because they can.

Regardless of age, the experimental children who carried through with the lie

TABLE 6.4
Correlation of Language Measures with Activity Reports by Group

Liars	Total MLU	Total Mean	Free Elab	Build Elab
Total MLU	1.00			
Total mean	**.75	1.00		
Free elab	−.38	−.18	1.00	
Build elab	−.17	−.06	*.60	1.00

Truth-tellers	Total MLU	Total Mean	Free Elab	Build Elab
Total MLU	1.00			
Total mean	**.87	1.00		
Free elab	*.76	*.79	1.00	
Build elab	.10	−.22	.09	1.00

Control group	Total MLU	Total Mean	Free Elab	Build Elab
Total MLU	1.00			
Total mean	***.81	1.00		
Free elab	*.45	*.36	1.00	
Build elab	−.10	−.05	.22	1.00

$*p < .05; **p < .01; ***p < .001.$

provided significantly shorter descriptions of their activities than did the control children. There are many possible explanations for the liars' brief reports. The first, of course, is that they simply had less to say because they had not actually experienced the event. Another explanation comes from Piaget's work on children's judgments of lies, in which 6- to 10-year-olds used the length and plausibility of statements in making their determinations, with one child reporting that a lie is worse if you tell "lots of things, not just one sentence but a long one" (Piaget, 1932/1965, p. 153). It is possible that the children in our study said little due to similar beliefs that the more they said, the "worse" their trick would become. It did appear that some children wanted to tell the lie in as few words as possible. For example, when asked what had been built, one 4-year-old replied:

CHILD: I built a house with it.
INTERVIEWER: What kind of house was it?
C: [no response]
I: Was it big?
C: [nods]
I: Yeah? A really big house?
C: [nods]

Some children, like this 6-year-old, tried to lie by giving evasive answers:

I: Did you play with that toy?
C: Yes.
I: What did you do with it?
C: Well. . . .
I: Did you build something?
C: Yes, sort of.
I: You did?
C: Umm Hmm.
I: What'd you build?
C: A house.
I: What else?
C: I forgot.

Although the children did provide reports of this nonexperienced event, their accounts were still clearly lacking, in comparison with the children who had indeed participated in the event. Compare the following transcripts:
Experimental Child, 5 years old:

I: Did you play with that toy?
C: Uh huh.
I: What did you build?
C: Well, I made that. (points to picture on box)
I: You made a car?
C: Uh huh.
I: How'd you do that?
C: Well, just looked at it and then I made it.

Control Child, 5 years old:

I: What'd you do with this?
C: See, you, magnets, they're magnet things and they can. . . . Take this off (the box lid). I made an elephant with it, and I'll make a lion.
I: How would you make a lion?
C: I can't make a lion, but I'll show you how to make an elephant. (demonstrates)

Control Child, 5 years, 5 months:

C: All I could do was some little figures and I couldn't do any of the things that are on the pack.

It was frequently quite easy, for a variety of reasons, to detect the children who were lying. Although initially it was difficult to determine whether or not this 7-year-old had actually participated in the experiment at all, the child's switch from ardent denial to exaggerated claims of what had been built with the toy made his deception obvious.

I: Did you play with any of these toys?
C: [shakes head no]
I: You didn't play with *any* of these?
C: Uh-uh.
I: Did you look at any of these books?
C: Well . . . no. I didn't even *see* any of those.
I: You didn't? (investigator is beginning to wonder if child had really participated in experiment)
C: Uh-uh.
I: How 'bout these masks? Did you put on any of these masks?
C: No. I didn't see 'em.
I: What about this book? (book used for expressive language test) Did you look at this book?
C: Yes.
I: Was it a good book?
C: Yes.
I: Did you play with this toy? (target toy)
C: Uh huh.
I: You did?
C: Uh huh.
I: What did you do with that toy?
C: I built this. (points to picture on box)
I: You built that man?
C: Uh huh.
I: Ooh, that looks like it would be hard to build.
C: It's easy.
I: Oh yeah?
C: Uh huh.
I: Did you build anything else?
C: Nods. This and this. (points to two pictures on box)

Neither was it a difficult task to determine that the following 5-year-old was lying about playing with the target toy.

I: What did you play with in here today?
C: Well, that. (points to target toy)
I: What did you do with this game? (target toy)
C: We tricked you!

I: You tricked me?

C: Yeah. That we, that we really didn't.

As the previous examples illustrate, there were qualitative differences in the activity reports of the children who lied and those who did not. The control group was more elaborate both with number of words and number of details in both reports (free and building) of their activities. Within age groups, language abilities did not seem to be responsible for differences. It does not appear that the more expressive children were more elaborate liars. The difference in elaboration appears largely among the older children. This may be true for a variety of reasons. The younger children may have exhibited a floor effect for verbal expressiveness. The reports of the control children were already so brief that it may have been virtually impossible for the children to shorten them further. Further, there may be a real age difference not just in verbal memory but in the understanding of the lie. Based on our current data, we cannot tell if this difference is simply a floor effect or not.

CONCLUSIONS

In summary, our results suggest that children can be coached into providing false statements (at least in the context of a harmless trick), but the coaching does not work very well or last very long for the majority of children. Our post hoc findings indicate that coaching seems to work best if the children know the coach. It is likely the coaching would be more successful if it was conducted by a parent or trusted other. The children might also have been more successful in carrying through with the lie if they had been more motivated to do so. Compliance with the request of the adult coach and self-aggrandizement were the only motives present in our study, although there did seem to be some motivation or "duping delight" arising from the excitement of playing a trick. Our preliminary results are open to many interpretations, and thus we must strongly caution about leaps to applications to children's coached statements of sexual or physical abuse. However, we will suggest a few possible issues and applications from our study for consideration.

First, as previously mentioned, several authors have proposed a developmental sequence for lying. DePaulo and Jordan (1982) suggested that the earliest lies to emerge are those told to escape imminent punishment. Next are lies told to obtain rewards (first material, then social), and finally lies to protect or hurt another person. Previous research has focused on children's spontaneous lies rather than children's abilities to tell a lie in response to an adult's request. It would be difficult to accommodate a lie told by a child in response to adult coaching into this developmental progression. If such lies fit at all, our suggestion is that they are told more to obtain the approval (or avoid the punishment) of the coach than they are designed to "get the accused" in trouble. Obviously, further research on the age of emergence of these types of lies is required.

Second, it is seemingly "common wisdom" among social workers, child psychologists, and others, that young children "simply do not lie" about sexual abuse, not only because they are believed to be more honest than older children (Leippe & Romanczyk, 1987) but because they are thought to lack the motivation to lie and the requisite knowledge about sexual behavior (Ross et al., 1990). Two questions come to mind about this assumption. How elaborate do children really need to be in allegations of sexual abuse? Moreover, can children be given adequate preparation by the adult coach to appear knowledgeable? It may be very difficult to provide adequate information from which a child can construct a convincing account on some topics (e.g., sexual abuse).

As previously noted, age appears to be used as one criterion to determine whether reports of sexual abuse are credible (Everson & Boat, 1986). Is it possible that older children are unfairly maligned? Simply because older children may have greater deceptive abilities in some contexts, one should not assume that they will necessarily engage in more deceptive behavior, especially in the context of falsely reporting sexual abuse. In our study, older children were more likely to carry through with the trick. However, if it had been a harmful lie the older children might have been more aware of the possible consequences of the lie and, as a result, more hesitant to carry through. As DePaulo and Jordan (1982) point out, the abilities that augment success in lying can be counteracted by an "increase in emotionality about the moral and interpersonal ramifications of deceit." Vasek (1986) also suggested that the very "skills which make deception possible also seem responsible for developing the more positive social skills such as empathy and compassion. Thus perspective taking may act as a natural check on a person's more antisocial deceptive practices . . ." (1986, p. 289).

We have spent considerable time criticizing the ecological validity of other research and must at this time acknowledge that our study also suffers from limited generalizability to children's false allegations of abuse. Although previous researchers have failed to examine the means by which the lie is accomplished we have failed to account for motivational level. It is difficult for any of us, due to ethical considerations and practical restrictions, to conduct research that accurately and completely reflects the context in which allegations of abuse are made. The first author is currently planning a continuation of this study with more children and also differing motives for the children to carry out the coaching. Hopefully we can come closer and closer to approximating the situations in which such lies occur so that we can provide more informative answers to those who must deal with children's allegations of abuse, particularly those who must decide if a child's report is credible.

ACKNOWLEDGMENTS

This research was funded in part by a North Carolina State University Faculty Emeritus award to the first author. We would like to thank the children, families, and staff of the St. Nicholas and Ridgedale preschool programs for their cooperation. Additionally, we are deeply indebted to Gregory A. Tate for editorial assistance, Kathy Hulse-Trotter for her indefatigable assistance in data collection, and to Jeannie Gillian for her meticulous data transcription.

REFERENCES

Ceci, S. J., DeSimone, M., Putnick, M. B., Toglia, M., & Lee, J. M. (March, 1990). Motives to lie. In S. J. Ceci (chair), *Do children lie? Narrowing the uncertainties.* Symposium conducted at the AP–LS/Division 41 biennial convention, Williamsburg, VA.

Chandler, M., Fritz, A. S., & Hala, S. (1989). Small-scale deceit: Deception as a marker of two-, three-, and four-year-olds' early theories of mind. *Child Development, 60,* 1263–1277.

DePaulo, B. M., & Jordan, A. (1982). Age changes in deceiving and detecting deceit. In R. S. Feldman (Ed.), *Development of nonverbal behavior in children* (pp. 151–180). New York: Springer-Verlag.

de Villiers, J. G., & de Villiers, P. A. (1978). *Language acquisition.* Cambridge, MA: Harvard University Press.

DiAngelis, T. (1990, September). Panel calls child abuse a "national emergency." *APA Monitor,* 18–19.

Ekman, P. (1989). *Why kids lie.* New York: Macmillan.

Everson, M., & Boat, B. (1986, May). *Lying about sexual abuse: In the eye of the beholder?* Paper presented at the fourth National Conference on Sexual Victimization of Children, New Orleans.

Goodman, G. S. (1991). Commentary: On stress and accuracy in research on children's testimony. In J. Doris (Ed.), *The suggestibility of children's recollections* (pp. 77–82). Washington, DC: American Psychological Association.

Goodman, G. S., Aman, C. J., & Hirschman, J. (1987). Child sexual and physical abuse: Children's testimony. In S. J. Ceci, M. P. Toglia, & D. F. Ross (Eds.), *Children's eyewitness memory* (pp. 1–23). New York: Springer-Verlag.

Goodman, G. S., Bottoms, B. L., Herscovici, B. B., & Shaver, P. (1989). Determinants of the child victim's perceived credibility. In S. J. Ceci, D. F. Ross, & M. P. Toglia (Eds.), *Perspectives on children's testimony* (pp. 1–22). New York: Springer-Verlag.

Hall, G. S. (1891). Children's lies. *Pedagogical Seminary, 1,* 211–218.

Hartshorne, H., & May, M. A. (1928). *Studies in the nature of character: Vol. 1. Studies in deceit.* New York: Macmillan.

Haugaard, J. J., Reppucci, N. D., Laird, J., & Nauful, T. (1991). Children's definitions of the truth and their competency as witnesses in legal proceedings. *Law and Human Behavior, 15,* 253–271.

Horgrefe, G. J., Wimmer, H., & Perner, J. (1986). Ignorance versus false belief: A developmental lag in attribution of epistemic states. *Child Development, 57,* 567–582.

Hulse-Trotter, K. (1990). *Do children believe in their own believability?* Unpublished master's thesis, University of Tennessee, Chattanooga.

Jones, D., & McGraw, J. M. (1987). Reliable and fictitious accounts of sexual abuse in children. *Journal of Interpersonal Violence, 2,* 27–45.

Kohlberg, L. (1963). The development of children's orientations toward a moral order: I. Sequence in the development of moral thought. *Vita Humana, 6*, 11–33.

Krout, M. H. (1931). The psychology of children's lies. *Journal of Abnormal and Social Psychology, 26*, 1–27.

Krout, M. H. (1932). *The psychology of children's lies.* Boston: Gorham Press.

Leippe, M. R., & Romanczyk, A. (1987). Children on the witness stand: A communication/persuasion analysis of jurors' reactions to child witnesses. In S. J. Ceci, M. P. Toglia, & D. F. Ross (Eds.), *Children's eyewitness memory* (pp. 155–177). New York: Springer-Verlag.

Leonard, E. A. (1920). A parent's study of children's lies. *Pedagogical Seminary, 27*, 105–136.

Lewis, M., Stanger, C., & Sullivan, M. (1989). Deception in 3-year-olds. *Developmental Psychology, 25*, 439–443.

Moses, L. J., & Flavell, J. H. (1989, April). *Inferring false beliefs from actions and reactions.* Paper presented at the biennial meeting of the Society for Research in Child Development, Kansas City, MO.

Perner, J., Leekam, S. R., & Wimmer, H. (1987). Three-year-olds' difficulty with false belief: The case for a conceptual deficit. *British Journal of Developmental Psychology, 5*, 125–137.

Peters, D. (1990). In S. J. Ceci (chair), *Do children lie? Narrowing the uncertainties.* Symposium conducted at the AP–LS/Division 41 biennial convention, Williamsburg, VA.

Peters, D. (1991). The influence of stress and arousal on the child witness. In J. Doris (Ed.), *The suggestibility of children's recollections* (pp. 60–76). Washington, DC: American Psychological Association.

Piaget, J. (1965). *The moral judgment of the child.* New York: Collier. (Original work published 1932)

Riggio, R. E., Tucker, J., & Throckmorton, B. (1987). Social skills and deception ability. *Personality and Social Psychology Bulletin, 13*, 568–577.

Ross, D. F., Dunning D., Toglia, M. P., & Ceci, S. J. (1990). The child in the eyes of the jury. Assessing mock jurors perceptions of the child witness. *Law and Human Behavior, 16*, 5–23.

Sodian, B. (1989, April). *Development of the ability to intentionally deceive.* Paper presented at the biennial meeting of the Society for Research in Child Development, Kansas City, MO.

Stern, C., & Stern, W. (1909). *Erinnerung, aussage und luge in der erst kindheit* [Remembrance, utterance, and deception in the first childhood]. Leipzig, Germany: Barth.

Tate, C. S., & Warren–Leubecker, A. (1989, April). *Effects of adults' coaching on children's willingness to provide false reports.* Paper presented at the biennial meeting of the Society for Research in Child Development, Kansas City, MO.

Tate, C. S., & Warren–Leubecker, A. (1990, March). Can young children lie convincingly if coached by adults? In S. J. Ceci (chair), *Do children lie? Narrowing the uncertainties.* Symposium conducted at the AP–LS/Division 41 biennial convention, Williamsburg, VA.

Tudor–Hart, B. E. (1926). Are there cases in which lies are necessary? *Pedagogical Seminary, 33*, 586–641.

Vasek, M. E. (1986). Lying as a skill: The development of deception in children. In R. W. Mitchell & N. Thompson (Eds.), *Deception: Perspectives on human and nonhuman deceit* (pp. 271–292). Albany: State University of New York Press.

Wakefield, H., & Underwager, R. (1989). Evaluating the child witness in sexual abuse cases: Interview or inquisition? *American Journal of Forensic Psychology, 7*, 43–69.

Wigmore, J. H. (1940). *Evidence in trials at common law* (3rd ed.). Boston: Little, Brown.

Wimmer, H., & Perner, J. (1983). Beliefs about beliefs: Representation and constraining function of wrong beliefs in young children's understanding of deception. *Cognition, 13*, 103–128.

7 Children's Lying and Truthfulness: Implications for Children's Testimony

Kay Bussey
Macquarie University

The number of children who could potentially serve as witnesses in criminal court proceedings is escalating as a result of the increased reporting of child sexual abuse (Haugaard & Reppucci, 1988). In most cases, it is necessary for children to testify about their alleged abuse, inasmuch as there are rarely witnesses and the medical evidence is often not conclusive. As the numbers of actual child witnesses have increased, concerns about their competence to serve as witnesses have grown. In particular, sensationalized media reports of alleged multiple abuse in day-care settings (e.g., McMartin case in the United States and Mr. Bubbles case in Australia) have fueled considerable debate among the general public and professionals alike about the competency of young children to serve as witnesses.

Such debates are not new. In 1895, the U.S. Supreme Court ruled that children could not be deemed incompetent to testify on the basis of age (*Wheeler v. United States*, 1895). At that time, the court held that trial judges were to determine, case-by-case, children's competence to testify. Judges were to determine the "capacity and intelligence of the child, his appreciation of the difference between truth and falsehood, as well as his duty to tell the former" (*Wheeler v. United States*, 1895, pp. 524–525). No standard competence test (or *voir dire*) has been adopted to the present day. To qualify as a witness, "a child must possess certain characteristics, including the capacity to observe, sufficient intelligence, adequate memory, the ability to communicate, an awareness of the difference between truth and falsehood, and an appreciation of the obligation to speak the truth" (Myers, 1987, p. 54), as determined by the presiding judge.

There has been mounting criticism, however, of the validity of the *voir dire* (Melton, 1987). Consequently, in the United States, the majority of states have abolished the requirement of establishing competency prior to testimony by a child. Instead, Federal Rule of Evidence 601, which states that "[e]very witness is presumed competent to testify" (677 F.2d at 1028) has been adopted. This does not mean, however, that all witnesses have an incontrovertible right to testify: In states that have adopted Rule 601, judges and defense attorneys may use Federal Rule of Evidence 403 to challenge the child's competence if it can be shown that "its probative value is substantially outweighed by the danger of unfair prejudice, confusion of the issues, or misleading the jury. . . ." Ultimately, even in those jurisdictions that have abolished the *voir dire,* the judge still determines whether the child witness's evidence can be admitted as well as the weight and credibility given to it.

Children are encouraged to disclose abuse and this is the goal of the various protective behavior programs taught in schools. Yet when they arrive at the adult-oriented venue of the courtroom to tell about their abuse, they incur challenges to the veracity of their testimony that are rarely directed at adults' testimony. Children's ability to report witnessed events accurately and their honesty are both doubted. It is therefore essential that judges and jurors who deal with child witnesses have informed knowledge of children's competence as witnesses.

Most of the developmental psychology research has addressed children's competency in terms of memory, differentiation of fact from fantasy, and vulnerability to suggestive questioning (see Ceci, Toglia, & Ross, 1987). However, the judge's appraisal of children's ability to differentiate truth from falsehood, and their understanding of the duty to tell the truth is a major component in the determination of children's competence to provide testimony. It is only recently that developmental psychologists have begun researching the psycholegal aspects of children's lying and truthfulness (Ekman, 1989). In this chapter, general psychological research issues regarding children's competence are considered before turning to a more specific discussion of one aspect of competence: children's understanding of lying and truthfulness. For a more complete understanding of these concepts, not only is research on children's *understanding* of lying and truthfulness examined, but their *actual* lying and truthfulness is looked at as well.

PSYCHOLOGICAL RESEARCH ON CHILDREN'S COMPETENCY TO TESTIFY

There is a wide range of expert and lay opinion about the competency of child witnesses. Some argue that child witnesses are in fact more reliable than adult witnesses and others insist that the evidence of children under 6 should be dismissed. This latter opinion is supported by the writings of two of the leading early theorists of child development: Freud and Piaget. Freud (1909/1955) wrote: "The untrustworthiness of the assertions of children is due to the predominance of their imagination, just as the untrustworthiness of the assertions of grown-up people is due to the predominance of their prejudices" (pp. 102–103). Piaget (1932/1965) echoed Freud's viewpoint even more strongly in *The Moral Judgement of the Child*. How do the views of these major theorists sit with current psychological theorizing and empirical investigations into the competence of child witnesses?

The impossibility of conducting controlled studies in the legal context has contributed to the continuing debate associated with this topic. Recently, researchers have resorted to analogue studies capitalizing on naturally occurring stressful events experienced by children to elucidate the processes associated with the reliability of children's eyewitness reporting. That research has focused on children's memory for eyewitnessed events and the degree to which children are vulnerable to suggestion, particularly when asked leading questions. Goodman and her colleagues, for example, have studied children's suggestibility in simulated investigations of child abuse (e.g., Goodman, Hirschman, & Rudy, 1987). The research findings have countered conclusions drawn earlier this century by Binet (1900) that children are highly suggestible. On the basis of these studies from Goodman's laboratories with children as young as 3 in which they "have been trying to produce false reports of abuse, particularly sexual abuse," the conclusion is drawn that "If children are as suggestible as former research might lead us to believe, this should not be a difficult task. We find, however, that it is!" (Goodman et al., 1987, p. 3).

Goodman's studies have provided invaluable information about children's eyewitness capabilities particularly when they are participants in an event. The findings that children can remember more about central than peripheral elements of an event and that they are less vulnerable to suggestion and leading questions about such events than shown by previous research, indicates that participant-victim witnesses are potentially more reliable witnesses than their nonparticipant witness counterparts. Although these studies reveal that children *can* provide reliable evidence even when subjected to highly suggestive questioning, this does not mean that they always *will* provide reliable and truthful evidence. To conclude that children *never* fabricate abuse on the basis of these studies needs more cautious consideration. In most of Goodman's studies there has been no reason to lie. When asked to recall events associated with a stressful medical procedure, such as receiving an inoculation, why would a child be motived to distort events intentionally, that is, to lie?

To demonstrate that children never or rarely lie about abuse demands a level of honesty that is not expected of adults. When adults serve as witnesses in court cases it is presumed that by taking the sworn oath they will not perjure themselves. However, adult witnesses do sometimes lie and it is the role of the jury to adjudicate the truthfulness of the witness' testimony. To expect children to always be truthful even about such important issues as abuse is unreasonable in view of the many faces of adults' deception.

Although a child might be capable of accurately reporting abuse, or a crime that they have witnessed an adult commit, they may not do so. From the perspective of social cognitive theory (Bandura, 1986, 1991), different factors govern what individuals *can* do and what they *will* do or *do* do. It is argued here that an important determinant of whether or not a child will report a witnessed event depends on the outcome anticipated for reporting that information (Bandura, 1986, 1991).

In order to examine children's competence in relation to lying and truthfulness it is first necessary to establish if children know the difference between a lie and a truthful statement.

LYING AND TRUTHFULNESS

Children's Knowledge About Lying and Truthfulness

As a result of the paucity of relevant psychological research on children's lying and truthfulness, legal professionals have principally relied on Piaget's (1932/1965) accounts of children's lying, reported almost 60 years ago in *The Moral Judgement of the Child*. Piaget's writings have reinforced jurors' and judges' skepticism about the testimony of young children. For example, he wrote that for young children:

> Without actually for the sake of lying, i.e. without attempting to deceive anyone, and without even being definitely conscious of what he is doing, he distorts reality in accordance with his desires and his romancing. To him a proposition has value less as a statement than as a wish, and the stories, testimony and explanations given by a child should be regarded as the expression of his feelings rather than of beliefs that may be true or false. (p. 157)

Thus, from the Piagetian perspective, whether or not children are even capable of intentionally telling a lie is an issue. This is because lying involves deception, and young children, according to Piaget (1932/1965), are not capable of such intentional deception. Rather, the child "lies" in order to avoid adult censure. According to Piaget, the child's evaluation of an action is dependent on the adult's reaction to it, rather than on any inherent value of the action.

Piaget's (1932/1965) investigation into children's lying was part of a larger project on moral reasoning. His research was, "dominated by the notions of intentionality and objective responsibility" (p. 134). He was particularly concerned with age differences in children's definitions of lies to establish whether or not they understood that lying was a witting and intentional betrayal of the truth.

Children's Definitions and Evaluation of Lying

Piaget's Legacy. According to Piaget (1932/1965), up until age 6, children's definition of lying is overinclusive. Their definition encompasses swearing, and every kind of false statement, including mistaken guesses. Between ages 6 and 10, however, children define a lie as something that is not true and children of this age do not differentiate between intentional and unintentional statements: "a lie is what does not agree with the truth independently of the subject's intention" (p. 141). By 10 or 11, intentionality is accommodated and only those false statements that are intended to be false are defined as lies.

Apart from investigating age differences in children's definitions of lies, Piaget (1932/1965) also investigated age differences in children's evaluations of lies. As with children's definitions of lies, he reported that objective responsibility is replaced by subjective responsibility with increasing age: The older the child, the more likely intentionality is taken into account in evaluating lies. For children below 6, the more a lie departs from reality the worse it is judged. Exaggerations, such as saying that a dog is as big as a cow, are judged more harshly by younger than older children. For acts of clumsiness, however, even older children judge the seriousness of the lie in terms of the material consequences. For example,

> A little boy upset an ink-pot on the table. When his father came back the boy told him it wasn't he who knocked over the ink-pot. He told him it was the cat! Was it a lie?—Yes. Naughty or not naughty?—Naughty. Why? Because he made a big stain. (p. 153).

Because even the older children were more likely to judge the seriousness of the lie on the basis of the material consequences or damage incurred, paying little attention to the intentions of the person committing the naughty action, lies involving misdeeds were excluded from Piaget's research investigations.

Contemporary Research. Contemporary researchers have shown that children's knowledge and understanding of lying and truthfulness is indeed greater than is apparent from Piaget's writings (Bussey, 1992; Peterson, Peterson, & Seeto, 1983; Wimmer, Gruber, & Perner, 1984, 1985). By focusing on lies about misdeeds, a lie type excluded in Piaget's research, it has been found that 7- and 10-year-olds were completely accurate in their identification of lies and truthful statements and that even 4-year-olds were highly accurate (88%) in their identification of such statements (Bussey, 1989). This is perhaps not surprising in view of Stouthamer-Loeber's (1987) findings that mothers reported the most frequent reason their 4-year-olds lied was to conceal a misdeed to avoid punishment. Lies about misdeeds were also the most frequent that children aged 4 to 12 themselves reported telling (Bussey, 1990b). It seems likely that children's understanding of lying may emanate from lies told about misdeeds. Hence, recent studies that have focused on these more ecologically valid lie types have demonstrated that children have a more sophisticated knowledge of lying and truthfulness than was evidenced in earlier studies involving lies that were more removed from most children's daily experience. Investigations of these lie types also provide information most relevant to the court context because most children's testimony hinges on them being about to report truthfully on another's or their own misdeed.

It is important to assess not only children's understanding of lying but also their ability to correctly identify truthful statements as well as their ability to understand the importance of truthfulness. Previous research has focused on children's appraisals of lies, paying little attention to truthfulness (Peterson et al., 1983; Piaget, 1932/1965). Parenting practices encourage children's truthfulness and the legal system emphasizes children's understanding of truthfulness as well as lying. Also, although Piaget was mainly concerned with the role of intentionality in children's judgments of lying, other factors, such as belief and punishment, may play an equally important part in influencing children's definitions and evaluations of lying and truthfulness. Statements (lies and truths) about misdeeds, and analogously the statements of abused victims, meet with belief or disbelief and sometimes punishment. Does the presence of these factors alter children's, particularly younger children's, definitions and evaluations of lies and truthful statements? These issue were addressed in a study in which children heard stories about other children who either lied or told the truth about a misdeed they had committed (Bussey, 1992). Results from that study showed that second ($M = 97.5\%$) and fifth ($M = 98.8\%$) graders were more accurate in their identification of both lies and truthful statements than preschoolers ($M = 71.3\%$), although the preschoolers' correct identifications were significantly above chance. These correct identifications were not affected by whether the lie was believed or not or whether the child's statement, lie or truth, met with punishment for the misdeed. Further, children's evaluative judgments of lies and truthful statements revealed that even the 4-year-olds were more disapproving of lies than of truthfulness. In addition, contrary to Piaget's findings, this study demonstrated that children across the three ages evaluated lies significantly more negatively than the misdeeds that led to the lies. Truthful statements, however, were not evaluated more favorably than the misdeed itself by the preschoolers. Thus, although younger children appreciated the naughtiness of lying, it was more difficult for them to appreciate the value of truthfulness where misdeeds were involved.

Punishment affected the evaluative judgments of the preschoolers, but not the older children. Consistent with both cognitive–developmental theory (Piaget, 1932/1965) and social cognitive theory (Bandura, 1986), preschoolers evaluated statements leading to punishment for the misdeed more negatively than statements not leading to such punishment. The older children were less swayed than their younger counterparts by the presence or absence of punishment for the misdeed in their evaluative judgments of lies and truthful statements. For the preschoolers, any statement, either a lie or a truthful one, that led to punishment for the misdeed was evaluated more negatively than a comparable lie or truthful statement that did not lead to punishment. Although stories in which the character was punished for the misdeed were rated more negatively than stories in which such punishment was not incurred, these children did not use the presence of punishment as the sole basis for forming their evaluative judgments. Lies were rated as worse than truthful statements, irrespective of punishment for the misdeed.

Piaget (1932/1965) also argued that younger and older children evaluate lies differently, depending on whether or not they are believed, with older children evaluating lies that are believed as worse than lies that are not believed and the reverse for younger children. In contrast, Bussey (1992) found that neither preschoolers nor, second and fifth graders evaluated lies believed versus those not believed differentially.

Can these findings be generalized to all lies or are they specific to lies involving misdeeds? Peterson et al.'s (1983) research shows that lying is not a unitary category and that children's understanding of lying varies as a function of lie type.

Children's Definitions and Evaluations of Lies and Truths as a Function of Content

According to Piaget (1932/1965), the further a lie departed from reality the worse it was judged by children up to age 9 or 10; he wrote that they "evaluated the lies, not according to the intentions of the liar, but according to the greater or lesser likelihood of the lying statement" (p. 144). Peterson et al.'s (1983) results offered little support for this position as lies involving misdeeds were evaluated more negatively than lies involving exaggeration.

As well, a study investigating children's ability to identify and evaluate lies and truthful statements about misdeed, tact, and trick events lends little support to Piaget's position (Bussey, 1989). Pretend lies or trick lies accounted for a large percentage of the lies that 5-year-olds reported telling (Bussey, 1990b) and tact lies, or "white lies," have been rated as the most innocuous lie type by adults (Lindskold & Walters, 1983; Peterson et al., 1983). Although second and fifth graders were almost totally accurate in identifying all lies and truthful statements, the preschoolers were less accurate ($M = 73.5\%$), but still scored significantly above chance. In contrast to the older children, the preschoolers' correct identifications varied across lies and truthful statements of differing content. They were highly accurate in identifying statements, lies, or truths, associated with a clear behavioral referent such as a misdeed. On the other hand, statements associated with appraisal (tact-related lies and truthful statements) or that were imaginary (trick lies) were more difficult for the younger children to identify correctly.

Children were also clearly influenced by the content of the lie or truthful statement in forming their evaluative judgments. Lies were judged as worse than truthful statements when associated with misdeeds and tricks, but not when they were associated with tact. Thus children, like adults, rated tact lies or white lies as the most innocuous type of lie. Further, a truthful statement associated with a tact issue (e.g., "I don't like your new hairdo") was rated as reprehensible as the lie about the same content (e.g., "I do like your new hairdo," when really they didn't like it), and the most negative of all three truthful statements. This is not surprising as parents either out of fear of offending or to avoid embarrassment to themselves often encourage children to lie in certain social situations. For example, children are sometimes coached to say they like a present when they do not. Children may thus rate such truthful statements negatively as a result of being discouraged for such truthfulness. The lack of evaluative differentiation for lies and truthful statements about tact related issues indicates that truthfulness and lying are not necessarily the inverse of each other. An important determinant of whether or not an individual lies or tells the truth may depend not only on their evaluation of lying but also on their evaluation of truthfulness. It is possible that the less favorably truthfulness is evaluated in comparison to lying, the less likely individuals are to be truthful.

In this section, it has been shown that children's correct identification of lies and truthful statements is well above chance for children as young as age 4. Their accuracy rates are particularly high for statements involving misdeeds. It seems that for preschoolers it is easier to identify lies and truthful statements associated with a clear behavioral referent such as a misdeed. On the other hand, statements associated with appraisal (tact-related lies and truthful statements) or that are imaginary (trick lies) are more difficult for young children to correctly identify. Other studies (Haugaard & Crosby, 1989) have also shown that when children as young as 4 y are provided with salient events relevant to their everyday situations, they are able to differentiate statements that are truthful from those that are not. These findings are particularly important for the courts where as a legacy from Piaget it is often suggested that children are unable to make this differentiation until many years later. Although it still remains that younger children may have an overinclusive definition of "a lie" in comparison with older children and adults in that even an unintentional false statement is designated a lie (Strichartz & Burton, 1990) they are quite capable of differentiating a lie from a truthful statement, particularly when the statement has a specific behavioral referent. But the court requires more than the child's being able to differentiate a lie from a truthful statement. It is necessary that children understand the importance of telling the truth and not lying. Again, the research demonstrates that even 4-year-olds evaluate lying more negatively than truthful statements (Bussey, 1992; Bussey, 1989).

Although 4-year-olds can distinguish lies from truthful statements and judge lies as morally worse than truths, this knowledge does not necessarily guide children's actual lying and truthfulness. The link between knowledge and behavior is tenuous for adults, and not surprisingly, it is weaker for children (Blasi, 1980; Henshel, 1971). Thus it is important to consider not only children's knowledge of lying and truthfulness, but also their actual lying and truthfulness.

ACTUAL LYING AND TRUTHFULNESS

How frequently do children lie? Few studies have addressed this intriguing question. Those studies that have addressed it have relied on self-report data usually from adults, teachers or parents. A study with 4-year-olds, based on the records kept by their parents reported an average of 4.9 lies per week (Stout-hamer-Loeber, 1987). However, it is difficult to establish the accuracy of this estimate because of the covert nature of lying. Reliance on parent's correct identification and reporting of such lies suffers from difficulty in establishing accuracy of detection. Stouthamer-Loeber and Loeber (1986) have reported results in support of a developmental decline hypothesis: Older boys told fewer lies than younger boys as measured by parent and teacher reports. It may be, however, that older children are better able to conceal their lies than their younger counterparts. If individuals become progressively more adept at concealing their lies, detection is confounded with age. As a result, researchers have turned to more direct observational measures to assess children's propensity for lying.

Observational Measures

Lewis, Stanger, and Sullivan (1989) investigated 3-year-olds' actual lying. Despite Piaget's doubts about the deceptive capabilities of 3-year-olds, Lewis et al. (1989) suggest that anecdotal reports of "young children who deny that they have eaten a cookie when there are signs of the cookie on their mouths" (p. 439) may reflect the deceptive capabilities of these young children. To investigate this systematically, Lewis et al. (1989) instructed 3-year-olds not to look at a toy placed behind them. The majority of these young children (88%) *did* look during a 5-minute observation period. Of those who did, an equal number admitted their transgression (38%) as denied it (38%). It is tempting, without comparative data from older children and adults, to be concerned at the high percentage of children who "lied" in this situation. However, 62% of the children who looked either owned up to their transgression or simply did not respond when asked if they looked. Thus, the majority of the children in this study did not actively try to deceive the experimenter. It is important to recall that for a statement to qualify as a lie (Bok, 1978; Piaget, 1932/1965) the speaker must intend to deceive the listener by inducing a false belief. Although the children who denied their transgression in this study provided a false statement, it is difficult to conclude from these data that intentional deception was involved. Whether intentional deception is even within the capabilities of 3-year-olds is a moot point.

The majority of findings show that it is not until about 4 years of age that children understand the concept of false belief and are therefore capable of intentional deception (Flavell, 1989; Gopnik & Astington, 1988; Perner, Leekam, & Wimmer, 1987; Sodian, 1989). Hence, the young children in Lewis et al.'s (1989) study may have provided a false statement to avoid punishment without necessarily being intentionally deceptive (Stouthamer–Loeber, 1987). It is possible that, as in other domains of development, children engage in a particular practice (deceptive-like comments/behavior) before they have the cognitive capabilities for understanding that practice (i.e., intentional deception). Is an understanding of the concept of false belief a necessary prerequisite for intentional deception? How does the acquisition of the concept of false belief relate to children's engagement in deception?

In an attempt to address this question, children aged 3 and 5 were tested in a similar setting to the 3-year-olds in Lewis et al.'s (1989) study (Bussey, 1990a). Results obtained for the 3-year-olds' were virtually identical to those reported by Lewis et al. (1989). For the 5-year-olds, it was found that 66% transgressed; fully 95% of these denied their transgression. Children's understanding of the concept of false belief was assessed using a measure similar to that of Gopnik and Astington (1988). All the 5-year-olds has mastered this concept, whereas few of the 3-year-olds had. Mastery was related to age rather than to denial or not of the transgression. Although mastery of this concept makes it more likely that deceptive practices were intentional, other factors, particularly motivational ones, were clearly important in determining whether this skill was used or not. Before examining the motivations for using one's deceptive skills, the development of this skill is first examined.

The Development of Deceptive Skills

Two skills critical to the development of deception have been isolated for consideration: verbal and nonverbal skills.

Verbal Deceptive Skills. It is necessary for children first to master the concept of false belief before they can provide intentionally false statements, that is, lies. Children's understanding of this concept appears minimal before 3 (Wimmer et al., 1984). They find it difficult to understand that another person falsely believes that some factual state of affairs is different from what the child knows it to be (e.g., when a chocolate is hidden in Drawer A and the child but not the bystander sees it moved to Drawer B, the child finds it difficult to understand that the bystander falsely believes it is still in Drawer A). Without a clear understanding of the concept of false belief, it is difficult to entertain that children intentionally engineer false statements. That they do make false statements at this age is not in dispute (Lewis et al., 1989); however, whether their false statements are deceptive or not is debatable. Chandler, Fritz, and Hala (1989) argued that 2½-year-olds are capable of employing deceptive strategies and are capable of acting deceptively. Deception includes not only statements but acts that are intended to mislead others into thinking that what is false is true. Using a novel hide-and-seek board game children as young as 2½ were observed to employ deceptive strategies. They wiped away the tracks of a puppet who hid a "treasure" in one of several different containers to remove the clues for the adult who later searched for the treasure. Some of the children not only destroyed the evidence leading to the treasure's container, but also made a false trail to another container. Even if children so young can use such deceptive strategies, whether or not they can bring them to bear to produce deceptive statements and how credible those statements will be, remains unanswered.

Once children acquire the concept of false belief and understand that they have successfully to convince another about the veracity of the false statement to become a successful liar, lies are more plausible and real feelings are concealed. Four-year-olds' lies typically take the form of simple denial ("No") or misleading confirmation ("Yes") rather than the more sophisticated elaborations of older children's and adults' lies (Bussey, 1990b; Stouthamer-Loeber, 1987). Over time, however, as children are exposed to more lies, from adults and peers, they learn to generate plausible lies themselves. The child told to tell Grandma that he or she likes his or her disliked Christmas present is learning not only how to lie but that lying is sometimes condoned.

Apart from learning the verbal skills that are necessary to be a successful liar it is also necessary to learn to hide one's true feelings.

Nonverbal Deceptive Skills. The majority of research on children's nonverbal deceptive skills has focused on their facial and sometimes their body cues. Morency and Krauss (1982) showed first and fifth graders pleasant and unpleasant slides. They were asked to pretend to be viewing a slide evoking the opposite reaction on half the trials. Children were more successful at deceiving their peers than their parents. Parents successfully detected the deception of the first graders on both the pleasant and unpleasant slides, but could only detect deception on the pleasant slides for the fifth-grade children.

Some support for Ekman and Friesen's (1969) theory of leakage and deception was obtained in a study by Feldman and White (1980), although the theory was more strongly supported for girls than boys. Children between the ages of 5 and 12 sampled good- and bad-tasting drinks and for half the trials attempted to convince others that the drink tasted opposite to its actual taste. In support of Ekman and Friesen's (1969) theory, with increasing age, girls' facial expression concealed their deception while their body movements became more revealing of deception. For the younger children, their true affect "leaked" out and their attempted deception was unsuccessful. Other studies have reported similar findings (Feldman, Jenkins, & Popoola, 1979): While first graders' attempts at deception were not credible to undergraduate raters, by seventh grade, children were successful liars in that they were capable of deceiving the adult judges.

There are plenty of opportunities in play contexts, for example, card games, board games, party games, and sports, for children to develop their nonverbal deceptive skills (De Paulo & Jordan, 1982). Deceit in these contexts is often not only condoned but encouraged. Thus, over the school years children become increasingly skilled at lying. Their verbal statements become more credible and their nonverbal leakage cues come under greater control so that observers are less likely to detect deception. Hence, during childhood most children develop the skills to be successful liars.

Having acquired deceptive skills, when will these be used? What are the factors governing children's lying and truth telling? Is it at a certain age that individuals can be relied upon to tell the truth, are some individuals more likely than others to be truthful, or is the situation the major determinant of an individual's truthfulness?

Determinants of Actual Lying and Truthfulness

Most theories of morality, including Piaget's, have focused on moral thought and have paid little attention to the application of such thought to moral conduct. In contrast, social cognitive theory (Bandura, 1986, 1991) pays considerable attention to the link between moral conduct and thought and posits that no one cause alone is responsible for an individual's truthfulness. "Within this conceptual framework, personal factors in the form of moral thought and affective self-reactions, moral conduct, and environmental factors all operate as interacting determinants that influence each other bidirectionally" (Bandura, 1991, p. 45). Knowledge about lying and truthfulness does not guarantee truth telling, just as telling the truth does not necessarily inform about knowledge of truthfulness. In this theory different factors govern what individuals *can* do and what they *will* do or *do* do in a particular situation.

Although a child might be quite capable of reporting abuse, or a crime that they have witnessed committed by an adult, an important determinant of whether or not they will report it is the outcome anticipated from reporting that information (Bandura, 1986, 1991). For example, some children might freely disclose abuse to a caring counselor but might be reluctant to report it in a court of law, either out of fear of retaliation from the accused (Bussey & Cashmore, 1990), or fear of being blamed themselves for the incident (Goodman 1984), or embarrassment (Saywitz, Goodman, Nicholas, & Moan, 1989). Thus, although children may be able to tell the truth about a particular event, whether or not they *will* tell the truth depends on their expectations of the outcome for truth telling. Neither adults nor children perform and do everything they know. Different factors are related to the acquisition of knowledge than to its performance (both verbal and behavioral). Thus, young children might know the difference between a lie and truthful statement and that it is wrong to lie and important to tell the truth; however, having acquired this information, there is no guarantee that they will tell the truth and not lie. Moral action is determined not only by moral knowledge (Bandura, 1991; Blasi, 1980; Kurtines & Greif, 1974); other factors, particularly cognitive motivational ones are important influencers of moral action (Bandura, 1991).

Cognitive Motivational Factors. One of the first cognitive motivational factors to develop and one that continues to influence conduct across the life span is provided by anticipated *social sanctions* for performing a particular behavior or providing a particular statement. These anticipated social sanctions or expectations associated with a particular course of action or statement provide the motivation for following that course of action or providing that statement. Not surprisingly, people tend not to perform activities they anticipate getting punished for, rather they engage in activities that bring some form of self-gain (Bandura, 1986, 1991).

Despite children and adults knowing that it is wrong to lie, many of them do lie. When questioned about lies they had told, adults and children reported that many of their lies were motivated by anticipated punishment for truth telling (Bussey, 1990b). The majority of lies (50%) were told to avoid punishment for a misdeed. Approximately 15% of lies were told for self-gain, and the remainder of lies were told either to avoid an activity, for fun, out of concern for others, or to be mean to others.

In many situations, children are motivated to lie when they have committed a misdeed and anticipate punishment for owning up to the misdeed (Bussey, 1990b). But what about the situation where the child witnesses a misdeed being committed by another? Are children differentially motivated to report or disclose such a transgression? To test this proposition, an attempt was made to influence children's lying and truthfulness by providing different motivations for lying about a witnessed misdeed (Bussey, Lee, & Rickard 1990).

In most court cases involving sexual abuse, the child witness provides testimony against an adult male. It has been suggested that in such instances the child may have been instructed by the accused not to report the incident, and this may undermine the child's ability to report the truth. Therefore, Bussey et al. (1990) investigated whether or not children of 3 and 5 years of age would lie about a transgression committed by an adult male who broke a "prized" glass and hid the broken pieces to cover up his "misdeed." The adult male appealed to the child in a number of different ways not to tell the female interviewer about what had happened. These conditions provided the motivations of gain, avoidance, concern for others, and for fun, which were established as the most significant motivations for lying in these age groups (Bussey, 1990b).

In the absence of the male who transgressed, the child's performance on a task was assessed. For those children who did not spontaneously disclose the transgression, the female interviewer asked several questions to encourage disclosure. Children who still did not disclose were finally asked directly whether or not the adult male had committed the transgression. In this study, across all conditions, approximately 76% of the 3-year-olds reported the witnessed event, whereas only 57% of the 5-year-olds did. Apart from the greater propensity of 3-year-olds to disclose the adult's transgression, the different types of appeal used to dissuade the child from disclosing impacted differentially on the 3- and the 5-year-olds. Specifically, the 3-year-olds were more likely to report the adult's transgression when the appeal was reward, concern, or when they were simply asked not to tell. Only about half the 3-year-olds instructed in a very stern manner not to tell, disclosed the adult's transgression.

The stern condition also reduced disclosure by the 5-year-olds, compared with the other conditions. Children from this age group were also less likely to report the incident if simply instructed not to tell than the 3-year-olds. Further, the 5-year-olds were more likely to disclose the transgression only after direct questioning about it, whereas the 3-year-olds were more likely to disclose the transgression spontaneously. The greater disclosure of 3-year-olds than 5-year-olds was confirmed in another study in which mothers requested their children not to report the mother's accidental breaking of a Barbie doll (Bottoms, Goodman, Schwartz–Kenney, Sachsenmaier, & Thomas, 1990).

Even though the 3-year-olds were more reluctant to report the adult's transgression when sternly requested not to, their level of disclosure was greater than that of the 5-year-olds. A reason for the higher level of disclosure on the part of the 3-year-olds might simply indicate that they find it more difficult than the older children to generate an alternative explanation of events. Hence, in a follow-up study employing a similar methodology, children were presented with a plausible false story to tell the female experimenter (Bussey & Lee, 1990). This enabled a test of the impact of "coaching" on children's accounts. Preliminary results indicate that a greater number of 5-year-olds than 3-year-olds succumbed to the coaching and hence did not report the transgression.

Results from these studies point to the increasing use of deception by those who have the skills to behave deceptively. With increasing age an individual's capacity for deception is greater as their leakage through nonverbal behaviors and verbal means diminishes. The data also lend support to the social cognitive view that anticipated outcomes (negative and positive) influence lying and truthfulness. Hence, 5-year-old children who have learned that they often get into trouble for admitting something witnessed, or their own transgression, are less likely to be truthful about such events than 3-year-olds who have not learned such a negative outcome for truthfulness (Bussey et al., 1990).

From the social cognitive perspective (Bandura, 1991) one other important cognitive motivational factor that regulates action is self-sanctions. With increasing maturation and social experience it is postulated that moral conduct is increasingly motivated and regulated by self-sanctions. Although 3-year-old and 4-year-old children may lie to avoid punishment for their misdeed (Lewis et al., 1989; Stouthamer-Loeber, 1987) lying and truth telling are expected to be increasingly regulated by anticipated self-sanctions associated with lying and truthfulness. Although much of human behavior is regulated by external outcomes, punishments and rewards, it is also regulated by people's "self-directive capabilities that enable them to exercise some control over their thoughts, feelings, and actions by the consequences they produce for themselves. Psychological functioning is, therefore, regulated by an interplay of self-generated and external sources of influence" (Bandura, 1986, pp. 335–336). People exercise their self-directive capabilities through setting standards for themselves and responding self-evaluatively to their own behavior. Once standards are established, the extent to which children behave in accord with their standards of valuing truthfulness and deprecating lying depends on the extent to which they anticipate positive self-reactions (feelings of pride, self-satisfaction) for truthfulness and anticipate negative self-reactions (guilt, self-censure) for lying. Research has shown that with increasing age anticipated self-reactions do contribute to children's ability to resist temptation (Grusec & Kuczynski, 1977), to resist behaving aggressively (Perry & Bussey, 1977, and to conform to gender-traditional stereotypes (Bussey & Bandura, in press).

Self-evaluative reactions associated with children's lying and truthfulness have also been charted (Bussey, in press). From preschool through the fifth grade, children projected greater anticipated self-censure to a story character after lying than truthfulness. However, only second and fifth graders anticipated characters feeling greater pride after truthfulness than lying. Thus, children first anticipate censure for lying and over time learn to anticipate feelings of pride and self-worth for truthfulness.

Although the development of anticipated self-evaluations have been shown to influence children's and adult's regulation of their own behavior, such self-influences do not control behavior unless they are activated (Bandura, 1986). Self-evaluations can be selectively activated or disengaged. Therefore, despite having acquired standards for judging right and wrong, even adults sometimes fail to anticipate negative reactions for wrongdoing such as lying. History dramatically demonstrates the possibility of disengagement of aversive self-reactions for immoral conduct through cognitive restructuring of the behavior to make it personally and socially acceptable. For example, "Nazi war criminals, Watergate participants, and a few Vietnam soldiers perpetrated crimes that might have violated their moral standards under other circumstances" (Perry & Bussey, 1984, p. 186). However, it is possible to structure situations to minimize disengagement of self-regulatory mechanisms. It would not be expected that young children would be capable of elaborate cognitive restructuring to enable disengagement of their self-evaluative reactions. However, concrete reminders to engage their standards, such as promising to tell the truth and not to lie in court and providing their testimony in front of the accused might facilitate children's conformity with standards of truthfulness. The impact of these factors on children's lying and truthfulness await future research.

IMPLICATIONS FOR THE COURTROOM

What are the implications from the psychological research reviewed here for the way that courts deal with child witnesses? As stated earlier, in the majority of U.S. states, children are rarely disqualified as incompetent to testify because of their age. In the minority of states where there is a statutory guideline that children under 10 or 14 years of age are presumed incompetent to testify, the competency of a child witness is established in the *voir dire*. Primary emphasis is placed "on the child's ability to differentiate truth from falsehood, to comprehend the duty to tell the truth, and to understand the consequences of not fulfilling this duty" (Melton, 1981, p. 74). It is obvious that in the *voir dire,* the court's focus is on the child's understanding of the moral principles of lying and truth telling rather than on the child's ability to apply such principles. Although it is possible for a child to tell the truth and to pass a competence exam, it is also possible for a child to pass a competence exam and not to tell the truth. Other than to provide additional information to the jury about a child witness' cognitive capabilities that might help in their assessment of the child's credibility as a witness, it is difficult to justify the use of the *voir dire* examination. In fact, Gary Melton (1987) wrote, "the court's time is wasted by a ritual that has very dubious value" (p. 193). There is no evidence that such a test is a valid assessment of the likelihood that the child will tell the truth.

If an understanding of lying and truth telling does not guarantee truth telling, what factors determine whether a child witness will provide truthful testimony? Is it at a certain age that individuals can be relied upon to tell the truth? Are some individuals more likely than others to be truthful? Does the situation primarily determine an individual's truthfulness? In this chapter, it has been argued that no one factor alone is responsible for an individual's truthfulness. Having acquired knowledge about lying and truthfulness does not guarantee truth telling, just as telling the truth does not necessarily inform about knowledge of truthfulness. Three-year-olds whose knowledge about lying and truthfulness was less advanced than older children were more likely to be truthful than their older counterparts (Bussey, 1990a). It was shown, however, that an important factor governing children's lying and truthfulness is the result they anticipate for either statement. The more censure children anticipate for truth telling, such as threat from an adult, the less likely they are to tell the truth. Children may have more to fear for truth telling than adults, especially in sexual abuse cases where they might be threatened with dire consequences for disclosure. Hence, it could be argued that special provisions are needed to promote truth telling in children, particularly when testifying about sexual abuse episodes where it is possible that they may have been threatened for disclosing the abuse.

Children under age 5 and older children under stress find it difficult to synthesize multiple pieces of information (Perry & Bussey, 1984). Hence, the salience of the accused who has threatened the child for truth telling may undermine the child's capacity for truthfulness. At this stage we do not know if children's truth telling is affected by the presence or absence of the accused. We are currently testing this proposition in our research. If the results indicate that this is a significant factor, then it would be important for the child not to be in the line of vision of the accused or for the child to be instructed to avert their gaze from the accused when they give their testimony. Several procedures have been proposed, for example, the use of video technology, or the use of a one-way vision screen where the child, judge and counsel are blocked off from the rest of the court.

Although some of these alternate procedures are gaining wide support, their basis in methodologically sound research is far from established (Melton, 1987). Legislators worldwide have introduced a barrage of new legislation essentially designed to eliminate face-to-face confrontation with the defendant and/or diminish the courtroom audience. The effectiveness of these modifications to courtroom procedures for improving the quality of children's evidence has not been assessed.

It is important to realize that most information about children's reactions to their courtroom experience relies almost exclusively on anecdotal reports. Although this is changing (Goodman et al., 1988) there is still a need to investigate children's reactions to their participation in the legal system to determine if testimony in the courtroom is traumatic for children and what aspect of it is most traumatic (e.g., facing the defendant, judge or jury, undergoing cross-examination, talking about the abuse, etc.). Despite the possible trauma of speaking before the accused, to "say it to the face of (the defendant)" may be more necessary on psychological than legal grounds in view of the Supreme Court's decision (*Maryland v. Craig*, 1990) that the essence of confrontation is cross-examination, not physical confrontation. However, the psychological necessity of facing the accused is still in doubt. Obviously, it is a more difficult task to face the accused for those who have been threatened by the accused for truth telling, but on the other hand it may be easier to maintain a false allegation if the accused is not confronted. Although the necessity of facing the accused to ensure truthfulness is well accepted in folklore, it lacks empirical verification.

Ultimately, there is no way to guarantee that individuals of any age will be truthful. Adults have a greater capacity for being deceitful and getting away with it, justifying their deceit (disengagement) and concealing it through providing minimal leakage cues. Competency examinations can do little to guarantee truthfulness from any age group, nor is there any evidence that expert witnesses are able to judge the veracity or mendacity of a witness' testimony.

It remains, however, stemming largely from the legacy of Piaget, that children are often viewed by the public and judiciary as more prone to lying than adults. There is mounting evidence, however, attesting that children are not convincing liars; they are not very skilled at masking their deception and hence their underlying affect leaks out (e.g., De Paulo & Jordan, 1982).

In conclusion, on the basis of the research presented in this chapter it is argued that it is important to allow children to testify in cases in which they are the sole witness. It is difficult to conclude that children would be any more capable than adults of intentionally and successfully leading a jury to a false understanding of a witnessed event. If anything, the inverse holds. Competence testing of young children, regardless of its purpose in different jurisdictions (i.e., for the prosecution to establish competence or for the defense to challenge the presumed competence of the child), seems to add little to the determination of whether a child should testify or not.

ACKNOWLEDGMENTS

The research described in this chapter was funded by a grant to Kay Bussey from the Australian Research Council. I gratefully acknowledge Kerry Lee, Karen Rickard, and Fiona Robertson for assistance in data collection. Special thanks to E. Jane Grimbeek for her helpful comments on this chapter.

REFERENCES

Bandura, A. (1986). *Social foundations of thought and action: A social cognitive theory.* Englewood Cliffs, NJ: Prentice-Hall.

Bandura, A. (1991). Social cognitive theory of moral thought and action. In W. M. Kurtines & J. L. Gewirtz (Eds.), *Moral behavior and development: Advances in theory, research and applications* (Vol. 1, pp. 45–103). Hillsdale, NJ; Lawrence Erlbaum Associates.

Binet, A. (1900). *La suggestibilité* [Suggestibility]. Paris: Schleicher Frères.

Blasi, A. (1980). Bridging moral cognition and moral action: A critical review of the literature. *Psychological Bulletin, 88,* 1–45.

Bok, S. (1978). *Lying: Moral choice in public and private life*. London: Quartet Books.

Bottoms, B., Goodman, G. S., Schwartz-Kenney, B., Sachsenmaier, T., & Thomas, S. (1990, March). *Keeping secrets: Implications for children's testimony*. Paper presented at the biennial meeting of the American Psychology and Law Society, Williamsburg, VA.

Bussey, K. (1989, April). *Children's definitions and evaluations of lies and truths involving a misdeed*. Paper presented at the meeting of the Society for Research in Child Development, Kansas City, MO.

Bussey, K. (1990a, August). *Adult influence on children's eyewitness reporting*. In S. Ceci (chair), *Do children lie? Narrowing the uncertainties*. Symposium conducted at the American Psychology and Law Society biennial meeting, Williamsburg, VA.

Bussey, K. (1990b). *The content and purpose of children's lies*. Manuscript submitted for publication.

Bussey, K. (1992). Lying and truthfulness: Children's definitions, standards, and evaluative reactions. *Child Development, 63*.

Bussey, K., & Bandura, A. (in press). Self-regulatory mechanisms governing gender development. *Child Development*.

Bussey, K., & Cashmore, J. (1990). *Children's conceptions of the witness role*. Unpublished manuscript.

Bussey, K., & Lee, K. (1990). *The effect of coaching on children's eye-witness reports*. Manuscript submitted for publication.

Bussey, K., Lee, K., & Rickard, K. (1990). *Children's reports of an adult's transgression*. Manuscript submitted for publication.

Ceci, S. J., Toglia, M. P., & Ross, D. F. (Eds.). (1987). *Children's eyewitness memory*. New York: Springer-Verlag.

Chandler, M., Fritz, A. S., & Hala, S. (1989). Small-scale deceit: Deception as a marker of two-, three-, and four-year-olds' early theories of mind. *Child Development, 60,* 1263–1277.

De Paulo, B., & Jordan, A. (1982). Age changes in deceiving and detecting deceit In R. S. Feldman (Ed.), *Development of nonverbal behavior in children* (pp. 150–180). New York: Springer.

Ekman, P. (1989). *Why kids lie: How parents can encourage truthfulness*. New York: Scribner's.

Ekman, P., & Friesen, W. V. (1969). Nonverbal leakage and clues to deception. *Psychiatry, 32,* 88–105.

Feldman, R., Jenkins, L., & Popoola, O. (1979). Detection of deception in adults and children via facial expressions. *Child Development, 50,* 350–355.

Feldman, R., & White, J. (1980). Detecting deception in children. *Journal of Communication, 30,* 121–129.

Flavell, J. H. (1989, April). *Young children's understanding of fact beliefs versus value beliefs*. Paper presented in the symposium on *Children's theory of mind* at the biennial meeting of the Society for Research in Child Development, Kansas City, MO.

Freud, S. (1955). Two case histories. In J. Strachey (Ed. and Trans.), *The standard edition of the complete psychological works of Sigmund Freud* (Vol. 10). London: Hogarth Press. (Original work published 1909)

Goodman, G. S. (1984). The child witness: Conclusions and future directions for research and legal practice. *Journal of Social Issues, 40,* 157–175.

Goodman, G. S., Hirschman, J., & Rudy, L. (1987, April). Children's testimony: Research and policy implications. In S. Ceci (chair), *Children as witnesses: Research and social policy implications*. Symposium presented at the Society for Research in Child Development, Baltimore.

Goodman, G. S., Jones, D. P. H., Pyle, E. A., Prado, L., England, P., Port, L. K., Mason, R., & Rudy, L. (1988). The child in court: A preliminary report on the emotional effects of criminal court testimony on child sexual assault victims. In G. Davies & J. Drinkwater (Eds.), *The child witness: Do the courts abuse children? Vol. 13. Issues in criminological and legal psychology* (pp. 46–54). Leicester, England: British Psychological Society.

Gopnik, A., & Astington, J. W. (1988). Children's understanding of representational change and its relation to the understanding of false belief and the appearance–reality distinction. *Child Development, 59,* 26–37.

Grusec, J. E., & Kuczynski, L. (1977). Teaching children to punish themselves and effects on subsequent compliance. *Child Development, 48,* 1296–1300.

Haugaard, J. J., & Crosby, C. (1989, March). *Children's definitions of the truth and their competency as witnesses in legal proceedings.* Paper presented at the Southeastern Psychological Association Conference, Washington, DC.

Haugaard, J. J., & Reppucci, N. D. (1988). *The sexual abuse of children: A comprehensive guide to current knowledge and intervention strategies.* San Francisco: Jossey-Bass.

Henshel, A. (1971). The relationship between values and behavior: A developmental hypothesis. *Child Development, 42,* 1997–2007.

Kurtines, W., & Greif, E. B. (1974). The development of moral thought: Review and evaluation of Kohlberg's approach. *Psychological Bulletin, 81,* 453–470.

Lewis, M., Stanger, C., & Sullivan, M. W. (1989). Deception in 3-year-olds. *Developmental Psychology, 25,* 430–438.

Lindskold, D., & Walters, P. S. (1983). Categories for acceptability of lies. *Journal of Social Psychology, 120,* 129–136.

Maryland v. Craig, 110 S. Ct. 3157 (1990).

Melton, G. B. (1981). Children's competency to testify. *Law and Human Behavior, 5,* 73–85.

Melton, G. B. (1987). Children's testimony in cases of alleged sexual abuse. In M. Wolraich & D. K. Routh (Eds.), *Advances in developmental and behavioral pediatrics* (Vol. 8, pp. 179–203). Greenwich, CT: JAI Press.

Morency, N., & Krauss, R. (1982). Children's nonverbal encoding and decoding of affect. In R. S. Feldman (Ed.), *Development of nonverbal behavior in children* (pp. 181–202). New York: Springer-Verlag.

Myers, J. E. B. (1987). *Child witnesses: Law and practice.* New York: Wiley.

Perner, J., Leekam, S. R., & Wimmer, H. (1987). Three-year-old's difficulty with false belief: The case for conceptual deficit. *British Journal of Developmental Psychology, 5,* 125–137.

Perry, D. G., & Bussey, K. (1977). Self-reinforcement in high- and low-aggressive boys following acts of aggression. *Child Development, 48,* 653–658.

Perry, D. G., & Bussey, K. (1984). *Social development.* Englewood Cliffs, NJ: Prentice Hall.

Peterson, C. C., Peterson, J. L., & Seeto, D. (1983). Developmental changes in ideas about lying. *Child Development, 54,* 1529–1535.

Piaget, J. (1965). *The moral judgement of the child.* Harmondsworth, England: Penguin Books. (Original work published 1932)

Saywitz, K., Goodman, G. S., Nicholas, E., & Moan, S. (1989, April). Children's memories of genital examinations: Implications for cases of child sexual assault. In G. S. Goodman (chair), *Can children provide accurate eyewitness testimony?* Symposium presented at the biennial meeting of the Society for Research in Child Development, Kansas City, MO.

Sodian, (1989, April). *The development of deception in young children.* Paper presented at the biennial meeting of the Society for Research in Child Development, Kansas City, MO.

Stouthamer-Loeber, M. (1987, April). *Mothers' perceptions of children's lying and its relationship to behavior problems.* Presented at the annual meeting of the Society for Research on Child Development, Baltimore, MD.

Stouthamer-Loeber, M., & Loeber, R. (1986). Boys who lie. *Journal of Abnormal Psychology, 14,* 551–564.

Strichartz, A. F., & Burton, R. V. (1990). Lies and truth: A study of the development of the concept. *Child Development, 61,* 211–220.

Weinstein, J., & Berger, M. (1988). *Weinstein's evidence.* New York: Matthew Bender Co.

Wheeler v. United States, 159 U.S. 523 (1895).

Wimmer, H., Gruber, S., Perner, J. (1984). Young children's conception of lying: Lexical realism—moral subjectivism. *Journal of Experimental Child Psychology, 37,* 1–30.

Wimmer, H., Gruber, S., Perner, J. (1985). Young children's conception of lying: Moral intuition and the denotation and connotation of "to lie." *Developmental Psychology, 21,* 993–995.

Other Minds, Obligation, and Honesty

Owen Flanagan
Wellesley College

INTRODUCTION: EPISTEMIC AND MORAL ISSUES

Two philosophical issues arise persistently in discussions of children and lying. First, there are epistemic issues—issues of what sort of knowledge the child must possess in order to lie. Second, there are issues of moral psychology— issues of how and when children learn that it is wrong to lie, and in what they understand the wrongness of lying to consist. My argument is this: On the epistemic side, lying is a type of action that requires a rich understanding of other minds, of the connections between belief and action, and in particular, of the way mental representations can be transformed into misrepresentations. Children can lie without being able to correctly define the term *lie*. But they cannot lie without having solved the philosophical problem of other minds.

What I call a *minimal lie* requires that the perpetrator believes that "X" but does something (or omits to do something) with the intention of making another think "not X." Being a minimal lie is not sufficient for being a *bona fide* lie. Many practical jokes satisfy the two conditions set forth but are not lies. Furthermore, if I believe that 'X' and try to make you believe "not X" whereas unbeknownst to me "not X" is, in fact, true, then I have satisfied the conditions for a minimal lie. But I have not lied, only attempted one. Although being a minimal lie is not sufficient for being a bona fide lie, it is necessary. The purpose of marking off the concept of a minimal lie is to capture the idea that *at a minimum* we require of *bona fide* lies that *mental* misrepresentation be intended.

Children who have not yet reached the point where they possess the knowledge that (a) other persons have beliefs and that (b) they themselves possess causal powers to create false beliefs in others can simulate lies. But they cannot even produce minimal lies. A child may be able to mislead others so long as he or she has correctly surmised how to do certain things that have the effect of misinforming and misleading others. That is, before a child has learned to lie he or she can aim to mislead. Producing this behavioral effect may normally require producing a false belief in one's audience. But children need not intend to produce this false belief, even though in fact they do so. Before children know what false beliefs are, or that they have the capacity to produce them, they may *know how* to produce them. Those who have learned to lie know what a false belief is, intend to create a false belief in their audience, and know how to do so.

With regard to moral psychology, things are substantially more complicated than is acknowledged in the literature devoted to lying. It is standardly thought that children are taught that lying is wrong simpliciter. But that is not true. To put things in the most contentious way, it would be better to say that children are taught norms of politeness, privacy, reticence, and loyalty that teach them that there is no categorical obligation to tell the truth. We hear that honesty is the best policy. But "honesty" has a complex meaning for us. And the policy is by no means set forth as a categorical one. Rational self-interest, the need for privacy, self-esteem, and self-respect compete with honesty and are thought, in some cases, to override the requirement to be honest. Kindness, politeness, tact, and the demands of friendship and loyalty also compete with honesty, and they too, in certain cases, override the requirement to be honest. Socialization in honesty involves the acquisition of what Aristotle called *phronesis*—practical wisdom. The honest person is the person who knows when to tell the truth, and does so in the right circumstances, in the right way, and to the right persons. There is no known algorithm that can be taught and that will produce the requisite set of moral sensitivities.

THE SEMANTICS OF 'LIE'

What does the child need to know in order to tell a lie? The answer to this question depends in part on what is meant by *lie*—by the semantics of the term. The semantics specify what conditions must be met for an action to be a bona fide lie. Once the relevant conditions are specified, psychologists can tell us whether children satisfy the relevant conditions. What are the relevant conditions?

It is tempting to think that in order to lie the child must know what a lie is, and that this is equivalent to saying that the child must possess the concept of a lie. But a trap lurks in this way of speaking. A child no more needs to have the concept of a lie in order to lie, than he or she needs to have the concept of consciousness in order to be conscious. Certainly, the child needs to be capable of engaging in acts that satisfy our concept of a *lie* in order to lie, but he or she herself need not possess the relevant concept.

What is our concept of a lie? The classical view is that the extension of a concept consists of a set of conditions that are jointly necessary and sufficient for the correct application of the concept. A child lies just in case he or she meets the necessary and sufficient conditions. This idea has two problems. First, like most concepts, the concept of a lie does not admit of characterization in terms of jointly necessary and sufficient conditions. One might think that expressing a falsehood, knowing it is false, and intending to mislead by expressing this known falsehood are jointly necessary and sufficient conditions for lying. The trouble is that a speech act can express a falsehood, be known by the speaker to express a falsehood, be intended to deceive and not be a bona fide lie. Practical jokes, as I have said, are examples.

Actually, even the assumption that a lie must involve a speech act is problematic if one sticks to the straight and narrow in characterizing speech acts. The philosopher Sissela Bok (1978), for example, defined a lie as "an intentionally deceptive message in the form of a statement" (p. 15). But surely pointing someone in the wrong direction can count as a lie even though no statement is involved at all.

The problem of defining *lie* is like the problem of defining *knowledge*. For centuries, philosophers thought that Plato had succeeded in providing a definition of knowledge in terms of necessary and sufficient conditions. S knows that "X" if and only if S believes that "X"; S is *justified* in believing "X"; and "X" is *true*. But in the 1960s a series of counterexamples to the justified-true-belief analysis of knowledge created a philosophical industry of seekers for the additional necessary condition. No satisfactory additional condition was ever discovered that, together with justified-true-belief, was immune to counterexamples.

Wittgenstein's idea that conceptual structure is normally rooted in family resemblance rather than necessary and sufficient conditions helps explain why exceptionless definitions for nontechnical terms almost never exist. The psychological theory of prototypes has vindicated the core idea. Indeed, even concepts such as "even number," which do have strict necessary and sufficient conditions, display prototype structure, that is, 2 is a better exemplar of an even number than 1,224, in the mind of an ordinary speaker.

With lies all the putative necessary conditions — saying something false, knowing that it is false, and intending by one's utterance to deceive — matter in our determination of some act as a lie. But these conditions can be satisfied and a lie not be told due to subtle features of the context or to the speaker's overall intentional state. Again, certain jokes fit this mold straightforwardly. More counterintuitively, one can tell a lie by telling the truth. Indeed, one lying strategy is to tell an abridged version of the truth knowing that one's audience will elaborate its meaning in exactly the wrong direction. If one's concept of "lie" has as a necessary condition the requirement that one says what is false, then such lies are not real lies. The concept of a minimal lie can accommodate lies that involve speaking the truth since the characterization given involves the intention to create a false belief. The means of generating the false belief are left unspecified. This is why I have some hope that the notion of a minimal lie captures a necessary but not a sufficient condition for a bona fide lie, where by a "bona fide lie" I mean "lie" as construed by experts, say, by moral philosophers. The core idea that, at a minimum, a lie requires intent to deceive does not capture a necessary condition of the concept "lie" as used by all ordinary speakers because some speakers, especially young children, think of objective falsehood as the most important feature of a lie. Intent to produce false belief figures negligibly, in some cases not at all, in their understanding of the concept of "lie." This is true, for example, of children who think that mistakes are lies. The claim that intent to produce false belief is a necessary condition of a bona fide lie is a normative semantic claim, not a descriptive sociolinguistic claim.

With lying, unlike with knowing, moral features are relevant in the determination. So-called *benevolent lies* will be thought by some to not be *real* lies at all. The best explanation for this is that for some individuals bad moral intent is the most important determinant of a lie. Inasmuch as a benevolent lie is a false utterance intended to mislead with good moral intent, it is not really a lie. But our semantic intuitions pull in both directions here. We might be tempted to say of a speech act intended to save a life that it is not a real lie or, equally sensibly, that it is a lie but is excusable.

The upshot is this: Knowing what counts as a lie is no simple matter of knowing a definition. Lies have prototypical structure (Burton & Strichartz, this volume). Almost all the research shows that objective falsity has greatest saliency in determining whether something is a lie for very young children, and thus that for them mistakes are considered lies (Peterson, Peterson, & Seeto, 1983; Piaget, 1932; Wimmer, Gruber, & Perner, 1984). Furthermore, contrary to one standard expectation neither preschoolers nor older children seem to lay much stock in whether a falsehood is believed or not in determining whether a lie has been told. Stating a falsehood is normally enough for the ascription of a lie (Bussey, this volume).

Definitions and ascriptions come apart in important ways. Coleman and Kay (1981) found that objective falsehood was the main feature given by adults when asked to define *lie*. But it "turned out consistently to be the least important element by far in the cluster of conditions" in actually determining whether a lie is ascribed (Lakoff, 1987, p. 72). Other important elements in the cluster of conditions relevant to the determination of whether some act is a lie include believing the opposite of what one says, and intending to deceive. All the research shows that both of these factors increase in saliency over time in determining whether a lie is attributed, despite the fact that they do not display similar saliency in attempts to give definitions of the word "lie." For many adults, objective falsehood reigns supreme for the definitional task, even as its power wanes in determining ascriptions. Suppose that I, unaware that my partner in crime has changed the location of your pilfered fortune, accidently send you in the right, rather than in the wrong, direction. Have I lied or not? Our semantic intuitions tug in two directions. I have said what is true while I intended to say what is false. If objective falsehood is the main determinant I have not lied. Whereas if intention to deceive and belief that what I said is false are more salient, then I lied but failed to mislead.

Learning the semantics of a term involves learning in the first instance how to use it, rather than how to define it. We might wonder whether children will ascribe lies, something they are taught is wrong, when there are countervailing pressures to do what are, under normal circumstances good things, for example, obeying adults and being loyal to friends. The answer appears to be that they will. Haugaard and Reppucci (this volume) found that most young children correctly attributed a lie when they were given a vignette in which a child protected a classmate who violated an order to stay in from recess. On the basis of this study and several related ones, they have concluded that "most young children understand that a child who purposefully makes an inaccurate statement, either at the request of a parent or in order to protect a friend, is telling a lie." The evidence suggests that the ability to use the term *lie* correctly, and to ascribe lies on the basis of a complex set of properties—even when these properties occur in situations that might be thought to undermine their saliency—matures earlier than the ability to define a lie in terms of these very properties.

What about self-ascription of lies? Attribution theory provides good evidence of a self-serving bias. The self-serving bias warrants the prediction that third-person attributions of lies and self-attributions will diverge in identical circumstances. Not surprisingly, children powerfully tempted to transgress some rule will do so, but will deny that they have done so. Children who peek at a toy lie when asked if they did (Lewis, Stanger, & Sullivan, 1989). It is unlikely that the children think that they did not peek. In fact, it is well known that both children and grown-ups often construe certain circumstances as mitigating in their own case (which would not be mitigating for others), and thus offer self-serving construals of their own lies as not real lies. The child who is caught in a lie and says sheepishly, "I was only kidding," may well believe her own, after the fact, self-attribution to a far greater extent than perfect memory of her actual prior intent would permit.

The upshot so far is that an individual can possess, as it were, first-order competence at lying, and even attribute lies correctly (especially third-personally), without being able to provide a definition in terms of jointly necessary and sufficient conditions (there are none), nor even a definition that captures what properties that individual thinks, in practice, constitute the most important factors in the determination of whether some act is a lie. Competent use of the term *lie* is best measured against the preferred prototype in the linguistic community in contexts where ascription, rather than definition, is called for. Ability to define the term *lie* is a bad test for adults as well as for children (Coleman & Kay, 1981). That said, the evidence indicates that the preferred prototype in which belief in something other than what is conveyed and intent to deceive have greater weight than objective falsehood is not fully acquired until the teen-age years—and even then it is somewhat unstable (Burton & Strichartz, this volume).

Why does intent eventually take top billing in our conception of a lie? It has to do, I think, with the distinctively moral character of lying. Lying is asymmetrical with truth telling in this respect. That is, even though we are taught that it is right to tell the truth and wrong to lie, all lies are moral violations, whereas most truthful utterances have nothing to do with morality. To inform another truly about the weather, one's health, what's on TV, or the latest finding about neuro-transmitters, is not conceived of as doing something that falls within the domain of the moral. If you lie about these things you do what is morally wrong. But the converse is not true: When you say what is true in these domains you do not do something morally good or praiseworthy. You simply do what is expected.

Focusing on the moral component of our prototype helps explain one respect in which practical jokes differ from lies. When you say something false with the intention of deceiving me in order to get me to open the door with the bucket of water on top it, you satisfy the conditions of intent, belief, and falsehood. The temptation to say that you have not really lied comes from the fact that you intend fun, not harm.

The general semantic model I favor is a network theory. We possess elaborate cognitive models for terms, with nodes and links to other terms, which them-selves have elaborate connections to other concepts. The holism of conceptual structure explains why subtle or novel features of a situation can kick off novel semantic intuitions. Strictly speaking, any unmarried male is a bachelor. But "Is the Pope a bachelor?" is a question that produces in many a mental cramp. Similarly, a white lie is a lie; it has "lie" as a proper part of its name, after all. But if I say of your disgustingly gaudy new dress—"Oh Jane, what a colorful new outfit!"—fully intending to make you think I like it, have I lied? Our semantic intuitions tug in two directions, producing a cramp similar to the question about the Pope.

Paradigm case lies involve speech acts. Is intentionally pointing someone in the wrong direction a speech act? If it is, then doing so is a lie. If it is not a speech act, then doing so is not a lie. What counts as a lie depends on how things are fitted together in our semantic network. Normally, there will be a significant amount of shared structure and thus shared meaning within a relatively homoge-neous linguistic community. But identical terms will often diverge somewhat in meaning even within a relatively homogeneous community of speakers. The fact that the concept of "lie" is bound up with a moral conception suggests a special complication. The moral conceptions that the term is tied to may well differ among speakers of the same language. Insofar as meaning is rooted in the overall semantic relations of a term, the meaning of lie will have a different meaning for different speakers depending on their moral background theory. Imagine a strict Kantian for whom all intentional falsehoods are lies and for whom no lies are excusable. For such a person, "benevolent lies" are just as good exemplars of bona fide lies as are straightforward self-serving lies, and both are equally bad. If one disagrees with the usage of the term *lie* of this strict Kantian, it is tempting to revert to sociolinguistic facts about preferred usage (as I have done at several points), and claim that she doesn't understand the meaning of lie. But we should be clear, when we do so, that all we have then done is pointed to where linguistic power lies. We have not hashed out the real issue that involves a substantive disagreement about morality.

The upshot is simply that to know what *lie* or any other term in the language means, and to understand how to ascribe it correctly, involves possessing an elaborate theory, not just of lies and lying but of *all* their semantic relations besides. In the case of "lie," these relations include connections to an elaborate moral theory. There are no purely semantic facts about the meaning of "lie" that stand sequestered from our views about substantive moral matters.

Indeed, despite whatever heterogeneity in background moral conception affects use of the term *lie,* it seems fair to say that the term has a moral component for all speakers. A lie requires that the perpetrator of the intentional falsehood intends harm. The Kantian simply has very strict criteria of when harm is intended.

So far we have isolated several components of our shared prototype: falsity, belief, intent to deceive, intent to produce harm by this deception. To be a competent liar, a child needs to know how to express falsehoods, he or she must be capable of believing "*X*" while expressing or otherwise indicating "not *X*." One must be capable of intending to deceive another, and one must be capable of intending, as part of the deception, to do moral harm (i.e., to protect oneself from being caught in some rule violation, to evade responsibility, to inconvenience or injure another, etc.). To possess this competence, to be capable of telling a *moral lie,* requires more than does the capacity to tell a minimal lie because it requires in addition to the intent to deceive the intent to do harm by this deception. I return to the more specifically moral dimensions of lying after saying something more specific about the epistemic competencies required for successful lying.

LYING AND KNOWLEDGE OF OTHER MINDS

When does the child know enough to really lie? The answer, I said at the start, is when he or she has solved the problem of other minds. Of course, I was exaggerating because the problem of other minds is, in one sense, a problem no one ever solves. Other minds never lose all their opacity. Furthermore, insofar as we do solve the problem of other minds, that is, insofar as we learn to treat others as mental beings and to make inferences about their mental states, we do not solve the problem all at once. Indeed, it is a lifelong project to become better and better at reading other minds. Nonetheless, there is a clear, but attenuated, sense in which lying requires solution of the problem of other minds. This comes out by reflecting on what sort of knowledge needs to be imputed for a minimal lie to be ascribed. A minimal lie requires that the perpetrator believes that "*X,*" but intends to make another think "not *X.*" A minimal lie requires that one intends to produce in another the effect of *mental* misrepresentation. To intend to produce some effect *E,* requires that one comprehends the nature of *E,* in this case the nature of mental misrepresentation, at least to some degree. The construct of a minimal lie is meant to highlight the fact that in order to lie the child must know something about the nature of false beliefs and about how to produce them.

Misleading does not require possession of this knowledge about false beliefs. A child can know how to mislead by pointing, by sabotage, by laying false tracks, and so on, without comprehending how he or she is producing this desired effect (Chandler, Fritz, & Hala, 1989; Sodian, 1991). Susan Leekam (this volume) rightly points out that "the use of a deceptive strategy does not always entail *intention* to influence *belief* at the time of the deception." As she points out, children may have lots of rules of thumb, such as "say 'no' if accused of a misdeed." They may recognize that these rules of thumb have some degree of success, but not have a clue as to how they produce these successes. Insofar as young children think that certain generalizations obtain, they might think of them as straightforward generalizations linking certain behaviors on their part with certain behaviors on the part of others. The child might operate on the basis of purely behavioral generalizations without being fully consciously aware of these generalizations, and more importantly, without entertaining any views what-soever about what mediates the behavior of his or her audience—indeed without any idea that there is reason to posit mental representations in the audience. According to the distinction between minimal lies and misleading, the same speech act, for example, "No, I didn't look at the toy when you were out of the room," motivated by the same self-serving intention, may be a case of mislead-ing (with no intention to create a false belief) or a lie (with that intention).

Leekam suggests that in mature lying the "speaker might not only have an intention about the listener's *belief* of the *statement.* She might also have an intention about the listener's *belief* of her own *intention* or *belief.*" This seems right. Being a good liar requires competence both at producing false belief in one's audience and in making the audience think that one is being helpful and cooperative and speaking the truth. To be capable of producing a minimal lie one needs only to be capable of believing "*X*" and intending to make one's audience believe "not *X.*" But one can produce a minimal lie, in this sense, without being at all successful at duping one's audience. Success at lying requires that one have some understanding of how others read faces, voices, and bodily gestures in testing for sincerity. Unless one realizes that one's audience is assessing what one says in the context of how one says it, as well as in the context of the current situation—is the situation ripe for acts of self-protection?—and in terms of an overall assessment of one's character, one will not be good at lying.

The competencies required for successful lying require a very elaborate understanding of other minds. Children must understand that other persons are repositories of intentional states, such as beliefs and desires, and that beliefs can be manipulated. They must also understand that they themselves are being read for sincerity, reliability, and motivational state by their audience, and must know what markers need to be deployed to give the desired impression of these things. Saying what is false with the intention of producing false belief is rarely sufficient to produce false belief in a savvy audience.

We might put the general point this way. There are minimal lies, and the set of competencies required to produce them, and there are mature minimal lies, which require additional competencies. Successful liars have as a constitutive part of their aim the production of two false beliefs: a false belief about some state of affairs and a false belief about their sincerity in portraying that state of affairs. Leekam, Bussey, and Tate and Warren (all in this volume) have illuminating things to say about how the production of the impression of sincerity is produced.

A minimal lie requires seeing others as intentional systems (Dennett, 1971), interpretable in terms of belief-desire psychology. Unlike misleading, a minimal lie requires understanding the complex relation between misleading actions (pointing in the wrong direction, speaking falsely) and the production of false beliefs in one's audience. When do children achieve the competence to tell minimal lies?

Children begin to use words such as "think," "know," "remember," "mean," and "guess" soon after their second birthday (Wellman, 1990). But the evidence is pretty convincing that they lack mastery of the concept of false belief until they are 3.5 or 4. Because linguistic competence can lag behind conceptual competence, the evidence for this comes from imaginative experiments that ask children to predict where an individual who wants the candy, and who believes it is still in the kitchen, will look, given that, unbeknownst to the child, it has been moved to the living room. Children under 4 consistently predict that the individual will look where the candy *really* is, rather than where she should believe it is, whereas children over 4 correctly predict that the individual's misrepresentation will guide his or her action (Wellman, 1990, p. 63).

It is somewhat obscure why the concept of *false belief* is so hard for children to master. Children engage in imaginary and pretend play at very young ages. Such play would seem to involve holding false beliefs, and treating one's playmate as going along with these false beliefs. So what is missing and why? One possibility is that children do not conceive of imaginary thought or pretending as involving false beliefs at all, but simply as imagining and pretending—activities with their own internal nontruth functional logic. The idea is not incredible. Indeed, it is not obvious that adults think of imagination and pretense as involving falsehood in any straightforward sense. Imaginative fiction expresses deep truth, despite the fact that each sentence of a work of fiction is false, strictly speaking.

One theory is that when it comes to belief (but not imagination) children think that the mind is a mirror of nature, and therefore hold a "direct copy understanding of reality-oriented representations" (Wellman, 1990, p. 263). Minds mirror the way the world is through beliefs. Therefore, when asked to track the beliefs of a puppet or a friend who has been intentionally deceived about the whereabouts of some candy or a pencil, children under 4 will ascribe a belief, qua "reality-oriented" representation, that corresponds to where the candy or pencil actually is, rather than one that misrepresents, no matter how clear (to us) that that is the right surmise given the evidence available to the puppet or friend. It is as if it is part of the essential nature of beliefs that they represent reality. This is the default theory. It only gradually yields in the face of mountains of anomalies.

Children master the problem of other minds to a considerable extent during the third and fourth years of life. They deploy belief-desire psychology, and the mental verbs that are its stock, with increasing sophistication between their second and fourth birthdays. But mastery of the concept of false belief is a consistent laggard. Perhaps the explanation just offered is the right one for why this is so.

But false belief is not the only piece of the puzzle of other minds still not in place in children between 3 and 4. Children are seriously deficient in the use of trait-ascriptions, in deploying the vocabulary of lay personality theory (Wellman, 1990, p. 119). Adults read other minds in part by ascribing stable character traits to individuals. Indeed, one of the main ways we assign initial probabilities to the utterances of others involves bringing complex characterological frames to these utterances.

Children understand minimal lies when they have mastered the concept of false belief, that is, around age 4. But they are not very good at lying until age 7 or so (Leekam, this volume). One plausible inference is that success at lying comes later than lying because it requires that children can think reliably about the effects of what they say and do on others, and, in particular, that they can think about what their occurrent actions and patterns of action cause others to think about them. Sophistication in thinking about what another thinks about oneself (one's intentions, motives, and character) requires skills of character appraisal, so one can judge the other, and an understanding of the logic of character inference, so one can judge how the other is appraising oneself (see Tate & Warren, this volume, on the difficulty of coaching youngsters to display successfully the requisite skills). If I am completely unreliable, realize this, and know that my audience knows that I am unreliable, then speaking the truth (for once) will produce the desired self-serving effect much better than stating yet another intentional falsehood. I tell a minimal lie because I believe that "X" and intend to make my audience believe "not X." But because my audience puts "not" before everything I say, I can best produce the desired effect by saying "X"!

SOCIALIZATION FOR HONESTY

The semantics of "lie," what lie means, depends on the network of semantic connections the concept has. One important set of connections involves the other moral terms one uses, the interpretation of these terms being fixed in complicated ways by the moral conception one abides. Relatedly, the epistemology of lying, what a child needs to know in order to tell a genuine lie, involves having solved the problem of other minds and knowing that lying is wrong. In this section I bring these connections to morality into clearer view.

When is an individual capable of telling a lie for which he or she is legitimately held morally responsible? Earlier I characterized a moral lie as involving the intention to cause harm. One might naturally think that culpability follows on the capacity to tell an intentional falsehood with the intention to cause harm. I think this is almost right. The child who knows full well that he or she harms a friend by denying knowledge of the whereabouts of the friend's toy, which he or she intends to keep for himself or herself, does what is morally wrong. We hold a child morally responsible when he or she understands the nature of harms and intends to produce one. However, it is not always easy to know when a child possesses this knowledge. The very same act may *cause* harm without involving the *intention* to cause harm. Imagine the child who lies to a friend simply in order to keep the friend's toy for himself, but who doesn't really understand that this harms the friend. This child, unlike the first child we imagined, causes harm to a friend but does not intend to do so. To make matters even more complicated, one might intend to cause harm without possessing a full understanding of the nature of harms, or even of the particular kind of harm one intends to produce. One might not completely understand, as we say, exactly what is wrong with the act in question or how it injures the other. The point is that our judgments of a child's culpability for a lie are tricky. Many more factors are considered mitigating for children than are considered mitigating for adults, and it is often unclear when a child possesses all the competencies required to be truly diabolical.

The competencies required for moral responsibility depend, in part, on an understanding of why lying is wrong and of the kinds of harms produced by lies. So we need to ask what children are taught about the immorality of lying. What exactly do we teach about the morality and immorality of lying? What do we teach about the different kinds of lies? How wrong do we teach that lying is? I cannot give a full answer to these questions here. But I can provide a sense for how complicated the full answers will be.

The answer to this cluster of questions is extremely important in the context of the present discussion because children's competence to testify in courts is standardly characterized as requiring evidence of two competencies: the epistemic competence to distinguish truth from falsehood, and the moral competence to understand the wrongness of lying. Apparently, the courts frame the second competence here as involving knowledge that one is obligated to speak the truth as a witness or "being sensitive to the obligations of the oath" (Haugaard & Reppucci, this volume). The competent witness is one who understands the "duty" to tell the truth (Bussey, this volume).

There are three points that will help get at the some of the complexities involved in the socialization for honesty. First, there is the issue of when children begin to receive instruction about the morality of lying, and what sort of prominence it is given in the overall structure of the morality that is being constructed in the mind of the child. Observations of normative interactions between mothers and children in their second year indicate that transgressions discussed in order of frequency involve issues of destruction/dirt, place/order, teasing/hurting others, politeness, and sharing (Dunn, 1987).

Lying itself is not a major issue before the second birthday. It is unlikely that parents engage in instruction about the wrongness of lying before children begin trying to lie. When does this occur? I'm not sure. But it seems plausible that the first "ecologically valid" lies are ones about misdeeds (Bussey, this volume), and that they start to occur with enough frequency to be noticed after the second birthday. We can presume then that children who already understand that certain actions constitute misdeeds, and who know that misdeeds are disapproved of, begin to be taught that lying about misdeeds is also disapproved of.

How disapproved of is it? There is, I think, no simple and clear-cut answer to this question. We teach children that it is wrong to lie about a misdeed. But we understand—and convey this understanding—that it is among the most natural things to try to cover up a misdeed. Furthermore, even as children are learning that lying about misdeeds is wrong, they are still in the process of learning what misdeeds are. Bunglings and accidents are sometimes discounted by adults. But they are not always discounted—at least not in the rush to anger. Thus children are rightfully wary about underestimating what the adult theory of misdeeds includes and does not include. Overgeneralizing is not a bad strategy.

Although many parents try to teach that lying is worse than the misdeed, children also realize that certain misdeeds are bad enough to be worth a try at covering up. The added marginal cost of being caught in the lie, as well as in the misdeed, is not so significant as to constitute a genuine disincentive to lying.

The first set of points can be summarized this way. Initial learning about the wrongness of lying is almost certainly tied to a certain class of lies—lies about misdeeds. Children are not exposed, at least at first, to anything like a general theory of lies and lying. Learning about the wrongness of lies about misdeeds comes after there has been prior instruction in the wrongness of certain characteristic misdeeds. How wrong the child thinks lying about misdeeds is, depends on how wrong adults convey that it is. But this is variable. It depends on how parents, caretakers, and preschool teachers treat lies. Do children learn that they are under an obligation or have a duty to tell the truth at this stage? I doubt it. Certainly talk of "duty" and "obligation" is not normally introduced to youngsters. Do children learn that it is unconditionally wrong to lie about misdeeds? Again, I think not. Sensitive adults convey to the child an understanding of why she has lied. In this way they convey the impression that they understand that there are certain conditions that make it hard not to lie, and that moderate, possibly even dissolve, judgments of wrongness.

The second point relates to the question of the development of the child's general understanding of the virtue of honesty and the vice of dishonesty. Most lies involve speech acts. It follows according to the network theory of meaning that both the nature and wrongness of lies need to be considered in relation to the norms governing speech acts more generally. Thinking of lies in this way imperils thinking about lies as a simple class to pick out, or as a class with simple norms governing wrongness. The philosopher, Annette Baier (1990), put the central point eloquently when she wrote that:

> Talk, as we teach and learn it, has many uses. It is not unrelievedly serious—it is often an extension of play and fun, of games of hide and seek, of peekaboo, where deceit is expected and enjoyed, of games of Simon says, where orders are given to be disobeyed, of games of tag, where words have magic power, of skipping games, where words are an incantation. Speech, as we teach and learn it is not just the vehicle of cool rational thought, and practical reason but also of fun and games of anger, mutual attack, domination, coercion, and bullying. It gives us a voice for our many moods, for deceit and sly strategy, as well as for love and tenderness, humor, play and frolic, mystery and magic. The child is initiated into all of this and gradually learns all the arts and moods of speech. Among these are the arts of misleading others, either briefly and with intent soon to put them straight ("I fooled you, didn't I!") or more lastingly to keep deceit going for more questionably acceptable purposes. (p. 262)

Exaggeration, politeness, tact, reserve in self-expression, omitting to say certain things, joking, and so on, all have to do with honest expression. Children are decidedly not taught that it is right, or even good, to be honest in the expression of all the matters that one could be honest about. The main point is that insofar as children are taught that there is an obligation to be honest, and thus not to lie, it is a complex, conditional, and culturally circumscribed obligation.

Consider in this regard the norms governing answers to polite queries about one's well-being. "If you ask me 'How are you?' and I reply 'Fine thanks, and you?' although I take myself to be far from fine, I have not lied" (Baier, 1990, p.

268). Such speech acts are "a form of consideration for others, a protection of them from undue embarrassment, boredom, or occasion for pity. Truth, let alone 'the whole truth,' is something we very rarely want told to us . . . veracity is knowing *when* one is bound to speak one's mind and then speaking it as best one can" (Baier, 1990, p. 268).

The third and final point relates to the implications of our style of socialization for honesty for the understanding of the special requirements of forensic contexts. In a culture of pure Kantians, children might learn that there is a categorical obligation to tell the truth (when the truth should be told, that is). In such a society, courts could count straightforwardly on children comprehending the obligation to tell the truth in a court of law. But, most children in this culture at least, are not raised to think of the obligation to tell the truth as a duty (notice the word itself has an almost archaic quality to it), or as a categorical obligation. This is not necessarily due to defects in our moral educational practices. It may as well be thought of, given what has just been said, as an accession to the complexity of moral life, and as based on the recognition that it is sometimes good, and not merely permissible, not to tell the whole truth.

But what this means is that children need to be taught explicitly that there are certain contexts in which the obligation to tell the truth is an unconditional duty, for example, when one is under oath in a court of law. This, no doubt, can be taught. I recall learning about this unconditional obligation watching "Perry Mason," while at the same time being exposed to the constant perjury the show's plot line required. But it is worth noting that the lesson of the solemnity of oath taking is harder now to learn and take seriously than it once was. This may have implications for the ease with which competing motives might lead a child to wonder whether it might be permissible to lie in court, say, to protect an abusive parent whom she, nonetheless, loves.

The point can be brought out this way. The raised right hand signifiying oath-taking followed by the words "I solemnly swear to tell the truth, the whole truth, and nothing but the truth" used to be followed by the phrase "so help me God" while the left hand was placed on the Bible. In Massachusetts the Bible is gone as is the phrase "so help me God." But the concept of a "solemn swear" is a religious one, and the removal of the religious underpinnings (in a very literal sense) makes our solemn swears different from traditional solemn swears with the original underpinnings. Within an orthodox setting in which the Bible and the phrase "so help me God" meant, among other things, that this was a context in which the demand to speak the truth could not be overridden by any other consideration, the expectation of complete veracity (especially if a child was socialized to fear hellfire and brimstone) might be reasonable. But in a more secular context, in which the practice lacks these underpinnings, the worry that loyalty to an abusive parent or fear of parental punishment might exert greater motivational force than a "solemn swear" is a legitimate one.

Hopefully, there are ways to create secular equivalents of solemn contexts in which truth telling is understood as an unconditional obligation. It would be a great cultural loss, a loss in our capacities to trust each other in close relations, and a loss in the ability of our social and political institutions to adjudicate certain conflicts, if we cannot reconstitute grounds for individuals, young and old, to feel the moral pull of such obligations.

CONCLUSION

Socialization for honesty is complex and culture-dependent. Children display honesty and dishonesty long before they are competent users of the relevant terms. Correct ascription, however, requires semantic competence. Proper use of the concept "lie" requires comprehension of a wide array of other concepts. These concepts include both the epistemic notions of belief, intent, and misrepresentation, as well as moral notions that specify, among other things, the sort of intent that counts as morally wrong and the sorts of situations in which dishonesty is wrong. The semantic task is not a simple one of learning, say, a dictionary definition. It involves the acquisition of an epistemic theory of other minds, as well as a moral theory. Because different moral conceptions construe the nature of lies, the kinds of lies, and the demands of honest expression in different ways, individuals will differ both in their ascriptions of lies and in their ascriptions of (degrees of) wrongness to different kinds of lies. In the end, the semantic problem of the meaning of "lie," the epistemic problem of coming to understand other minds as representational systems capable of containing misrepresentations, and the ethical task of coming to see oneself as a moral agent capable of doing good and harm (including the harms associated with creating misrepresentations in others) are inextricably intertwined. The sort of person that can be counted on to be honest will have had to learn many things, almost none of which is simple to teach. An honest character requires learning both our intricate theory of honest expression and caring that one exemplify that theory in one's life. Understanding other minds and comprehending the subtleties of our theory of honest expression is something the most manipulative cad needs to know as well as the saint. It is caring that one exemplifies this theory, that one be a person of a certain sort that makes all the difference. It is to this task of character formation and concern for one's own character that our moral community pays insufficient attention.

ACKNOWLEDGMENT

I am grateful to Debbie Zaitchik for helpful conversations on the issues discussed in this chapter.

REFERENCES

Baier, A. C. (1990). Why honesty is a hard virtue. In O. Flanagan & A. O. Rorty (Eds.), *Identity, character, and morality: Essays in moral psychology* (pp. 259–282). Cambridge, MA: MIT Press.

Bok, S. (1978). *Lying: Moral choice in public and private life.* New York: Random House.

Chandler, M., Fritz, A. S., & Hala, S. (1989). Small-scale deceit: Deception as a marker of two-, three-, and four-year olds' early theories of mind. *Child Development, 60,* 1263–1277.

Coleman, L., & Kay, P. (1981). Prototype semantics: The English verb *lie. Language, 57,* 26–44.

Dennett, D. C. (1971). Intentional systems. *Journal of Philosophy, 8,* 87–106.

Dunn, J. (1987). The beginnings of moral understanding: Development in the second year. In J. Kagan & S. Lamb (Eds.), *The emergence of morality in young children* (pp. 91–112). Chicago: Chicago University Press.

Lakoff, G. (1987). *Women, fire, and dangerous things: What categories reveal about the mind.* Chicago: Chicago University Press.

Lewis, M., Stanger, C., & Sullivan, M. W. (1989). Deception in three-year-olds. *Developmental Psychology, 25,* 439–443.

Peterson, C. C., Peterson, J. L., & Seeto, D. (1983). Developmental changes in ideas about lying. *Child Development, 54,* 1529–1535.

Piaget, J. (1932). *The moral judgement of the child.* London: Kegan Paul.

Sodian, B. (1991). The development of deception in young children. *British Journal of Developmental Psychology, 9,* 173–188.

Wellman, H. M. (1990). *The child's theory of mind.* Cambridge, MA: MIT Press.

Wimmer, H., Gruber, S., & Perner, J. (1984). Young children's conception of lying: Lexical realism-moral subjectivism. *Journal of Experimental Child Psychology, 37,* 1–30.

9 Commentary: On the Structure of Lies and Deception Experiments

Mark G. Frank
University of California, San Francisco

There is a particular structure to every situation in which a lie is told. There must be a liar, a person being lied to, a motive for the lie, a period spent conjuring the lie, a form to the lie, as well as stakes associated with successful or unsuccessful delivery of the lie. The value assigned to each of these structural features necessarily affects the likelihood that a person will choose to lie or tell the truth. For example, it is more tempting to lie to people who are poor lie detectors than to people who are good lie detectors; it is more tempting to lie for motives that justify a lie (such as avoiding harm), than for motives that don't justify a lie (to gain a reward that we don't deserve); it is more tempting to lie in situations in which there is little risk if caught in a lie, compared with situations in which terrible punishment awaits those caught lying, and so on.

The adult deception literature has looked at both lies and the structural features of lie situations as independent variables to answer the following two questions: "What are the behavioral clues to deceit?" and "How good are people at detecting these behavioral clues to deceit?" (see DePaulo, Stone, & Lassiter, 1985; Zuckerman & Driver, 1985, for reviews). For example, lying and truth telling are manipulated in order to determine behavioral clues to deceit (e.g., Ekman, Friesen, & O'Sullivan, 1988; Frank, 1989; Kraut & Poe, 1980); or certain structural features, such as characteristics of the liar and the stakes, are manipulated to determine their effect on observers' abilities to detect deception (e.g., DePaulo, Lanier, & Davis, 1983; Frank, 1989).

The topics of lying and the structural features of lie situations have received the same treatment in the child deception literature, with one big exception. In the child literature, lying appears not only as an independent variable (e.g., Feldman, Jenkins, & Popoola, 1979; Morency & Krauss, 1982), but also as a *dependent* variable (e.g., Ceci & DeSimone Leichtman, this volume; Chandler, Fritz, & Hala, 1989; Hartshorne & May, 1928; Lewis, Stanger, & Sullivan, 1989; Nigro & Snow, this volume; Tate & Warren, this volume). For example, structural features such as motives are manipulated to determine how they influence whether or not a child will lie (e.g., Ceci & DeSimone Leichtman, this volume), or features such as the characteristics of the liar and target are manipulated to ascertain their effects on whether or not a child will lie (e.g., Nigro & Snow, this volume).

These structural features are present in every deception scenario, regardless if the scenario presents itself in the real world or in the laboratory. In the laboratory, some of these structural features are experimentally manipulated and others are not; however, all of these structural features are present. When manipulated in an experiment, they have been shown to influence the probability that a child will lie (e.g., Ceci & DeSimone Leichtman, this volume; Nigro & Snow, this volume). It seems reasonable to presume that even when not manipulated, these structural features will still exert pressure on a child to lie or tell the truth.

This chapter attempts to incorporate the findings on children's lies presented in this volume into a general discussion of the structural features of both lies and the situations in which lies are produced. These structural features of a lie—such as deliberately misleading someone, and the structural features of a deception situation—such as the motive for the lie, the stakes for successful and unsuccessful deception, the relationships of the individuals involved, and so forth— are examined in order to speculate how the way in which each of these features are modeled or experimentally manipulated affects the likelihood that a person— in this case a child—will lie.

FEATURES THAT DEFINE A LIE

The definition of lying that has had the most utility for our research on adult deception was formulated by Ekman. He defined a lie as a deliberate attempt to mislead a person (target), without the target's prior consent to be misled (Ekman, 1985). This two-part definition has the most utility for our research because it distinguishes between deliberate and accidental behaviors, as well as between sanctioned and unsanctioned behaviors. It is these distinctions that have important implications for children's deception research.

A Deliberate Attempt to Mislead. The first part of Ekman's (1985) definition is the deliberate attempt to mislead on the part of the liar.[1] The liar chooses a

---

[1]The term *liar* is used as a shorthand term to describe the person telling the lie, even though the term *liar* has pejorative connotations. Because there are situations in which lying is justified (e.g., lying to a person who wants to murder your brother about his whereabouts), this term is intended to be connotatively neutral.

statement or course of action that the liar believes will create erroneous thoughts, actions, or beliefs in the target. Authors in this volume have discussed this concept under the term *intent;* their discussions are quite thorough and the reader is directed there for a fuller understanding of this term (e.g., chapters by Burton & Strichartz, Flanagan, and Leekam).

The deliberate attempt to mislead component of a lie is important because the word *deliberate* separates behaviors done with a purpose from behaviors done by accident. In other words, a child who deliberately misleads someone has *chosen* to mislead that person. In contrast, a child who misleads someone inadvertently or unconsciously by definition is not aware that he or she is misleading or being untruthful. If the child is unaware of the untruthfulness, then the consequences of consciously presenting untruthful information—that is, guilt, or fear of being caught in a lie, or fear of punishment for the act the lie was designed to conceal (all of which reduce the likelihood that an adult will lie, all other things being equal; Ekman, 1985)—would not be present[2] in proportions large enough to either inhibit or unmask a child's presentation of untruthful information. In this instance, the untruthful child should appear behaviorally no different from a truthful child.

This deliberate versus nondeliberate presentation of erroneous information is one of the key features that distinguish among the three types of nontruthful testimony outlined by Haugaard and Reppucci (this volume). Haugaard and Reppucci distinguish intentional presentation of erroneous information from both mistaken recall of an event and honest difference of opinion in that only in the former case does an individual intentionally present false and misleading information. In both latter cases the individual presents what he or she believes to be the truth. Notice that the law relies upon this distinction to make the presentation of false information prosecutable only when it is done deliberately (called fraud or perjury in legal proceedings). The presentation of the very same false information, but done unwittingly, is not a prosecutable offense.

Without the Prior Consent of the Target. The second aspect of Ekman's definition is that the liar does not give the target any prior notification that the liar is planning to deceive the target, so that the target cannot give his or her consent to being misled. Thus, an actor in performance is not lying to us; when we choose to view a performance we have given our tacit consent to the actors to mislead us into believing that they truly are the role they are playing (note that we even give awards to those actors who are the most effective in misleading us). However, an actor who engages us with an equally skilled performance *without*

---

[2]It should be noted that people do not need to lie to show guilt and fear. For example, we might feel guilty about killing someone in a car accident, even though it was not our fault. We can fear being punished for mistakenly giving inaccurate information on our tax returns, even though we did not deliberately choose to mislead the Internal Revenue Service.

our overt or tacit consent—the street corner confidence person or "con man"—
is lying to us.

Certain social contexts can serve to give both liar and target prior notification
that misleading information will be presented, and by entering these contexts,
targets and liars give their consent to being misled. For example, the individuals
involved in a bargaining situation do not truthfully state their final positions; this
is the norm for such situations that both participants understand and expect.
Likewise, many games—such as poker—require deliberately misleading someone as part of the game. As long as all the players understand that bluffing is part
of the game, then the players give their tacit consent to being misled when they
consent to play the game.

There are also some social contexts in which misleading others is less clearly a
norm, such as certain forms of politeness. When we receive a present, we tell the
gift giver that we really enjoy the present, regardless whether we actually like the
gift or not. We also tell the host of a party that we enjoyed ourselves, whether we
actually enjoyed ourselves or not. In these situations, we are sometimes, but not
always, truthful; however, we are not expected to be always truthful—we are
expected to be polite. Imagine the chaos unleashed upon our social gatherings if
we were entirely truthful all the time.

We can only assume that a potential liar—whether adult or child—will
be more likely to engage in misleading behaviors when the situation or the target authorize such behavior. After all, the integral part of a poker game
involves misleading one's opponents. This is in contrast to deliberately presenting misleading information in a courtroom, which if discovered, is a punishable
offense. It should be kept in mind, however, that just because a person or
situation authorizes the liar to present misleading information does not mean that
the liar will actually do so. It is just that the situation or the target permit the
potential liar to present misleading information with little or no penalty if the liar
so chooses.

What This Definition Does Not Assert. Ekman's definition of lying does
not assert that lies be spoken. Leekam (this volume) uses the term *listener* to
describe the person who is the object of the lie; this implies that lying must take
the form of a statement or be spoken (e.g., Bok, 1978). We believe along with
Bussey (this volume) and Flanagan (this volume) that deliberately pointing in a
wrong direction is as much of a lie as deliberately telling someone to head in a
wrong direction; thus, children who deliberately point in the wrong direction to
mislead someone are lying (e.g., Chandler et al., 1989). This is why the term
target is preferred to the term *listener*.

Included in this category of unspoken lies are situations in which a person
deliberately does not answer a question, or a person deliberately chooses not to
disclose information that he or she understands must be disclosed. An example of
the latter situation comes from Ekman (1989), who describes the son who lies by

not telling his father that he got kicked out of school; the son is lying because he knows that his father has made it clear in previous discussions that the disclosure of this type of information is mandatory. Ekman (1985) has called these types of lies *concealment lies*. Notice that by not answering a question, or by not volunteering information, the liar is still attempting to deliberately mislead a target, and again without the target's prior consent. This is why the abused child who does not respond when questioned about the abuse is lying. This is also why a child who knows that being touched on the genitals by a stranger is wrong and must be reported to a parent is lying when he or she has been touched on the genitals by a stranger and tells no one.

Ekman's definition of a lie also does not presume that the information contained in the lie be factually incorrect, even though others have reported this to be essential to the prototypical lie (Burton & Strichartz, this volume; Coleman & Kay, 1981). Flanagan (this volume) mentions how practical jokes can fall into this category. Take the following example of a practical joke: one person (target) asks to borrow a golf ball from another person (liar). The liar gives one of his joke exploding golf balls to the unwitting target, and the target asks, "Is this a good ball?", to which the liar responds sarcastically, "No, it explodes." Because the liar knows that the target would not expect the liar to admit it was an exploding ball if in fact it was, then the liar's factually correct response misleads the target. A target's startled reaction when he or she hits the ball and it explodes will confirm that the target was in fact misled. Ekman (1985) has called this *telling the truth falsely*, and it demonstrates that one can lie with factually correct information. However, it should be noted that this is a very sophisticated form of lying even by adult standards; thus, it is unlikely that a child would be sophisticated enough to use such a strategy.

Why This Definition. This definition allows us to eliminate the other types of untruthful testimony outlined by Haugaard and Reppucci (this volume)— memory deficits or distortions, as well as testimony that involves an honest difference of opinion. If we are trying to extrapolate to serious real-life situations such as courtroom testimony of sexual and physical abuse, then it appears as if this definition captures—both by what it requires, as well as by what it doesn't require—the contingencies that the legal community would also classify as a lie worthy of penalty.

In summary, the way an investigator defines a lie may influence the likelihood that a child will lie. An experimental task that involves whether or not a child will *accidentally* mislead someone tells us nothing about *lying*. Likewise, an experimental task that requires a child to present misleading information that both the child and the target know is part of a game or expected from a social context will most likely result in an overestimation of the likelihood that this child will tell a lie in situations in which the child's honesty is expected and required by the potential target. Only those statements or behaviors that meet the requirements of this definition of a lie[3] can begin to be generalized to questions involving the likelihood that a child will lie in situations such as the courtroom.

STRUCTURAL FEATURES OF A LIE SITUATION

Just as there are particular features shared by lies, there are also particular features shared by all lie situations—whether these situation occur in the real world or are created in the laboratory.

Many of the contributors to this volume have addressed the effects of a number of these structural features on a child's propensity to lie. For example, Bussey discussed motives for the lie, the form of the lie, and the stakes for the lie; Ceci and DeSimone Leichtman examined motives for the lie, and the interrelationships between the liar and the target; Nigro and Snow investigated the characteristics and interrelationships of liar and target; and Tate and Warren examined motives for the lie, the form of the lie, and the presence or absence of a coach. These chapters have demonstrated that when these features are manipulated as independent variables, they affect the likelihood that a child will lie. However, those features that are not manipulated must also influence—either intentionally or unintentionally—the likelihood that a child will lie or tell the truth.

The best way to illustrate the potential effects of each of the structural features is to draw them out into basic categories—the lie, the scenario, and the people—and then show or speculate how they might influence children's truthfulness. First, there are the structural features of a lie:

1. The type and form of the lie.
2. The motive behind the lie.

Then there are the structural features of the deception scenario:

1. The stakes for telling a lie and the stakes for telling the truth.
2. The interval between the event and the liar's presentation of his or her account of that event.

---

[3]However, this is where the study of children's lies has a distinct ecological validity advantage over the study of adults' lies. Because most young children do not know when they are in a deception experiment, they choose of their own volition whether or not to lie to a target whom the children believe has not authorized the lie (but in fact the target registers whether or not they lie). Thus, these lies (save "tricking" lies) usually conform with Ekman's (1985) definition of a lie. Conversely, adult subjects sign consent forms informing them that they will be asked to lie sometime over the course of the experiment; it can be argued that the experiment itself authorizes the lie and thus the lies produced by adult subjects do not conform with Ekman's definition of a lie.

And finally, there are the interpersonal structural features:

1. The characteristics of the liar.
2. The characteristics of the target.
3. The presence or absence of a coach.
4. The presence or absence of others.

It should also be kept in mind that more often than not these features interact with each other. However, in order to get a handle on these interactions we must first measure or predict the effects of these features separately. For this reason, and for the sake of clarity, these features are addressed individually.

The Features of a Lie

The features of a lie in this sense are different from those discussed in the previous section. Although the earlier discussion focused on issues involved in defining a lie, this section deals with the outcome of that definition—the form of the lie, and the motivation behind it.

The Type and Form of the Lie. Even though a lie can take many different forms, there are only two basic types of lies. First, there are the types of lies that require the fabrication of an event; these lies take the form of multiword statements (e.g., telling someone that you built something you didn't; Tate & Warren, this volume), one word responses (e.g., "Did you know who broke my toy?", "No"; Ceci & DeSimone Leichtman, this volume), or gestures (e.g., nodding or pointing in a misleading direction; Chandler et al., 1989). Second, there are the types of lies that require concealment of an event (Ekman, 1985); these lies take the form of an absence of behavior, either in response to a direct question or in response to a compulsory disclosure (e.g., not volunteering the fact that a "thief" gave the child a severe head rubbing; Peters, 1990).

The amount of behavioral sophistication needed to deliver the different forms of lies in all likelihood affect the probability that a child will lie. For example, it is probably more difficult for a 3-year-old child to fabricate an allegation than to conceal an allegation; the former requires constructing a false allegation, while the latter requires saying nothing (as pointed out by Tate & Warren, this volume). It may not even be in the behavioral repertoire of 2- to 3-year-old children to fabricate an account of an event via a multiword statement (let alone a plausible multiword fabrication). However, one-word responses, gestures, and concealment lies are all in the behavioral repertoire of 2- and 3-year-old children. Thus, a child most likely will have the ability to lie by concealing or giving one word answers before he or she has the ability to generate lies by multiword, multistate-ment accounts (see Leekam, this volume).

Because it is easier for a child to make a false statement by responding with a nod, a "yes," or a "no" than by responding with a narrative, a child may be more likely to lie when a target—via his or her line of questioning—constrains the form of a child's lie to these simpler forms. The following anecdote illustrates how this works. When I was 6 years old I heard it was dangerous to jump out of a second-story window; yet when I looked out of the second-story window of our house, this did not look very dangerous. I decided to jump. I survived unscathed, but feared greatly the punishment that I would receive if I told the truth as to why I jumped (my leap was discovered because I made the mistake of jumping out a window that was directly above the window where my mother and a neighbor were having coffee). While feigning injury (to forestall punishment), I debated whether or not I should lie or tell the truth (to avoid further punishment). Mean-while, my mother and grandfather concocted a story that explained how I could have *accidentally* slipped out the window, somersaulted, and miraculously land-ed on my feet unharmed. They then asked me if this is what happened. All I had to do in order to tell the lie was either nod or say "yes," which I did. However, had they asked me "what happened?", I doubt I would have lied; and, if I did lie, it certainly would not have been very convincing. In this case, the way the question was posed made it so easy for me to lie that I did (this lie was so successful that my mother will only discover it if she reads this chapter).

Thus, the form in which the lie is delivered—multiword, one-word, gesture, or concealment—must impact the likelihood that a child will lie. It appears that children may be more likely to show an inclination to lie—for whatever rea-son—when the form of their lie is a simple one-word or simpler concealment response than when they must verbally produce details of an event that has not happened.

The Motive Behind the Lie. There are many motives for a child to lie. For example, Ekman (1989) drew up the following list of motives for children's lies (note that these are much the same motives for adults' lies): to avoid punishment, to get something a child couldn't get otherwise, to protect friends from trouble, to protect self or others from harm, to win admiration of others, to avoid creating an awkward social situation, to avoid embarrassment, to maintain privacy, and to demonstrate power over authority. Ceci, DeSimone, Putnick, Lee, and Toglia (1990) also add the motive to sustain a game, and the motive to conform with a stereotype. However, it seems that sustaining a game involves the prior consent of the target, and thus would not be classified as a lie under the prior consent of the target condition of Ekman's definition (see earlier section on features that define a lie).

It has already been noted by Tate and Warren (this volume) that it is the failure to take motives into account that is partly responsible for why there is a debate as to when children develop the ability to lie.[4] The reason for this is that different motives often require different levels of behavioral complexity to deliver the lie. For example, considerably more complex thinking and behaviors are needed to create a lie to avoid an awkward social situation than is needed to merely gainsay the accusation of a punishable behavior (see chapters by Leekam and by Flanagan). For the former motive, a child must anticipate the feelings of the person who might feel awkward and then choose a course of behavior that will most effectively assuage the awkwardness of the situation, which may also require more verbal production and sophistication (Tate & Warren, this volume). This is in contrast to the latter motive, in which a simple denial or nonresponse to the accusation would suffice (see the section on the form of the lie).

Because the behaviors associated with these different motives require different levels of cognitive complexity, it is not surprising that the emergence and potency of each of these motives to lie seems to change with age for the child. For example, it has been reported that the majority of lies for 4-year-olds are lies to avoid punishment, while for 5-year-olds a greater percentage of their lies are trick or pretend lies (Bussey, 1990; Stouthamer-Loeber, 1987; both cited in Bussey, this volume). It is for these reasons that researchers have proposed that the ability and willingness of children to lie for these different motives follow a particular developmental progression from less to more complex; for example, children first generate lies for self-preservation (e.g., to avoid punishment and harm), and then add motives until they reach the level where they can generate lies for self-presentation (e.g., to win admiration), and finally complete their repertoire with the addition of altruistic lies (e.g., to avoid awkward social situations; Burton & Strichartz, this volume; Bussey, this volume; Ceci & DeSimone Leichtman, this volume; DePaulo & Jordan, 1982; Leekam, this volume; Tate & Warren, this volume).

The evidence from psychological experiments has suggested that children as young as $2\frac{1}{2}$ to 3 years of age will lie for a number of different motives; it has been shown that $2\frac{1}{2}$-year-old children will deceive if it is in the context of a game

---

[4]It is important to note that these structural features may inadvertently impact not only the question *when will a child lie,* but also the question *when can a child lie?* These are two are distinct questions. As we have seen, the *when will a child lie* question is answered by understanding the features of the lie, the situation, and the people involved, in order to determine the circumstances in which a child is more or less likely to lie, once he or she has the capacity to lie (other examples from this volume include Bussey; Ceci & DeSimone Leichtman; Nigro & Snow; and Tate & Warren).

The *when can a child lie* question is answered by understanding the child's mind to determine whether or not the child has the capability to lie, and at what age he or she gains this ability (examples from this volume: Burton & Strichartz; Flanagan; Leekam; and Haugaard & Reppucci). If a child *can't* lie, then the question whether he or she *will* lie becomes irrelevant. It is only at the age in which a child *can* engage in a particular kind of lie does the *will he or she lie* question becomes relevant. Even though it is beyond the scope of this chapter, we can speculate that the structural features described in this chapter impact *both* questions: the when *can* a child lie question, as well as the when *will* a child lie question.

(Chandler et al., 1989), or to trick someone (Tate & Warren–Leubacker, 1990, this volume); 3-year-olds will lie to avoid punishment (Lewis et al., 1989; Nigro & Snow, this volume), to protect a loved one, to get a reward, to sustain a game, and to conform with a stereotype (Ceci et al., 1990; Ceci & DeSimone, this volume). Eventually, by the time children reach the age of 6, they can and will lie for all of the motives mentioned in the beginning of this section (Ekman, 1989). Thus it seems that the ability and willingness of children to lie is contingent upon the specific motive to lie only when the children are between the ages of 2.5 and 6. To date, we know that children can lie to avoid punishment by the age of 3, and can lie to protect a loved one somewhere between 3 and 4, and so forth. However, the exact age at which children will lie to avoid creating an awkward situation, to avoid embarrassment, to maintain privacy, and to demonstrate power over authority, has yet to be determined. However, as Bussey (this volume) has noted, just because a child has the capacity for a particular behavior does not necessarily mean that he or she will implement this behavior.

Ceci and DeSimone (this volume) concluded that children *will* lie when the motivational structure of a situation is tilted toward lying. In one sense this means that children—like adults—will be more likely to lie when the motive for a lie is sanctioned rather than unsanctioned. Thus, "tricking" lies (Tate & Warren, this volume), or a "white lie," such as a child telling Grandma that he or she really loved the pajamas with the attached feet when in fact the child really wanted a Nintendo—are sanctioned lies. A child whose motive for lying involves taking the credit for a good deed that the child did not do is telling an unsanctioned lie (e.g., Ceci & DeSimone Leichtman, this volume).

It is also true that the motives that make a lie unsanctioned to a child may also make a lie sanctioned to an adult, and vice versa; for example, many children rate "white" lies as negative as other more invidious lies (Bussey, this volume). This suggests that researchers must first assess what a child feels about the motive behind the lie, and not just assume what a child feels, before proceeding to generalize the results of a deception study.

In another sense, the tilting motivational structure means that a child realizes that certain situations sanction certain motives for certain lies; for example, it is OK to lie to avoid harm if this harm stems from the neighborhood bully. It is not OK to lie to avoid harm when the harm emanates from a parental spanking for misbehavior.

Finally, a change in the child's perception of a motive can sanction a previously unsanctioned motive to lie. The motive to avoid punishment will not sanction a lie when the punishment stems from the parent. However, if the child believes that this parental punishment is unjustified or undeserved for the offense, he or she may decide that the unjust nature of the punishment justifies telling a lie (Ekman, 1989).

Thus, each motive to lie must be understood within the situation in which it is embedded, as well as the child's perception and understanding of the situation as well as the motive. Understanding the child's perception of a motive may help explain the results reported by Tate and Warren (this volume) that 5-year-old children were more likely to engage in a "tricking" lie than 2½-year-olds; 5-year-olds better understand that it is OK to "trick" people because the whole point of a tricking lie is to tell the target later that he or she was tricked (as Paul Ekman's 10-year-old daughter, Eve, has explained). Two-and-one-half-year-olds may not understand this, and to many of them this type of lie may be as "bad" (i.e., unsanctioned) as any other type of lie (see Bussey, this volume), which may explain their general reluctance to engage in a "tricking" lie.

The general point is that just because a 3-year-old is capable of lying to avoid punishment does not mean that he or she *will* lie to avoid punishment. Furthermore, because a 3-year-old will lie for one motive— for example, to avoid punishment —does not mean that he or she will lie for a different motive—for example, to avoid an awkward social situation. Bussey's argument (this volume) bears repeating: Children do not necessarily engage in all the behaviors in which they are proficient.

Scenario Structural Features

The features of a lie scenario are the product of many factors, such as the motives to lie and the people involved in the scenario. However, at this point it may be more useful to examine features of the scenario independent of the lie and the people.

The Stakes for Telling a Lie and for Telling the Truth. The patterns of rewards and punishments for lying or telling the truth—the *stakes*—remains one of the biggest obstacles to the ecological validity of deception paradigms (e.g., DePaulo et al., 1983; Ekman, 1985; Frank, 1989). Only recently has this feature of deception situations received attention in the area of children's deception research (e.g., Bussey, this volume; Ceci & DeSimone Leichtman, this volume; Peters, 1990). However, for reasons ranging from interest in low-stake scenarios to ethical prohibitions against high-stake situations, this feature has not been systematically explored, particularly with regard to the question as to whether or not a child will lie in high-stake situations.

The stakes for a deception scenario can be broken into separate rewards and punishments because each has opposite effects on the propensity to lie. For example, we can speculate that the more severe the threat of punishment for lying, the less likely the child is to lie. Likewise, Bussey (1990) and Peters (1990) have shown that the more severe the threat of punishment for telling the truth, the less likely the child is to tell the truth.

It is just as straightforward to propose that as the reward for successful lying increases, the child will be more likely to lie. We can also presume that situations in which the reward for truthfulness increases, so would the tendency to be truthful (e.g., an adult's smile to a 3-year-old girl increases her likelihood to be honest; Nigro & Snow, this volume).

However, rarely in the real world do rewards for successful lying occur independent of punishments for unsuccessful lying. Yet rewards for successful lying are presented in the laboratory without the complementary, counterbalanced threat of punishment for unsuccessful lying (e.g., Kraut & Poe, 1980). Thus, we do not know how high the rewards for successful lying must be in relation to the punishments for unsuccessful lying in order for the child to lie. Moreover, we also do not know how the relative weight of these two elements needed to induce a lie or truthful statement changes with the child's age.

Finally, the fear of being caught in a lie versus the fear of telling the truth highlights questions concerning children's perceptions of the consequences of lying, compared with the consequences of the act about which they are lying. That is, what do children learn about the trouble they may get into for lying? Burton and Strichartz, and Bussey, address some of this in their chapters. Yet, in many households lying is an offense worse than any other transgression (Ekman, 1989). Are there things that can be done to enhance the child's belief that to lie about serious matters, even to lie about major transgressions, may be in itself a worse transgression? We need to evaluate how each child views the severity of his or her lie in relation to the transgression it is designed to conceal in order to assess more accurately the likelihood that a child will lie in a given situation.

The Interval Between an Event and the Liar's Presentation of His or Her Account of That Event.

A child playing with his or her father's hacksaw breaks the blade. The father discovers this 2 hours later, and questions the child about possible involvement. What effect does this 2-hour interval have on the likelihood that the child will lie? What if the father questioned the child 5 minutes after it happened? What if it was 5 weeks? This time interval between an event and the initial inquiry—where the child may first have to actually tell a lie or the truth—is a feature of children's *deception* experiments that has received little attention to date (this is a key variable in children's *memory* research, however; e.g., Goodman, Aman, & Hirschman, 1987).

How do the laboratory manipulations of this interval compare with that found in the real world? As a general rule the procedure in laboratory research involves asking the child about an event within minutes after it has occurred (Ceci & DeSimone Leichtman, this volume, Lewis et al., 1989; Nigro & Snow, this volume; Peters, 1990; Tate & Warren, this volume). However, in typical abuse cases the initial interrogation of the child may not be for hours, days, weeks, or even months after the event (Mason-Ekman, 1989). What effect might this time interval have on the child's tendency to lie? We know that increasing intervals have an effect on adult eyewitness accuracy (Loftus, 1979). How might this decreasing memory of the event affect a young child's willingness to lie deliberately? We do not know this yet.

Interpersonal Structural Features

The final group of structural features that influence whether or not a child will lie is the nature of the interpersonal relationships between adults and children and the roles that each play in a deception situation. The child as well as the adult can accommodate the role of the liar, the target, the coach, or observer; moreover, each participant may play more than one role at a given time.

Characteristics of the Liar. It has been reported earlier that by the time children reach age 6 they will lie for all the motives mentioned earlier (Ekman, 1989). But are older children more likely to lie than younger children? Again, this may depend on the motivation to lie; for example, there may be no difference between older and younger children in their likelihood to lie to avoid punishment due to the fact that it is one of the first motives to emerge in the child, and it remains the most frequent motive to lie into adulthood (Bussey, 1990; Ekman, 1989). However, there are differences between younger and older children in the likelihood to lie to trick someone such that older children are more likely to engage in the trick lie (Tate & Warren, this volume). Thus, the motives to lie, as discussed earlier in this chapter as well as elsewhere in this volume (Bussey; Ceci & DeSimone Leichtman; Flanagan; Leekam; Tate & Warren), may influence age-related differences in the likelihood that a child will lie.

Are there personality factors that might influence a child to lie? Ekman's (1989) analysis of the Hartshorne and May (1928) study suggested that more intelligent children are less likely to lie because they are more likely to recognize the risks for getting caught; however, when the odds of being caught in the lie are negligible, the more as well as the less intelligent children seem as likely to lie. Machiavellianism also seems to be a personality trait that predisposes certain children to be more likely to lie; however, this trait does not seem to manifest itself until around the age of 10, and so may be irrelevant to this analysis (Braginsky, 1970). Therefore it seems as though Hartshorne and May's (1928) original conclusion is still valid—that situational factors such as the stakes for the lie, the motivation to lie, the sanctioned and unsanctioned nature of the lie, and so forth, tend to outweigh personality factors in predicting whether or not a child will lie.

The Characteristics of the Target. The child's perception of the target seems to influence the likelihood that a child will choose to lie. For example, preliminary results reported in Ceci et al. (1990) suggest that when the target is a negatively evaluated person the child is more likely to lie about this person's actions. The converse may also apply: It may be that children are less likely to lie if the target is positively evaluated by the child.

The target's age is another factor; children seem more ready to lie to children of their own age—in the context of tricks and games—than to adults (Tate & Warren, this volume). However, research has also shown that children are more likely to give erroneous and misleading information to adults than to children (Ceci, Ross, & Toglia, 1987). Again understanding motives may clarify this situation. For example, because adults are a more potent agent of punishment than children, a child may be more likely to lie to an adult to avoid punishment than to lie to another child to avoid punishment. However, a child may be more likely to lie to play a trick on another child than to play a trick on an adult.

The nature of the child (liar)–target relationship is also important to consider; generally speaking, if the child shares values with the target, or respects the target, he or she will be less likely to lie to the target due to the increased guilt the child would feel when lying (Ekman, 1989). A child who hates a target may not feel such guilt about lying to the target and may actually be more inclined to lie to a despised target. However, there are exceptions to these rules; Ceci and De-Simone Leichtman (this volume) have shown that a child is more likely to lie to a respected loved one when protecting this loved one from trouble. But if the child believes that the target is an effective lie-catcher, the child may also be less inclined to lie to this target (Ekman, 1985). Finally, the behavior of the target can differentially affect the likelihood that different liars (in this case, boys and girls) will lie; Nigro and Snow (this volume) have shown that 3-year-old girls are less likely to lie when the target smiles while questioning them, and 3-year-old boys are less likely to lie when the target stares while questioning them.

The actual presence, or implied future presence, of a target or assailant must also affect a child's truthfulness. Peters (1990) and Bussey (1990) have shown that a threatening person can inhibit a child's truthfulness. What if this person leaves the room, or is hidden behind a screen—is the child more likely to disclose honestly an event such as abuse? Might the opposite occur such that to keep the target out of the physical presence of the child increases the chance that a child might lie? This debate was at the heart of two recent Supreme Court rulings. In *Coy v. Iowa* (1988), the court ruled that placing a screen between a defendant and the child witness/victim violated the defendant's Sixth Amendment right to confront his or her accusers—based on the presumption of Justice Scalia that it is harder to lie to someone face to face than behind his or her back.[5] In *Craig v. Maryland* (1990), the court ruled that it is constitutional for a child to testify via closed-circuit TV from a room separate from the defendant as long as

---

[5]Justice Scalia stated: "It is always more difficult to tell a lie about a person 'to his face' than 'behind his back.' In the former context, even if the lie is told, it will often be told less convincingly. . . . The state can hardly gainsay the profound effect upon a witness of standing in the presence of the person the witness accuses, since that is the very phenomenon it relies upon to establish the potential 'trauma' that allegedly justified the extraordinary procedure in the present case. That face-to-face presence may, unfortunately, upset the truthful rape victim or abused child; but by the same token it may confound and undo the false accuser, or reveal the child coached by a malevolent adult" (*Coy v. Iowa*, 1988, pp. 1019–1020).

the judge and jury can see enough of the child's demeanor to weigh the credibility of his or her testimony. However, the effect of a physical or psychological barrier on a child's likelihood to tell the truth or lie has not been determined.

The Presence or Absence of a Coach. One specific role assigned to adults in lie situations is that of a coach (Tate & Warren-Leubacker, 1990; Tate & Warren, this volume). In the Tate and Warren studies, the coach was on friendly terms with the children and many of them chose to participate in the lie ("trick"). However, is it possible that an unfriendly or threatening coach could make a child fabricate a story about someone else, (e.g., a tricking lie)? What would happen if the coach was a parent who threatened the child against telling the truth? Studies have shown that a threatening target (coach?) can inhibit truthfulness in a child via concealment lies (Bussey, 1990; Peters, 1990). Could this threatening coach make a child lie about the actions of a loved one, such as one of the child's parents? Would a child be likely to maintain a coached lie designed to harm when the coach is one parent and the target another? Does a coach's effect on a child liar disappear when the coach is removed from all future contact with the child? These questions need to be examined in light of the surprisingly high number of child custody cases in which it appears as if the child had been coached to fabricate an abuse allegation (Jones & McGraw, 1987; Mason-Ekman, 1989).

Finally, we can ask the converse question: Can you coach a child to be truthful? What happens if you say to the child that it is very important that you tell the truth? What effect would that have on the children in the paradigms described in this volume? In other words, what is the antidote to coaching a child into a lie? How do we reduce the likelihood that a child will lie or inoculate the child against lying?

The Presence or Absence of Others. In order to obtain the most accurate prediction of whether or not a given child will lie in a given situation, the effect of other observers and participants on the child must be assessed. For example, in a sexual abuse case a number of different people are brought to bear on the child—that is, social workers, psychologists, police officers, a judge, and other family and friends, and so on. What effect do these people have on the child's propensity to be truthful or deceptive?

The presence of this investigatory team in an abuse case also creates a numerical disparity on the side of the case that believes that a crime has occurred. Only the defense attorney and the defendant/alleged perpetrator are on the side that believes a crime has not occurred. We do not know what effect a large number of people holding a certain expectancy has on the likelihood that the child will lie, or, if the child has initially lied, the likelihood that the child will buck the expectancies and recant before the case goes to trial. It seems reasonable to suggest that being surrounded by people who believe an offense has occurred will make the child who is concealing abuse be more likely to disclose this abuse; however, the converse may also apply in that it might be more likely for the child who has not been abused to claim that abuse has occurred.

Interaction of Features

It is important to reiterate that these features do not usually operate independent of one another. Many of the unanswered questions in the study of children's lies involve the interaction of a number of these structural features. For example, what do we know about the relationship between the stakes and the type and form of the lie? Is it the case that as the stakes increase linearly, the child is increasingly more likely to engage in a concealment lie? (such as a child concealing the truth; Bussey, 1990; Peters, 1990). Yet as stakes rise might it be the case that this relationship is curvilinear for one word or gestural forms of lies, and negatively related to multiword fabrications? We do not know what these relationships might be due to the fact that we do not have any systematic data from the high arousal end of the stakes continuum.

Now what happens if a third variable is added, such as motives? We can ask, "Will a 3-year-old child engage in a concealment lie to protect a loved one when the stakes for lying are so high as to create near paralyzing arousal levels?" Will a 3-year-old child engage in a multiword fabrication under these conditions, or is it the case that this child will only engage in a concealment lie for this motive at this arousal level? Now what if we add a coach to this equation, and ask, "Will a child lie to protect a loved one under extremely high arousal levels when the child is being coached by another adult loved one?". How much lower must the stakes be in order to allow this 3-year-old child to present a multiword fabrication as well as conceal? What if the motive was to avoid punishment, or to gain a reward? What form of lie could the child engage for this motive, and under what stakes? These are all questions that have remained unanswered to date.

An Example. An experiment reported in this volume illustrates how the structural-features-as-independent-variables effect and interacts with some of the nonmanipulated structural features. In Nigro and Snow's experiment, the independent variables were the characteristics of the liar (in this case, gender) and the characteristics of the target (smiling or staring teacher). The lies told in this experiment had a particular form (one word or gestural), a motive (to avoid punishment or trouble), particular stakes—a reward for successful lying (satisfying their curiosity without being punished), a punishment for unsuccessful lying (the possible anger of the experimenter), an interval between peeking at the toy and being asked to whether or not they peeked (within seconds of peeking, if they peeked), and all done in the presence of an inattentive observer (the child's parent was in the room).

Nigro and Snow report that 3-year-old boys were more likely to lie when they were smiled at by the experimenter, whereas 3-year-old girls were less likely to lie when smiled at. What happens if we change the focus of our analysis to the nonmanipulated structural features? What happens if we change the values assigned to these features? What might have happened if the children were asked, "Tell me everything you did when I was out of the room"? Now how many children would produce the narrative needed to lie? What if the experimenter told the children not to peek because the person who correctly guesses what the toy is wins a big prize? Would changing the motive for lying from avoiding punishment or disapproval to gaining a reward change the results such that both boys and girls would disclose that they peeked at equal rates, independent of the target's smiling? (Given that boys seem to be punished more for transgressions than girls [Sears, Maccoby, & Levin, 1957], avoiding punishment might have a slightly stronger potency for boys.) In other words, to what extent are these results for liar and target characteristics contingent upon just those experimentally manipulated variables, or do the other structural variables such as motive and time interval help create that particular result?

CONCLUSION

This chapter described a number of features that form the structure of both lies and deception scenarios, and showed, when the data permitted, and speculated otherwise, how these features may influence children's deceptive behavior.

The effects of these features are not limited to those features that undergo direct experimental manipulation. Because each one of these features appear in various forms in all deception situations, they cannot do anything but influence the likelihood of deception. So while measuring the main independent variables, it can be the case that the other structural features are exerting an equally strong effect on a child's tendency to lie or be truthful.

The effect of these structural features on whether or not an adult will lie has not been addressed in the adult deception literature because virtually no adult studies allow a subject to choose whether or not to lie. Certain experiments will allow subjects to choose when to lie, or which question to lie to (e.g., Frank, 1989), but do not allow the subject to choose whether or not to lie at all. Experiments have usually randomly assigned individuals to lie or tell the truth because these experiments have been more interested in clues to deceit and people's ability to detect deception than whether or not they will lie (e.g., Kraut & Poe, 1980).

In contrast, the children's literature has been focused more on the conditions under which the children will lie. Thus, clearly delineating the value of the structural features in children's studies takes on greater importance than in adult studies because the value assigned to these structural features directly impacts the dependent variable, whether or not a child will lie.

Finally, there are a number of benefits to listing, defining, and estimating the effect of each of these features on a child's propensity to lie. First, explicitly identifying these features ensures that each feature is not overlooked both when designing and interpreting deception research; in other words, so that we can be sure the rate at which children lie in an experiment is caused by the variables we think caused the effect. Second, it allows us to compare more easily the results of a laboratory experiment to the real-world situation it was designed to model by making a feature by feature comparison across both situations. And third, it allows us to predict more accurately the outcome of situations in which deception is a possible response; one can determine the value of each feature and estimate how it may compel or deter a child from lying.

What all these speculations and analyses suggest is that one ask the following 10 questions about any children's deception study in order to understand, generalize, or model deception experiments:

1. Is the child deliberately presenting misleading information, or is it merely a memory distortion or honest difference of opinion?

2. Has either the target or the situation presented the child with authorization to present misleading information?

3. Does the investigator word questions in such a way that a child has merely to respond with a one-word answer to lie, or must the child respond with some sort of narrative? Or, how does an investigator get a child to admit a fact in which he or she is concealing, without leading the child into presenting false information?

4. Are there motives for the child to lie, and if so, what are they?

5. What are the stakes? That is, what are the patterns of rewards for successful lying, risks or punishments for unsuccessful lying, rewards for truth telling, and risks and punishments for truth telling?

6. How long after the alleged event was the child questioned?

7. What are the characteristics of this particular child?

8. What are the characteristics of the target, is this target in the presence of the child, and what is the child's relationship to the target?

9. Is there a coach, and what is the child's relationship to him or her, either now or in the future?

10. Are there other people involved, how many are there, and how many hold what expectancies about the particular situation?

By no means should this list be considered an exhaustive list of questions to ask or list of structural features. Although every situation involves motives, stakes, people, and so forth, there are other characteristics which may affect a child's likelihood of lying. For example, what happens when a child is questioned about something that he or she has very limited knowledge, such as sexual behavior? However, the point here is that every deception scenario has in common each structural feature mentioned in this chapter.

Clearly, our knowledge of children's abilities and proclivities to lie is in its infancy. Hopefully the framework presented in this chapter revealed some of the holes in our knowledge, as well as raised a number of questions that will help guide future research piece together the entire picture of children's lies. It is only when we more fully understand how the values of these structural features influence the likelihood that a child will lie can we begin to generalize confidently the results of laboratory research to such dramatic and serious situations as children's courtroom testimony.

ACKNOWLEDGMENT

The author is supported by NIMH NRSA training grant No. MH09827. I would like to thank Paul Ekman for his insightful and influential comments on earlier drafts of this chapter.

REFERENCES

Bok, S. (1978). *Lying: Moral choice in public and private life.* New York: Random House.

Braginsky, D. D. (1970). Machiavellianism and manipulative interpersonal behavior in children. *Journal of Experimental Social Psychology, 6,* 77–99.

Bussey, K. (1990). Adult influence on children's eyewitness reporting. In S. J. Ceci (chair), *Do children lie? Narrowing the uncertainties.* Symposium conducted at the biennial meeting of the American Psychology/Law Society, Williamsburg, VA.

Ceci, S. J., DeSimone, M., Putnick, M., Lee, J. M., & Toglia, M. (1990). Motives to lie. In S. J. Ceci (chair), *Do children lie? Narrowing the uncertainties.* Symposium conducted at the biennial meeting of the American Psychology/Law Society. Williamsburg, VA.

Ceci, S. J., Ross, D. F., & Toglia, M. (1987). Age differences in suggestibility: Narrowing the uncertainties. In S. J. Ceci, M. P. Toglia, & D. F. Ross, (Eds.), *Children's eyewitness memory* (pp. 79–91). New York: Springer-Verlag.

Chandler, M., Fritz, A. S., & Hala, S. (1989). Small-scale deceit: Deception as a marker of two-, three-, and four-year-olds early theories of mind. *Child Development, 60,* 1263–1277.

Coleman, L., & Kay, P. (1981). Prototype semantics: The English verb *lie. Language, 57,* 26–44.

Coy v. Iowa. (1988). In *United States Law Week, 56.*

Craig v. Maryland. (1990). Cited from excerpts presented in the *New York Times,* June 28.

DePaulo, B. M., & Jordan, A. (1982). Age changes in deceiving and detecting deceit. In R. S. Feldman (Ed.), *Development of nonverbal behavior in children.* (pp. 151–180). New York: Springer–Verlag.

DePaulo, B. M., Lanier, K., & Davis, T. (1983). Detecting the deceit of the motivated liar. *Journal of Personality and Social Psychology, 45,* 1096–1103.

DePaulo, B. M., Stone, J. I., & Lassiter, G. D. (1985). Deceiving and detecting deceit. In B. R. Schlenker (Ed.), *The self and social life* (pp. 323–370). New York: McGraw-Hill.

Ekman, P. (1985). *Telling lies: Clues to deceit in the marketplace, politics, and marriage.* New York: Norton.

Ekman, P. (1989). *Why kids lie: How parents can encourage truthfulness.* New York: Scribner's.

Ekman, P., Friesen, W. V., & O'Sullivan, M. (1988). Smiles when lying. *Journal of Personality and Social Psychology, 54,* 414–420.

Feldman, R. S., Jenkins, L., & Popoola, O. (1979). Detection of deception in adults and children via facial expressions. *Child Development, 50,* 350–355.

Frank, M. G. (1989). *Human lie detection ability as a function of the liar's motivation.* Unpublished doctoral dissertation, Cornell University, Ithaca, NY.

Goodman, G. S., Aman, C. J., & Hirschman, J. (1987). Child sexual and physical abuse: Children's testimony. In S. J. Ceci, M. P. Toglia, & D. F. Ross (Eds.), *Perspectives on children's testimony,* (pp. 1–23). New York: Springer–Verlag.

Hartshorne, H., & May, M. A. (1928). *Studies in the nature of character: Vol. 1. Studies in deceit.* New York: Macmillan.

Jones, D., & McGraw, J. M. (1987). Reliable and fictitious accounts of sexual abuse in children. *Journal of Interpersonal Violence, 2,* 27–45.

Kraut, R. E., & Poe, D. (1980). Behavioral roots of person perception: The deception judgments of customs inspectors and laymen. *Journal of Personality and Social Psychology, 39,* 784–798.

Lewis, M., Stanger, C., & Sullivan, M. W. (1989). Deception in three-year-olds. *Developmental Psychology, 25,* 439–443.

Loftus, E. F. (1979). *Eyewitness testimony.* Cambridge, MA: Harvard University Press.

Mason-Ekman, M. (1989). Kids' testimony in court: The sexual abuse crisis. In P. Ekman, *Why do kids lie: How parents can encourage truthfulness* (pp. 152–180). New York: Scribner's.

Morency, N. L., & Krauss, R. M. (1982). Children's nonverbal encoding and decoding of affect. In R. S. Feldman (Ed.), *Development of nonverbal behavior in children* (pp. 181–200). New York: Springer-Verlag.

Peters, D. P. (1990). Confrontational stress and lying. In S. J. Ceci (chair), *Do children lie? Narrowing the uncertainties.* Symposium conducted at the biennial meeting of the American Psychology/Law Society, Williamsburg, VA.

Sears, R. R., Maccoby, E. E., & Levin, H. (1957). *Patterns of childrearing.* Evanston, IL: Row-Peterson.

Stouthamer-Loeber, M. (1987). *Mother's perceptions of children's lying and its relationship to behavior problems.* Presented at the annual meeting of the Society for Research on Child Development, Baltimore, MD.

Tate, C., & Warren-Leubacker, A. (1990). Can young children lie convincingly if coached by adults? In S. J. Ceci (chair), *Do children lie? Narrowing the uncertainties.* Symposium conducted at the biennial meeting of the American Psychology/Law Society, Williamsburg, VA.

Zuckerman, M., & Driver, R. E. (1985). Telling lies: Verbal and nonverbal correlates of deception. In A. W. Siegman & S. Feldstein (Eds.), *Multichannel integration of nonverbal behavior.* (pp. 129–147). Hillsdale, NJ: Lawrence Erlbaum Associates.

Commentary: The Occasions of Perjury

Lucy S. McGough
Louisiana State University Law School

THE INCIDENCE OF CHILDREN'S PERJURY

The legal concept of perjury is strikingly similar to the social science definition (Burton & Strichartz, Leekam, this volume). *Perjury* is a crime, typically defined as:

> [T]he intentional making of a false written or oral statement in, or for use in, a judicial proceeding, or any proceeding before a board or official, wherein such board or official is authorized to take testimony. In order to constitute perjury the false statement must be made under sanction of an oath or an equivalent affirmation, and must relate to matter material to the issue or question in controversy.
>
> It is a necessary element of the offense that the accused knew the statement to be false; but an unqualified statement of that which one does not know or definitely believe to be true is equivalent to a statement of that which he knows to be false. (Louisiana Revised Statutes 14:123, 1989; see, for similar statutes, e.g., Florida Statutes Annotated § 837.021; Washington Statutes 9a.72.020)

As this definition suggests, the witness must know that the statement is false and must intend to deceive the trier of fact. Though not explicit, the intended goal of the perjurious speaker must be to manipulate the belief of the trier of fact—to convince the court that the witness' version of the facts is the accurate one. False swearing on documents and statements made out of court are also crimes, but they are not considered as serious as perjury made in the course of a trial and usually carry lesser penalties (see e.g., Louisiana Revised Statutes 14:124 ["false swearing"]; Washington Statutes 9a.72.40 ["false swearing"]).

At the outset of this commentary, it is important to note that we simply do not know how often child witnesses commit perjury. A check of reported appellate decisions from all states for the past 40 years records only three prosecutions of children for perjury. Each of these cases apparently involved teen-agers, and two of the convictions were reversed. (*In re Appeal in Pima County Juvenile Action No. 61935–4*, Ariz. 1983 [Record does not reveal the exact age of the juvenile; conviction reversed]; *In re D.*, Okla. 1981 [13-year-old; conviction reversed]; *Griggs v. Venerable Sister Mary Help of Christians*, Ariz. 1951 [13-year-old, conviction for false swearing of rape affirmed.]) There are limitations in using case reports because only prosecutions that are appealed are reported. Although early precedent held that children could not be punished for the offense of perjury ("Note," 1953), now in all states, perjury when committed by a child witness is a "delinquent offense" permitting a prosecution in the juvenile court (e.g., Texas Family Code Annotated § 51.03 [c] [Vernon, 1986]; Uniform Juvenile Court Act § 2[2] [12987]). There are no known empirical studies of the incidence of perjury prosecutions of juveniles, and appeals from juvenile court judgments are rarely taken.

Opinion surveys, however, yield some rather shocking impressionistic data. As Tate, Warren, and Hess (this volume) report, college students believe that children under 6 are "highly prone to be liars, second only to politicians" (quoting Vasek, 1986). Lawyers divide, as might be expected, according to their professional roles. Although only 2% of responding prosecutors surveyed estimated that children knowingly give false testimony on a "frequent basis," one out of four defense counsel thought that children often committed perjury (Leippe, Brigham, Cousins, & Romanczyk, 1989). There is also some anecdotal evidence from therapists who have received confessions of perjury, such as in the homicide studies of Pynoos and Eth (1984):

> One adult we interviewed had testified at the age of 11 in the fatal shooting of her mother. She had been told by her stepfather to say the shooting was an accident, and she repeated that explanation in court. The stepfather was acquitted because there was insufficient evidence of willful intent. When she was 15, the girl began to reexamine her role as an unwitting accomplice. (p. 105)

There are suspicions that as many as 50% of allegations of sexual abuse are fictitious, based on incompatible polygraph examinations or independent evaluation of complaints (Raskin & Yuille, 1989, collecting reports). These studies, however, often fail to distinguish between child-generated and parent-generated complaints or to recount the history of the child's interactions with adults about the alleged abuse. A complaint may be "fictitious" and yet not result from the child's perjury or from that matter, from a child's lies. On the assumption that a child has given false testimony, there are three possible explanations: The child has spontaneously and voluntarily lied; the child has been compelled or even simply proselytized to lie; or the child has lost his or her ability to recall what really occurred in a blur of suggestive exchanges with family members or professional interviewers. In only the first possibility would the child have committed perjury.

Although the legal definition of perjury does not include a specific requirement that the witness must be acting voluntarily, free from the compulsion of another, that is a general requirement for the prosecution of any crime. A defense of justification arises when any crime, except murder in some jurisdictions, is committed due to "threats by another of death or great bodily harm, and the offender reasonably believes the person making the threats is present and would immediately carry out the threats if the crime were not committed" (e.g., Louisiana Revised Statutes 14:18). Because of children's greater vulnerability to threats and their special dependency, justification is far more likely to be asserted on behalf of a child than an adult witness. Furthermore, the range of threatening behavior would undoubtedly be expanded in the case of children beyond a threat of death or serious personal assault. In other contexts, courts have acknowledged that a threat to harm a family member or even a beloved pet may justify taking special procedures, such as shielding the child from the threat-maker while the child gives his or her testimony (*Craig v Maryland* (U.S. Sup. Ct. 1990) or declaring the child "unavailable" for giving any in-court testimony at all, thus permitting the child's hearsay statements to be reported (e.g., *State v. Bullock,* Utah 1989; *State v. Sorenson,* Wis. 1988).

Furthermore, in order to convict for perjury the willful misrepresentation of a material fact must be demonstrated; thus, a believable claim of memory lapse will defeat a perjury prosecution (*People v. Madden,* Ill. App. 1977). In view of the known fragility of children's memory, especially after a considerable period of time has elapsed before trial, this defense is quite likely to be asserted and be successful. In some states, a recanting of prior false statements under oath gives relief from prosecution for perjury (e.g., Missouri Revised Statutes 575.040, 1986; Maine Revised Statutes Annotated 17–A §452). Children seem quite likely to recant when challenged both before trial and during their testimony. For example, in *Mumphrey v. State* (Tx. App. 1989), when the penalties for perjury were explained to a 15-year-old witness, he broke down on the stand in tears and admitted that his older brother had forced him to confess to the brother's crime.

Both judges and prosecutors are reluctant to prosecute children for perjury even when there is a strong suspicion that a young witness has lied. In *State v. Edwards,* the trial court noted that in its opinion, the 8-year-old child had testified "like a well-oiled machine," but no charges of perjury were pressed. (La. 1982, p. 676) In *In re Marriage of Dall* (Ill. 1989), which presented a scenario strikingly similar to the more famous *Morgan-Foretich* child abuse litigation (4th Cir. 1988), the trial court placed a 7-year-old child in state custody for 90 days' insulation from both parents in an extraordinary attempt to discover whether the mother was in fact sexually abusing the child or the father was encouraging the child's perjury. In both examples, the trial court clearly chose to believe that the child witness had been subjected to manipulation by interested adults and declined to take any direct action against the child.

The conclusions drawn from the most widely publicized incidents of apparently false sex abuse accusations, the McMartin case in California (*People v. Buckey,* 1984; *Six Years of Trial by Torture,* 1990) and the "Sex Ring" investigation in Jordan, Minnesota (*Report on Scott County Investigations,* 1985), did not accuse the young child victims of intentional deception, but rather placed the blame on hysterically receptive parents, suggestive interviewers, and overzealous prosecutors. As Feher (1988) has observed:

> [T]he interviewing process is also a learning process and can actually change what exists in the child's memory. Once such a change takes place, it is virtually irreversible.
>
> Repeated interviewing reinforces these altered perceptions. The repeated reinforcement of these ideas creates in the child a "subjective reality" that an event did happen even if it never did. This enables the child to relate such experiences on the witness stand without "lying." She actually believes the event happened, and no conventional trial tactics should be able to show that she is "lying," because she is not. (p. 233)

In summary, we lack any solid data about the incidence of children's perjury in American trials. The legal definition of the crime of perjury will exempt from prosecution child witnesses who intentionally lie from fear of retribution or to protect a loved one as well as those who forget or who have been subjected to suggestive interviews. The reported case decisions of the past decade certainly suggest that we have sanitized this problem of conscious deception by children by characterizing the debate as one of the testimonial "reliability" of children. Although if pressed, lawyers and judges acknowledge that a child witness may purposively lie, they usually express confidence that current procedures are adequate to the discovery of such deceit.

In the past decade, many empiricists have conducted research on children's capacity for observation and for recollection. Elsewhere I have discussed the applications of those data for the reform of legal processes (McGough, in press). The studies published in this volume explore children's capacity for truthfulness, which is perhaps the more neglected, though equally vital concern of the legal system. In this commentary, I attempt to make some of the more obvious connections between these data and the legal processes of the oath administration, competency determination, and cross-examination. Haugaard and Reppucci note that we now have only a few bare handfuls of empirical data concerning if and when children lie; furthermore, Tate and Warren appropriately warn that there are dangers in extrapolating from what are laboratory studies to the specific context of the courtroom. Nevertheless, there would seem to be sufficient information upon which to suggest at least tentatively some rather simple adjustments in the legal procedures affecting child witnesses.

Bussey suggests that the relevant triple inquiry for empiricists is: "Can children lie?" "Will they lie?" and "Do they lie?" Building on her schema, I think that the question for the legal system is: "If a child is lying in giving testimony, are the current procedures adequate for discovering such falsity or more importantly, for encouraging the child to tell the truth?"

REFURBISHING THE OATH "CEREMONY"

A typical procedure for administering the oath to a child witness in any metropolitan court, even a juvenile court, goes something like this. A tired, harassed clerk of court half-rises from her desk, barricaded by a stack of dockets, files, and other papers and in a distracted manner breezes through the oath: "Do-you-solemnly-swear-that-the-testimony-which-you-are-to-give-in-this-cause-will-be-the-truth, the-whole-truth-and-nothing-but-the-truth, so-help-you-God?" To the ears of the infrequent witness, it sounds like one long, polysyllabic word uttered without pause or breath. Usually, counsel will have prepared the witness that at the clerk's pause he or she is then expected to respond simply, "I do." To the witness, testifying is a momentous event. To the clerk, the procedure has lost all meaning; this repetition is but one of hundreds of intonations that he or she will give during any heavy trial week. The judge may be shuffling papers trying to find the pleadings in this case or may be instructing some other clerk to find something. The judge rarely pays attention to the administration of the oath because it also has lost all meaning. It has become the white noise of a lawsuit or criminal prosecution.

This lack of ceremony, this trivializing of the oath's sanctity, is not a new phenomenon. In 1938, the American Bar Association's Committee on the Improvement of the Law of Evidence suggested rather modestly that in order to "ensure the maximum efficacy of the oath: (a) it should be administered by the judge, not the clerk; (b) it should be repeated word for word by the witness; (c) it should be administered anew to each witness on coming to the stand, not to a group and in advance; and (d) the judge and all persons in the courtroom should stand while the oath is pronounced" (Reports of the American Bar Association, 1938, p. 586). More recently, Weinstein and Berger (1990) indirectly paint a picture of current practices in making what they believe are adjustments more likely to be implemented:

> The main point to be observed in most courts is that the *clerk* who administers the oath take it seriously. He should stand upright, face the witness and repeat the oath from memory slowly and deliberately. While the oath is taken the judge should put

aside all his other work, face the witness and observe his demeanor in a way that makes it clear the court expects him to tell the truth. (p. 603–3, emphasis in original)

Over time and through different cultures (Williams, 1931–1932), preliminary assurance of a witness' truthfulness has been sought. Some methods, like the rack and screw, were very compelling; but all methods, including the modern oath, serve notice that truthful testimony is a societal expectation. The modern oath or affirmation ceremony does not, however, include a reminder to witnesses that they can be prosecuted for perjury if they give false testimony.

The administration of the oath ceremony can serve three functions: an *evidentiary* function to provide a record for any subsequent potential prosecution for perjury; a *cautionary* function to remind the witness of the enforceable demand for truth; and a *ritual* function to establish solemnity for the witness' forthcoming role in the trial's search for truth and to underscore the cautionary function. Unfortunately, only the barest lip service to the cautionary function occurs in the modern courtroom when, as is usually the case, a clerk drones perfunctorily and hurriedly through a litanized oath. The court may appropriately presume that an adult witness knows the law, including the significance of the oath and the prohibition against perjury. That same presumption ought not apply with equal vigor when a child witness is before the court.

Certainly today we can no longer safely assume that all children receive the same or even similar moral instruction. The homogenization process than traditionally has resulted from a child's exposure to such instruction in church or school appears to be breaking down (e.g., *Mozert v. Hawkins County Board of Education,* 6th Cir., 1987). In a series of cases striking down prayer (*Engel v. Vitale* (Sup. Ct. 1962), Biblical study (*Abington School District v. Schempp,* Sup. Ct. 1963) and the study of "Creationism" (*Edwards v. Aguillard,* Sup. Ct. 1987), schools have retreated from giving any moral instruction that may cross the line marking the separation of church and state. For example, in a New Jersey case, the trial court was faced with a 6-year-old who claimed to lack any formal instruction about the importance of truthfulness:

> **COURT:** Do you go to Sunday School?
> **D____:** (shakes her head No)
> **COURT:** You go to school, what grade are you in?
> **D____:** First.
> **COURT:** Does the teacher ever talk about telling the truth?
> **D____:** (shakes her head [No]) (*State v. Zamorsky,* N.J. App., p. 194)

The really intriguing finding of the studies of Clarke-Stewart, Thompson, and Lepore (1989, 1991, reported in Goodman & Clarke-Stewart, 1991) linking a child's individualized suggestibility to the importance of truthfulness inculcated by his or her parents may have even broader implications for deception. Thus, as a safeguard against the possibility that the child witness may not have internalized the importance of truthful testimony, the court must give some minimal instruction about that duty and that serious consequences stem from giving untrue testimony.

The first part of the oath ceremony for a child witness should be a two-pronged examination by the court: Can the child discriminate between telling the truth and falsity and does he or she appreciate the duty to give only truthful testimony in court. Baseline information about the child's understanding of the difference between truth and falsehood, a "conceptual awareness of truth and falsehood" (*State v. Zamorsky,* N.J. 1979, p. 195) is important to an assessment of the child's ability to testify. Even if we assume, as Bussey's data show, that most 4- and all 7- and 10-year-olds were completely accurate in identifying true from false statements of misdeeds, irrespective of whether punishments were meted out (Bussey, this volume), the court is surely entitled to the reassurance that this particular child witness has acquired such discrimination capability.

Given what we know about the gradual development of abstract thinking, questions should be posed by the trial court as simply and concretely as possible (Blank & Franklin, 1980; Blank, Rose, & Berlin, 1978). For example, the following exchange occurred between a North Carolina trial court and a 7-year-old:

Q. If I were to tell you that [t]his book right here was green, would that be the truth or a lie?
A. It would be a lie.

. . .

Q. Why would that be a lie?
A. Because it isn't green. It's red.
Q. It is red. Will you tell the truth about what happened to you, here in court?
A. Yes, ma'am. (*State v. Hicks,* N.C. 1987)

The court should then seek some information about the child's awareness that giving untruthful information, such as saying the book is green, would be misleading and thus, "wrong," at least while he or she is providing information to the court and jury. Seeking information from a child about what one's parents may have told him or her about the importance of telling the truth is perfectly appropriate.

Even if from this brief exchange the child demonstrates an internalized value of the importance of truthfulness, the oath ceremony should go further to instruct the child about the importance of complete truthfulness. Second, the court should inform any child witness, in words the child can comprehend, that he or she is expected to answer truthfully all questions asked. If, as the data suggest, understanding beliefs about beliefs does not emerge until between the age of 6 and 8 (Leekam, citing Perner & Wimmer, 1985), then it may be also useful to explain to young children the importance of their role as a witness. The court might well say to children that both judge and jury were depending on them to tell the truth because they were not present when the dispute occurred and can only rely upon the accuracy of those witnesses, including the children who were present. Third, the court should instruct children explicitly that if they do not understand a question, they should ask to have it clarified by either the lawyer or by the court (Brennan & Brennan, 1988; Saywitz, 1988).

Fourth, the court should inform children that if they do not know the answer to any question, the court will expect them to say that they do not know the answer rather than to guess about what might have happened. A substantial body of research on child interviewing shows that children often misperceive a duty to supply an answer to every question. Although empirical data demonstrate this tendency in children, researchers disagree why it occurs. Some attribute this tendency to the "demand characteristic" of all direct questions (Dent & Stephenson, 1979; others attribute this tendency to the child's developing ability to make inferences; Hughes & Grieve, 1983). While knowledgeable counsel already may have given this third instruction to a child witness (Myers, 1987, p. 46), it is important to the ritual function of the oath ceremony for the court to underscore the importance of this duty to say "I don't understand" or "I don't know the answer."

Fifth, the court should also reassure children that they should not worry about how others receive what they have to say nor attempt to please the lawyers, the judge, or anyone else in giving testimony. Instead, they should give only those facts that they personally remember. The child is not responsible for the outcome of the trial; he or she is responsible only for telling accurately what he or she knows about the dispute.

Sixth and finally, the court should instruct the child that the law punishes any witness who gives false testimony in court. Young children are often unaware that consequences attach to perjurious testimony:

Q. . . . . What if nobody knew that you were telling a lie? Only you knew that you were telling a lie, and if you did come in here and tell a lie, what would happen to you? Would anything happen?
A. I don't know.

. . . .

Q. Okay, If nobody else found out about it?
A. I don't know.

. . . .

Q. Okay. Now, let's just suppose for a few minutes that you came in here and put your hand on the Bible and raised your right hand and told a lie, and your mama and your daddy didn't know about it. Would would happen to you?

A. Nothing.

Q. So if your mama and daddy didn't know about it, you could lie and nothing would happen to you at all?

A. Right. (*State v. Hicks*, 1987, p. 426)

The data on the earliest emergence of spontaneous deception around age 3 (Bussey, citing Stouthamer-Loeber, 1987), and particularly the finding that children tell lies to avoid punishment for misdeeds, suggest that the child witness ought to be informed about the penalties that can be imposed if the court finds that he or she has given false testimony with knowledge that it is false: the "misdeed" is misleading the court; the "punishment" is being brought before the juvenile court as a delinquent. Occasionally, trial courts attempt this instruction. In *Payne v. State* (Ala. Cr. App. 1986, p. 263) the court gave this admonition to a mentally impaired 15-year-old witness:

I want you to listen carefully. There is such a thing in law called perjury. And perjury is the giving of testimony that is false, once one has taken an oath in Court to tell the truth, nothing but the truth. If one, having sworn and taken an oath, that they will tell the truth before a Court, then intentionally misrepresents the facts by telling a lie, to any question asked in the Court, he can be found guilty of the crime of perjury, and for that offense as an adult could be imprisoned, or as a juvenile could also be detained, the equivalence of being imprisoned. So, I instruct you that is the penalty for the offense of perjury. You are expected to tell the truth at all times to all questions that are asked you.

While these sentences are too convoluted and the words too sophisticated for complete understanding by a child, this case is remarkable because the trial court did attempt to communicate with the child and to underscore his duty as a witness.

In recommending such an instruction about perjury, I do not mean to suggest that it be terrifying, heavy-handed or that it otherwise increase the trauma of the child's appearing in court. Rather, the model envisioned is that developed by most parents when faced with a child who they suspect is covering a misdeed with denial. Assurance can be given that the punishment for compounding a misdeed with lying is far greater than any feared retribution for the misdeed itself. In a gentle way, the court can help a very young child realign his or her emerging values system to place the highest premium on a truthful account. The court should instruct children that telling a lie or failing to answer questions completely and truthfully is a serious matter which, if proved, could result in their being taken before the juvenile court. Such an admonition, coupled with assurances of the court's protection against the effectuation of any threat, seems essential to reinforce the significance of the child's court appearance. In reality, as we have seen, few children are ever prosecuted for perjury. Cautioning of the potential of prosecution might, however, still have some deterrent effect.

Today in most American courts, the administration of the oath is more of an incantation than a ritual ceremony. As a result, an important opportunity to educate children about their role as a witness, to reinforce their obligation, to dispel some of the more common misperceptions of acceptable responses, and to counter any improper pressures that might otherwise incline them to shade the truth. Of course, data that the child witness can distinguish between truth and falsehood and can appreciate that lying is wrong and punishable do not wholly ensure that the child will give truthful testimony. The question, it seems to me, is not whether as an abstraction children are capable of lying or lie more than adults. Instead, it is whether a properly cautioned child witness is more likely to tell the truth than a child who is not.

DETERMINATIONS OF COMPETENCY

The task of any witness in a legal proceeding is to give an accurate account of an accurate perception of some past event. A commitment to tell the truth is meaningless unless the witness could originally form a perception of the observed event accurately. So, too, perceptual accuracy is meaningless unless the witness agrees to speak truthfully when summoned to the witness stand. Historically, the law has used the *voir dire*, or preliminary examination, as a screening device to test both the cognitive skills and the truthfulness of a witness. Once that hurdle is crossed, the law then primarily depends on rigorous cross-examination to dislodge any misperception or deceit.

Under British law until late in the 18th century, no witness was permitted to give testimony unless he or she clearly demonstrated an understanding of the significance of taking an oath (*The King v. Brasier,* 1779). That rule of law meant that children under 14 were absolutely disqualified due to their moral naïveté, and even adolescents were subjected to a searching inquiry into their appreciation of the theological implications of an oath. Charles Dickens, a lawyer turned novelist, contributed much to the reform of the law, including the law's treatment of child witnesses. In *Bleak House,* he penned this description of the competency *voir dire* of Little Jo, a crossing sweeper who is called at a coroner's inquest into the mysterious death of a lodger with whom he reputedly had met several times:

> Name, Jo. Nothing else that he knows on. Don't know that everybody has two names. Never heerd of sich a think. Don't know that Jo is short for a longer name.

Thinks it long enough for *him*. *He* don't find no fault with it. Spell it? No. *He* can't spell it. No father, no mother, no friends. Never been to school. What's home? Knows a broom's a broom, and knows it's wicked to tell a lie. Don't recollect who told him about the broom, or about the lie, but knows both. Can't exactly say what'll be done to him after he's dead if he tells a lie to the gentlemen here, but believes it'll be something wery bad to punish him, and serve him right—and so he'll tell the truth.

"This won't do, gentlemen!" says the coroner, with a melancholy shake of the head.

"Don't you think you can receive his evidence, sir?" asks an attentive juryman.

"Out of the question," says the coroner. "You have heard the boy. " 'Can't exactly say' won't do, you know. We can't take *that* in a Court of Justice, gentlemen. It's terrible depravity. Put the boy aside." (Dickens, 1852, chap. 11, emphasis in original)

In more modern times, the growing appreciation of young children's capabilities is perhaps best illustrated by comparing two Supreme Court cases separated by nearly a century. In *Wheeler v. United States* (1895), the court affirmed a finding that a 5-year-old witness to his father's murder was competent although it commented as an aside that "[N]o one would think of calling as a witness an infant only 2 or 3 years of age" (p. 524). In *Idaho v. Wright* (1990), the court went out of its way to note that it was bowing to the parties' failure to challenge a trial court's determination that a $2\frac{1}{2}$-year-old was incompetent and hence, unavailable as a trial witness. Today most states have dropped any specific age requirements and instead authorize the court to permit the questioning of any child offered as a witness. Thus, even a $2\frac{1}{2}$-year-old might show himself competent to testify (e.g., *State v. Hunsaker*, Wash. App. 1984; *State v. Colwell*, Kans. 1990).

With the promulgation of the Federal Rules of Evidence in 1979, the preliminary competency examination was dropped for all witnesses in the federal court system, including children. Instead, opposing counsel has only the general grounds for the challenge of any witness—that the witness' testimony is not based on personal knowledge, is irrelevant to the resolution of the dispute being tried (Fed. R. Evid. 401), would cause prejudice or confusion of the issues, or is redundant and thus, inefficient because the court has already heard similar evidence (Fed. R. Evid. 403).

Like the federal system, all states have now abandoned the requirement of a threshold showing of competency for *adult* witnesses in their courts. However, despite the substantial regularizing influence of the Federal Rules of Evidence, only slightly more than one third of the states have followed the "no competency inquiry" of the Federal Rules' model insofar as child witnesses are concerned (Weinstein & Berger, § 601[06], 1990). This is a point often lost in social science analyses. Thirty-six American jurisdictions retain either a "full inquiry" or "oath understanding" preliminary examination when any child is offered as a witness. Thus, whether children should be singled out for such a special showing of testimonial capability is still a quite lively topic of legal debate (McGough, 1989; cf. Melton, 1981).

In those jurisdictions adopting the "full inquiry" rule, counsel or the court can ask any questions about either the child's perceptual ability or his or her appreciation of the importance of truthful testimony. Children can be questioned about their proper orientation in time and space ("What day of the week is today?"); their academic learning ("What is two plus two?"); their memory ("Do you remember whether this automobile wreck you saw was on a hot or cool day? During the summer or winter?"). Its vice lies in the potentially limitless range of topics of proper inquiry that may well produce little information bearing on the child's ability to have perceived correctly the original events, to recollect them with accuracy, and to relate truthfully all that then occurred.

Thus, many *voir dires* conducted under the "full inquiry" rule are a wasteful, intrusive, and meaningless use of a trial court's time and can unnerve a child struggling to provide truthful testimony. Furthermore, this type of *voir dire* can fuel arguments that a child who stumbles in providing answers during the warm-up is incompetent to provide important information relevant to the dispute at trial. In *Edmondson v. United States* (D.C. App. 1975, p. 516), the defendant asserted successfully to the trial court that the failure of a 7-year-old witness to recall, during *voir dire,* the name of her kindergarten teacher who had taught her the previous year demonstrated her incompetency. Rejecting this argument, the appellate court observed that the proper test was the "child's ability to recollect the events about which she was to testify."

In states adopting the "oath understanding" test, the preliminary examination is more focused on the child witness's appreciation of the distinction between telling the truth and telling a lie and what Wigmore called "moral responsibility," defined as a "consciousness of the duty to speak the truth" (Wigmore § 506, p. 712, 1979). However, the "oath understanding" rule is broad enough to permit a trial court to question a child about whether he or she attends Sunday school or otherwise has received moral instruction about the importance of truthfulness (*Commonwealth v. Tatisos,* Mass. 1921; Stafford, 1962). The child's responses are deemed sufficient if the child indicates that lying means "not going to heaven" or "I be bad" (*State v. Interest of R,* N.J. 1979); that "It's good to tell the truth" (*State v. Barber,* N.C. 1986; Perry & Tepley, 1984–1985, citing other cases); or that "I'd get a whipping" (*Knopp v. State,* Ga. App. 1989). Pursuing the oath understanding rule, some courts even take a philological tack by inquiring literally into whether the child understands the meaning of the word "oath" (*Zilinmon v. State,* Ga. 1975). As Melton has persuasively argued, "[A]sking a child to tell the meaning of 'truth,' 'oath,' or 'God' probably tells more about his or her intellectual development than about the child's propensity to tell the truth" (1981, p. 79).

Furthermore, trial records of *voir dires* suggest that oath understanding is not always taken very seriously. In a 1980 Alabama murder prosecution, the state offered a 5-year-old witness. After preliminary inquiry by the court, defense counsel renewed its motion to suppress the child's testimony because "[h]e has shown no knowledge of God, and that God awards for the truth and avenges for falsehood. He has no comprehension of the solemnity of the oath. . . ." At this point, the trial court resumed control of the *voir dire:*

> **COURT:** Okay. Dennis, do you know what it means to tell the truth?
> (No answer from the witness)
> **COURT:** Do you know what it means to swear to tell the truth and to take an oath?
> **WITNESS:** Uh-huh.
> **COURT:** What do you do when you swear to tell the truth?
> **WITNESS:** When you tell the truth you have got to tell the truth.
> **COURT:** Okay. Anything else from the State?
> **[STATE'S COUNSEL]:** I don't have anything.
> **COURT:** All right, come down.
> (Witness leaves the witness stand)
> **COURT:** Okay, I am going to overrule your motion. I am going to allow him to testify.

On appeal, this perfunctory examination was upheld as sufficient to satisfy the oath understanding rule (*Harville v. State,* 1980).

It is difficult to defend either the "full inquiry" or the oath understanding competency examination as both are currently employed. Indeed, it is now fashionable to cry for the elimination of any *voir dire* procedure, denigrating it as a waste of time, "a ritual that has very dubious value" (Bussey, this volume; Melton, 1987, p. 193). Nevertheless, criticizing the use of the *voir dire* process as a misfocused, often-abused procedure hardly justifies its wholesale rejection. The fundamental question is whether there are any purposes that a pretrial preliminary examination could efficiently serve when the witness is a child.

Depending on whether other adjustments are made in pretrial processes, there are four potential uses of the *voir dire*. First, there should be some process for ensuring that the child can distinguish between truth and falsehood and understands the importance of providing completely truthful testimony. What then may be thought of as an *instructive* function can be met by either a more elaborate oath administration process, as previously proposed, or an oath understanding *voir dire*. Using either process, the responsibilities of a witness can be communicated to the child. Certainly those states that have adopted the oath understanding rule or use the full inquiry rule to underscore the importance of truthful testimony are motivated by a proper, even paramount, concern.

An instructive function can be optimized only if a subtle shift takes place in the trial court's role. In almost all states, the trial judge assumes no role in the oath administration ritual. In most states, in a *voir dire,* the trial judge assumes only a slightly more active role as an arbiter of disputes arising out of the examination and cross-examination of the child by counsel and of the ultimate issue of the child's competency. As practiced in most courtrooms, counsel for the child assumes the role of instructor-adviser by including some instruction in his or her direct examination: for example, "Do you understand, Leslie, that you are expected to tell the truth about what happened to you?" This instructive function should more properly be allocated to the trial judge. Basic understanding of the court's expectations and acceptance of the responsibilities of being a witness ought not to be the subjects of either partisan presentation or adversarial debate. This preliminary inquiry could be used by the trial judge to engage in a meaningful dialogue with the child and to ensure that the child understands the obligations as a witness. On balance, revitalizing the oath administration as an educational exchange between the court and the child witness is a more efficient means of achieving the instructive function than an adversarial, counsel-controlled oath understanding *voir dire.* However, as long as some instruction is given by the court before the child is questioned by counsel, the procedural label attached to the exchange doesn't much matter.

The second function that can be met in a *voir dire* is a *competency screening* function. The chapters in this book strongly suggest that even very young children of 3 or 4 can make true–false discriminations and can understand the importance of truthful testimony. From those data, we can, therefore, project that most children would be deemed competent following either a full oath administration inquiry or an oath understanding *voir dire.* However, the *voir dire* could be used to winnow out those few who are incapable.

At least in criminal prosecutions, constitutional problems are encountered if we were to attempt to shift this function from the trial lawyers to the court. In *Kentucky v. Stincer* (1987), the trial court conducted its own in-chambers competency examination of two child witnesses, from which the defendant had been excluded, though he was represented by counsel. The court held that an accused must be afforded the right to conduct a full and complete cross-examination of a witness' competency in order to effectuate the commands of the confrontation clause of the Sixth Amendment and the due process clause of the Fourteenth Amendment. *Stincer* does not require that a competency *voir dire* be conducted; these constitutional guarantees may be satisfied by cross-examination on competency issues at trial. Because, according to *Stincer,* the due process clause is implicated by competency determinations, probably in both civil and criminal cases the competency screening function can only be fulfilled by extending the opportunity for cross-examination.

The only issue that remains is whether procedural efficiency is better served by a pretrial *voir dire* vis-à-vis examination at trial. A study of reported case decisions reveals that few child witnesses are ever found to be incompetent. Furthermore, the empirical data displayed by the chapters in this book are very persuasive that few children should be eliminated on this basis. Consequently, there is little substance to support a claim that the *voir dire* should be used as a competency screening procedure. Instead, a child witness should be permitted to give his or her testimony at trial, subject to cross-examination, which could press any claims of incompetency as well as claims of perjury.

The third function that can be met by a *voir dire* process is the *reliability screening* function. The chapters in this volume do not address the testimonial problems created by lengthy trial delays and suggestive pretrial interviewing of the child or for that matter, less formal interactions with the child. Thus, though the reliability screening function is the most important potential function of a *voir dire,* a thorough discussion of this issue is beyond the scope of this commentary. Only a brief sketch of that analysis can be set out. As I have argued elsewhere (McGough, 1989, in press), the potential distorting effects of memory-fade, fantasization, and suggestibility upon a child witness' account deserve to be treated as substantial matters for serious pretestimony inquiry. In litigation lacking a videotaped record of a child's early statement, the *voir dire* is the next best mechanism available for determining if such distortions exist, albeit after the fact.

If substantial time has elapsed since the observed event, the trial court should properly be concerned about a child's recall ability. If coaching is suspected, the court also should permit the questioning of any adults suspected of having influenced the child's account. The two major reliability risks of memory-fade and suggestibility appear so prevalent that pretrial screening is more than amply justified.

The fourth and final function that might be met by a *voir dire* is a *perjury screening* function. Haugaard and Reppucci correctly note that "making a statement that the child defines as the truth but which most adults would not define as the truth" is primarily a question of competency. In contrast, they argue that the question of whether a child is "purposively lying" is more properly characterized as a question of credibility (this volume). A witness' competency depends on his or her ability or capacity to perceive, recollect, and communicate, and as Wigmore wrote, "consciousness of the duty to speak the truth" (Wigmore § 506, p. 712, 1979). Thus, the instructive screening and, most importantly, the reliability screening functions are appropriate matters for the *voir dire*.

However, the *voir dire* process is a cumbersome and inefficient procedure for the testing of perjury. Determining whether the child witness is intentionally deceiving the court requires hearing actual testimony and comparing it with other evidence adduced at trial. Thus, this issue is more appropriately resolved after his or her direct and cross-examination at trial (e.g., *People v. McCaughan*, 1957).

In sum, of the four potential functions a *voir dire* might serve, only the instructive and reliability screening functions survive close scrutiny, and the instructive function can be better met by revising the oath administration ceremony. The *voir dire* can effectively be utilized to screen for reliability risks and to exclude those child witnesses whose recall accuracy has been seriously compromised, but it is likely to be an ineffective means to test for perjury.

CROSS-EXAMINATION AT TRIAL

Though the undoing of a deceitful witness by deadly cross-examination at trial is the most dramatic means of combatting perjury, it is misleading to think of cross-examination as the only such means or even the only trial method. Testing for possible perjury probably occurs with the child's first report of his experience to an adult. The child certainly will be screened for deceptiveness by every professional with whom he or she comes in contact, such as the police, a child abuse investigator, a therapist, lawyers in civil disputes, or the prosecutor in a criminal case. For example:

> [A]n 8-year-old boy whom we saw at the police station the night of his mother's fatal beating . . . told the police a rehearsed story of his father's efforts to revive his drunken wife. Within minutes, however, he drew a picture of a man being arrested for killing an unprotected woman. We later learned that the father had his son wear the belt used in the crime in order to hide the evidence. (Pynoos & Eth, 1984, p. 99)

Any child witness who passes those hurdles still bent on deception must be not only hardy but extremely skillful, even cunning. This may help explain why there such few perjury prosecutions of child witnesses.

As Leekam's analysis points out, the legal dilemma posed by child witnesses is that although there is a developmental trend for increased perceptual accuracy, there is also a parallel trend toward acquiring the skills necessary for intentional deception. Because children who appear as trial witnesses are typically 4 or older and thus above the developmental stage at which the perceptions and skills of lying are acquired, the possibility of deceptive testimony must be taken into account. Certainly, research supporting the naïveté of 3-year-olds—that conscious deception apart from game-playing behavior manipulations (Chandler, Fritz, & Hala, 1989) does not begin until around age 4—perversely would lend support to a rule *permitting* very young children to testify. However, the enhanced risks of suggestibility and memory-fade in such very young children cut in the opposite direction (e.g., Ceci, DeSimone, Putnick, & Nightingale, in press).

The trial of a dispute provides many different means of attacking the credibility of any witness, including a child witness. In fact, the perjury of one witness may not become apparent until all relevant evidence is received, and counsel for both sides submit the cause for resolution by the court or jury. The direct examination of other eyewitnesses may discredit a prior witness' testimony. Tangible evidence may refute a witness' testimony. Special witnesses may be called who cast doubt upon a witness' character for truthfulness or impugn his or her testimony on grounds of potentially perjurious bias or motive. Cross-examination, though only one method for challenging the credibility of a witness, is the most typical.

Lawyers ascribe superheroic powers to the process of cross-examination. According to Wigmore's eloquent paean to cross-examination, later enshrined in numerous Supreme Court precedents:

> [Cross-examination] is beyond any doubt the greatest legal engine ever invented for the discovery of truth. . . . The fact of this unique and irresistible power remains, and is the reason for our faith in its merits. . . . [C]ross-examination, not trial by jury, is the great and permanent contribution of the Anglo-American system of law to improved methods of trial procedure. (Wigmore, 1940, § 1367, quoted, e.g., in *California v. Green*, S.Ct.1970)

The chief aim of cross-examination is to destroy the credibility of a witness. Though its tone may be pleasant, even reassuring, its purpose is hostile. Even the Supreme Court uses martial metaphors to describe this dark art: "weapons," "blows of truth," "warring," "clash" (e.g., *California v. Green*, 1970). The most devastating cross-examination is that which elicits details that can be disproved by recorded fact. Short of complete devastation, a witness' credibility can be undermined by revealing internal contradictions among his or her assertions on direct examination or contradictions between his or her account and the recalled version of some other witness. Unfortunately, unrelenting cross-examination can also shake the confidence of truthful witnesses, causing faltering, confusion, and self-doubt even for adults. Studies of occupational stress of police officers identify "giving evidence" as a principal stressor (Carson, 1990; Davidson & Veno, 1980).

Consequently, there are costs stemming from the practice of cross-examination in an adversarial system, especially when the target of interrogation is a child who is attempting to give truthful testimony. However, there is little evidence to suggest that cross-examination is not an effective process for ferreting out perjury in either adult or child witnesses. Most trial-technique treatises strongly caution lawyers to employ softer strategies in cross-examining a child (e.g., Myers, 1987, §§ 4.25–4.36; Stone, 1988, pp. 186–187). Defense attorneys stoutly maintain that brutalizing a child witness, even one suspected of lying, is counterproductive. As one such attorney observed, "You have to be very careful with a kid. You press to a point and then you quit while you're ahead. If you press too far, suddenly 12 angry pairs of eyes are focused on you, wanting to know why you're riding roughshod over the child" (Barry Plotkin, quoted in Girdner, 1985, p. 90).

Nevertheless, even a low-key cross-examination is undoubtedly perceived by the child as more threatening and aggressive than questioning methodologies used by empiricists to test the resilience of deceitful children. The authors in this book unanimously agree that the effects of such hostile attacks on the child's credibility cannot be assayed in the laboratory within the strictures of ethical treatment of subjects. Thus, even though the data presented in this volume suggest that a significant number of children do succumb to pressures to lie, we do not know nor can we know whether cross-examination is an effective means of dislodging perjury.

CONCLUSION

As pointed out in the introduction to this volume, the study of children's lying has been only sporadically studied by social scientists for the past 80 years. In contrast, legal scholars have had to worry about perjury for centuries. A trial is a reconstruction of an historical event, which usually is played out by eyewitnesses. Through verbal testimony, these witnesses re-enact what happened before a judge and jurors who were not present and must wholly rely on both the witnesses' accuracy of re-enactment and truthfulness.

All of the chapters in this volume suggest that even kindergartners can lie, will lie, and do lie. Like every other human trait, deception is an acquired skill. Those data suggest that the potential perjury of child witnesses should be taken seriously. Though identifying a potential problem is essential, the more difficult task is to figure out how the legal system should be changed to encourage and facilitate truthful testimony by child witnesses. Where the American legal system fails child witnesses is in its lack of encouragement to be truthful and in its failure to empower them to be effective. In approving the use of screening devices to shield a child from the accused in a criminal proceeding, the Supreme Court has taken an important first step toward encouraging a child to be truthful, who otherwise might be attempted to soften the force of his or her accusation (*Maryland v. Craig,* 1990). More remains to be done. Trial judges must play a more active role in instructing each child witness about the awesome responsibilities of serving as a witness.

The forms suggested by this commentary are simple and easy to implement with current resources, although they rest on what is perhaps a rather naïve assumption that many properly instructed children can be made at least as impervious to perjury as adult witnesses. This chapter also assumes that if a properly instructed child persists in deceit, he or she will be unmasked by cross-examination at least as often as is the adult witness.

Any more pervasive reform that may be necessary will ultimately turn on further study of the general or special motivations that prompt children to lie so that they may be defused by appropriate legal processes. Unlike the comparatively pallid dilemmas that laboratory experiments can produce for a would-be dissembler, in a trial, financial ruin, the disposition of the family farm, imprisonment or even death can depend on telling the truth. The more we know about human frailty for deceit, the more likely we are to achieve justice in our courts.

REFERENCES

Blank, M., & Franklin, E. (1980). Dialogue with preschoolers: A cognitively-based system of assessment. *Applied Psycholinguistics, 1,* 127–150.

Blank, M., Rose, S. A., & Berlin, L. J. (1978). *The language of learning: The preschool years.* New York: Grune & Stratton.

Brennan, M., & Brennan, R. E. (1988). *Strange language.* Wagga Wagga, Australia: Riverina Murry Institute of Higher Education.

Bussey, K. (1990, March). *Adult influence on children's eyewitness reporting.* Paper presented at the biennial meeting of the American Psychology and Law Society, Williamsburg, VA.

Carson, D. (1990). *Professionals and the courts.* Birmingham: Venture Press.

Ceci, S. J., DeSimone (Leichtman), M., Putnick, M. E., & Nightingale, N. N. (in press). The suggestibility of children's recollections. In D. Cicchetti & S. Toth (Eds.), *Child abuse, child development, and social policy.* Norwood, NJ: Ablex.

Chandler, M., Fritz, A. S., & Hala, S. (1989). Small-scale deceit: Deception as a marker of two-, three-, and four-year-olds' early theories of mind. *Child Development, 60,* 1263–1277.

Davidson, M., & Veno, A. (1980). Stress and the policeman. In C. Cooper & S. Marshall (Eds.), *White collar and professional stress.* Chichester: Wiley.

Dent, H., & Stephenson, G. M. (1979). An experimental study of the effectiveness of different techniques of questioning child witnesses. *British Journal of Social and Clinical Psychology, 18,* 41–51.

Dickens, C. (1852). *Bleak house.* Boston: Lothrop.

Feher, T. L. (1988). The alleged molestation victim, the rules of evidence, and the Constitution: Should children really be seen and not heard? *American Journal of Criminal Law, 14,* 227.

Girdner, B. (1985). *California Lawyer* 57–90 (June).

Goodman, G. S., & Clarke-Stewart, A. (1991). Suggestibility in children's testimony: Implications for sexual abuse investigations. In J. Doris (Ed.), *The suggestibility of children's recollections* (pp. 92–105). Washington, DC: American Psychological Association.

Hughes, M., & Grieve, R. (1983). On asking children bizarre questions. In M. Donaldson, R. Grieve, & C. Pratt (Eds.), *Early childhood development and education.* Oxford: Basil Blackwell.

Leippe, M. R., Brigham, J. C., Cousins, C., & Romanczyk, A. (1989). The opinions and practices of criminal attorneys regarding child eyewitnesses: A survey. In S. J. Ceci, D. F. Ross, & M. P. Toglia (Eds.), *Perspectives on children's testimony* (pp. 100–130). New York: Springer-Verlag.

McGough, L. S. (1989). Asking the right questions: Reviving the voir dire for child witnesses, *Georgia State University Law Review, 5,* 557–589.

McGough, L. S. (in press). *Fragile voices: The child witness in American courts*. New Haven, CT: Yale University Press.

Melton, G. B. (1981). Children's competency to testify. *Law and Human Behavior, 5,* 73–85.

Melton, G. B. (1987). Children's testimony in cases of alleged sexual abuse. In M. Wolraich & D. K. Routh (Eds.), *Advances in developmental and behavioral pediatrics* (Vol. 8, pp. 179–203). Greenwich, CT: JAI Press.

Myers, J. E. B. (1987). *Child witness law and practice*. New York: Wiley.

Note: The competency of children as witnesses (1953). *Virginia Law Review, 39,* 358–370.

Perner, J., & Wimmer, H. (1985). "John thinks that Mary thinks that . . .": Attribution of second-order beliefs by 5–10-year-old children. *Journal of Experimental Child Psychology, 39,* 437–471.

Perry, N., & Tepley, L. (1984–1985). Inteviewing, counseling, and in-court examination of children: Practical approaches for attorneys. *Creighton Law Review, 18,* 1369–1426.

Pynoos, R. S., & Eth, S. (1984). The child as witness to homicide. *Journal of Social Issues, 40,* 87–108.

Raskin, D. C., & Yuille, J. C. (1989). Problems in evaluating interviews of children in sexual abuse cases. In S. J. Ceci, D. F. Ross, & M. P. Toglia (Eds.), *Perspectives on children's testimony* (pp. 184–207). New York: Springer-Verlag.

Reports of the American Bar Association. (1938). Vol. 63.

Saywitz, K. J. (1988). The credibility of child witnesses. *Family Advocate, 10,* 38–41.

Six years of trial by torture. (1990, January 29). *Time.*

Stafford, C. F. (1962). *Washington Law Review, 37,* 303–324.

Stone, M. (1988). *Cross-examination in criminal trials*. London: Butterworths.

Stouthamer-Loeber, M. (1987, April). *Mothers' perceptions of children's lying and its relationship to behavior problems*. Paper presented at the annual meeting of the Society for Research on Child Development, Baltimore.

Vasek, M. E. (1986). Lying as a skill: The development of deception in children. In R. W. Mitchell & N. Thompson (Eds.), *Deception: Perspectives on human and nonhuman deceit* (pp. 271–292). Albany, NY: SUNY Press.

Weinstein, J. B., & Berger, M. B. (1990). *Weinstein's evidence* (Vol. 3). New York: Matthew Bender.

Wigmore, J. H. (1940). *Evidence* (3rd ed.). Boston: Little, Brown.

Wigmore, J. H. (1979). *Evidence in trials at common law* (J. Chadbourn, Rev. ed.). Boston: Little, Brown.

Williams, F. E. (1931–1932). Note: The oath as an aid in securing trustworthy testimony. *Texas Law Review, 10,* 64–67.

CASES

California v. Green, 399 U.S. 149 (1970).

Commonwealth v. Tatisos, 130 N.E. 495 (Mass. 1921).

Craig v. Maryland, _____U.S._____, 110 S.Ct. 3157 (1990).

Edmondson v. United States, 346 A.2d 515 (D.C. App. 1975).

Edwards v. Aguillard, 482 U.S. 578 (1987).

Engel v. Vitale, 370 U.S. 421 (1962).

Griggs v. Venerable Sister Mary Help of Christians, 238 S.W.2d 8 (Mo. App. 1951).

Harville v. State, 386 So.2d 776 (Ala. Crim. App. 1980).

Idaho v. Wright, _____U.S._____, 110 S.Ct. 3139 (1990).

In re Marriage of Dall, 548 N.E.2d 109 (Ill. 1989).

In re Appeal in Pima County Juvenile Action No. 61935–4, 669 P.2d 1345 (Ariz. 1983).

In re D., 625 P.2d 114 (Okla. Crim. App. 1981).

Mozert v. Hawkins County Board of Education, 827 F.2d 1058 (6th Cir. 1987). *Certiorari denied,* Mozert v. Hawkins County Public Schools, 484 U.S. 1066 (1988).

Kentucky v. Stincer, 482 U.S. 730 (1987).

(The) King v. Brasier, 1 Leach 199, 168 Eng. Rep. 202 (1779).

Knopp v. State, 378 S.E.2d 703 (Ga. App. 1989).

Morgan v. Foretich, 846 F.2d 941 (4th Cir. 1988).

Mumphrey v. State, 774 S.W.2d 75 (Tx. App. Beaumont 1989).

Payne v. State, 487 So.2d 256 (Ala. Crim. App. 1986).

People v. Buckey, No. A-750900 (Ca. Crim. Dist. Ct., 1984).

People v. Madden, 368 N.E. 2d 384 (Ill. App. 1977).

People v. McCaughan, 317 P.2d 974 (Calif. 1957).

School District of Abington Township v. Schempp, 374 U.S. 203 (1963).

State v. Barber, 346 S.E.2d 441 (N.C. 1986).

State v. Bullock, 791 P.2d 155 (Utah 1989), *certiorari denied,* Bullock v. Utah, ———U.S.———, 110 S.Ct. 3270 (1990).

State v. Colwell, 790 P.2d 430 (Kans. 1990).

State v. Edwards, 420 So.2d 663 (La. 1982).

State v. Hicks, 352 So.E.2d 424 (N.C. 1987).

State v. Hunsaker, 693 P.2d 724 (Wash. App. 1984).

State in the Interest of R., 398 A.2d 76 (N.J. 1979).

State v. Sorenson, 421 N.W.2d 77 (Wis. 1988).

State v. Zamorsky, 406 A.2d 192 (N.J. App. 1979).

Wheeler v. United States, 159 U.S. 523 (1895).

Zilinmon v. State, 216 S.E.2d 830 (1975).

STATUTES

Florida Statutes Annotated §837.021.

Louisiana Revised Statutes 14:124;14:18.

Maine Revised Statutes Annotated 17A §452

Missouri Revised Statutes 575.040 (1986)

Texas Family Code Annotated §51.03(c) (Vernon, 1986)

Uniform Juvenile Court Act §2(2) (1987)

Washington Statutes 9a.72.40

Author Index

A

Abington School District v. Schemp, 152, 167
Aman, C., 30, 44, 71, 72, 74, 86, 138, 146
Anderson, N. H., 18, 27
Astington, J. W., 98, 108

B

Baier, A. C., 123, 124, 126
Bandura, A., 92, 94, 100, 101, 103, 106
Baum v. State of Wyoming, 32, 44
Baxter, J., 1, 8
Benedek, E. P., 35, 44
Bennett, J., 48, 61
Berger, M., 31, 45, 109, 151, 157, 166
Berlin, L. J., 153, 165
Binet, A., 91, 106
Birnbaum, D. W., 66, 67
Blank, M., 153, 165
Blasi, A., 97, 101, 106
Block, J. H., 64, 68
Boat, B., 71, 85, 86
Bok, S., 48, 49, 51, 61, 98, 107, 113, 126, 130, 145
Bottoms, B. L., 2, 8, 42, 44, 73, 86, 102, 107
Bowden v. State of Arkansas, 32, 44
Boyes-Braem, P., 13, 28
Braginsky, D. D., 139, 145

Brainerd, C. J., 1, 8
Brennan, M., 154, 165
Brennan, R. E., 154, 165
Brigham, J. C., 148, 165
Burton, R. V., 15, 17, 18, 23, 27, 28, 30, 34, 41, 43, 44, 45, 67, 68, 96, 108, 114, 116, 129, 131, 135, 138, 147
Bussey, K., 2, 5, 7, 8, 67, 93–95, 97–99, 101–105, 107, 108, 114, 119, 122, 130, 132, 135–142, 145, 151, 153, 155, 159, 165
Butterfield, P., 66, 68
Byrne, R. W., 48, 61

C

California v. Green, 163, 166
Campos, J. J., 66, 68
Cantor, N., 13, 27
Carson, 163, 165
Cashmore, J., 101, 107
Ceci, S. J., 1, 2, 8, 65, 68, 71, 72, 74, 85–87, 90, 107, 128, 132–140, 145, 162, 165
Chandler, M., 54, 61, 70, 74, 86, 99, 107, 118, 126, 128, 130, 133, 136, 145, 162, 165
Cheney, D. L., 48, 61
Chisolm, R. M., 50, 59, 61

169

Clarke-Stewart, A., 152, 165
Cohen, R. L., 30, 44
Coleman, L., 14, 17, 27, 30, 34, 40, 44, 49, 61, 114, 116, 126, 131, 145
Commonwealth of Massachusetts v. Corbett, 32, 44
Commonwealth of Massachusetts v. Tatisos, 158, 166
Cousins, C., 148, 165
Coy v. Iowa, 140, 145
Craig v. Maryland, 140, 146, 149, 166
Croll, W. L., 66, 67
Crosby, C., 96, 108
Culver, C., 66, 68
Cuneo, D. O., 18, 27

D

Davidson, M., 163, 165
Davis, T., 127, 137, 146
de Villiers, J. G., 75, 86
de Villiers, P. A., 75, 86
Deaux, K., 66, 67, 68
DeJong, A. R., 29, 44
Dennett, D. C., 119, 126
Dent, H., 154, 165
DePaulo, B. M., 72–74, 80, 84–86, 100, 106, 107, 127, 135, 137, 146
DeSimone, M., 2, 8, 72, 74, 86, 128, 132–140, 145, 162, 165
DiAngelis, T., 71, 86
Dickens, C., 156, 157, 165
Doran v. United States, 31, 44
Driver, R. E., 127, 146
Dunn, J., 122, 126
Dunning, D., 71, 85, 87
Durant v. Commonwealth of Virginia, 32, 44

E

Edmondson v. United States, 158, 166
Edwards v. Aguillard, 152, 166
Ekman, P., 63, 68, 72, 73, 77, 86, 90, 99, 100, 107, 127–134, 136–140, 146
Emde, R. N., 66, 68
Engel v. Vitale, 152, 166
England, P., 105, 107
Eth, S., 148, 162, 166
Everson, M., 71, 85, 86

F

Feehan, T. D., 50, 59, 61
Feher, T. L., 30, 44, 150, 165
Feinman, S., 66, 68
Feldman, R. S., 100, 107, 127, 146
Fivush, R., 66, 68
Flanagan, O., 67, 129–131, 135, 139
Flavell, J. H., 70, 87, 98, 107
Florida Statutes Annotated §837.021, 147, 167
Fodor, J. A., 13, 27
Frank, M. G., 127, 137, 143, 146
Franklin, E., 153, 165
French, R. D., 13, 27
Freud, S., 90, 107
Friesen, W. V., 63, 68, 74, 99, 100, 107, 127, 146
Fritz, A. S., 54, 61, 70, 86, 99, 107, 118, 126, 128, 130, 133, 136, 145, 162, 165

G

Girdner, B., 164, 165
Goodman, G. S., 2, 8, 30, 42, 44, 71–74, 86, 91, 101, 102, 105, 107, 108, 138, 146, 152, 165
Gopnik, A., 98, 108
Gray, W., 13, 28
Greif, E. B., 101, 108
Grieve, R., 154, 165
Griggs v. Venerable Sister Mary Help of Christians (Arizona), 148, 166
Gruber, S., 12, 13, 17, 28, 34, 45, 93, 99, 109, 114, 126
Grusec, J. E., 103, 108

H

Hala, S., 54, 61, 70, 74, 86, 99, 107, 118, 126, 128, 130, 133, 136, 145, 162, 165
Hall, G. S., 69, 86
Harnick, M. A., 30, 44
Harris, P. L., 54, 62
Hartshorne, H., 67–69, 86, 128, 139, 146
Harville v. State of Alabama, 159, 166
Haugaard, J. J., 2, 8, 30, 35, 39, 43, 44, 73, 86, 89, 96, 108, 115, 122, 129, 131, 135, 150, 161

Haviland, J. M., 66, 68
Henshel, A., 41, 45, 97, 108
Herscovici, B. B., 73, 86
Hess, T. M., 119, 120, 128, 132–141, 148, 150
Hirschman, J., 30, 44, 71, 72, 74, 86, 91, 107, 138, 146
Horgrefe, G. J., 70, 86
Howe, M. J., 1, 8
Hughes, M., 154, 165
Hulse-Trotter, K., 72, 86
Huston, A. C., 64, 68

I

Idaho v. Wright, 157, 166
In interest of C.B. (Wyoming), 32, 45
In re Appeal in Pima County Juvenile Action (Arizona), 148, 167
In re D. (Oklahoma), 148, 167
In re Marriage of Dall (Illinois), 149, 167

J

Jenkins, L., 100, 107, 127, 146
Johnson, D., 13, 28
Jones, D. P. H., 72, 86, 105, 107, 141, 146
Jordan, A., 72–74, 80, 84–86, 100, 106, 107, 135, 146

K

Katz, J. J., 13, 27
Kaufer, D. S., 59, 61
Kay, P., 14, 17, 27, 30, 34, 40, 44, 49, 61, 114, 116, 126, 131, 145
Kelleum v. State of Delaware, 31, 45
Kentucky v. Stincer, 160, 167
(The) King v. Brasier, 156, 167
Klinnert, M. D., 66, 68
Knopp v. State of Georgia, 158, 167
Kohlberg, L., 24, 27, 70, 87
Krauss, R. M., 99, 108, 127, 146
Kraut, R. E., 137, 138, 143, 146
Krout, M. H., 47, 61, 69, 87
Kuczynski, L., 103, 108
Kurtines, W., 101, 108

L

Lacayo, R., 35, 45
Laird, J., 2, 8, 35, 44, 73, 86
Lakoff, 114, 126
Lanier, K., 127, 137, 146
Lassiter, G. D., 127, 146
Lee, J. M., 72, 74, 86, 134, 136, 139, 145
Lee, K., 101–103, 107
Leekam, S. R., 17, 28, 56, 57, 59, 61, 62, 67, 70, 87, 98, 108, 118–120, 129, 130, 134, 135, 139, 147, 154, 162
Leichtman, M. D., *see DeSimone*
Leippe, M. R., 85, 87, 148, 165
Leon, M., 18, 27
Leonard, E. A., 69, 87
Lepore, R., 152
Levin, H., 143, 146
Lewis, H., 64, 68
Lewis, M., 54, 61, 63–66, 68, 70, 74, 75, 87, 97–99, 103, 108, 115, 126, 128, 136, 138, 146
Lindskold, D., 95, 108
Loeber, R., 97, 108
Loftus, E. F., 1, 8, 138, 146
Louisiana Revised Statutes, 14:18, 149, 167
Louisiana Revised Statutes, 14:124, 147, 167

M

Maccoby, E. E., 23, 28, 143, 146
Maine Revised Statutes Annotated 11-A §452, 149, 167
Major, B., 67, 68
Malatesta, C. Z., 66, 68
Martin, J. A., 23, 28
Maryland v. Craig, 105, 108, 164
Mason, R., 105, 107
Mason-Ekman, M., 138, 141, 146
Mauthner, N., 54, 61
May, M. A., 67–69, 86, 128, 139, 146
McGough, L. S., 150, 158, 161, 165, 166
McGraw, J. M., 72, 86, 141, 146
Melton, G. B., 43, 45, 89, 104, 105, 108, 158, 159, 166
Mervis, C. B., 13, 28
Mezzich, J., 13, 27
Michell, G., 67, 68
Missouri Revised Statutes 575.040, 149, 167
Mitchell, R. W., 48, 51, 61

Moan, S., 101, 108
Morency, N. L., 99, 108, 127, 146
Morgan, E. v. Foretich, E., 149, 167
Moses, L. J., 70, 87
Mozert v. Hawkins County Board of Education, 152, 167
Mumphrey v. State of Texas, 149, 167
Myers, J. E. B., 89, 108, 154, 163, 166

N

Nauful, T., 2, 8, 35, 39, 44, 73, 86
Neisser, U., 13, 28
Nicholas, E., 101, 108
Nightingale, N., 2, 8, 162, 165
Nigro, G. N., 128, 132, 135, 136, 138, 140, 142, 143
Nosanchuk, T. A., 66, 67
Note (1953), 148, 166

O

O'Sullivan, M., 63, 68, 127

P

Payne v. State of Alabama, 155, 167
People v. Buckey, 150, 167
People v. Madden (Illinois), 149, 167
People v. McCaughan, 161, 167
Perner, J., 12, 13, 17, 28, 34, 45, 53, 54, 56, 57, 59, 61, 62, 70, 75, 86, 87, 93, 98, 99, 108, 109, 114, 126, 154, 166
Perry, D. G., 103–105, 108
Perry, N., 158, 166
Peskin, J., 54, 61
Peters, D. P., 2, 5, 7, 8, 72, 74, 87, 133, 137, 138, 140–142, 146
Peterson, C. C., 12, 13, 28, 33, 45, 93–95, 108, 114, 126
Peterson, J. L., 12, 13, 28, 33, 45, 93–95, 108, 114, 126
Piaget, J., 11–13, 24, 28, 30, 33, 45, 69, 70, 81, 87, 90–98, 100, 106, 108, 114, 126
Plotkin, B., 164
Pocatello v. United States, 32, 45
Poe, D., 127, 138, 143, 146

Popoola, O., 100, 107, 127
Port, L. K., 105, 107
Prado, L., 105, 107
Putnick, M., 2, 8, 72, 74, 86, 134, 136, 139, 145, 162, 165
Pyle, E. A., 105, 107
Pynoos, R. S., 148, 162, 166

R

Raskin, D. C., 148, 166
Reed, R. S., 30, 44
Report on the Scott County Investigations, 150, 166
Reports of the American Bar Association, 151, 166
Reppucci, N. D., 2, 8, 30, 35, 39, 44, 73, 86, 89, 108, 115, 122, 129, 131, 135, 150, 161
Reyna, V., 1, 8
Rickard, K., 101–103, 107
Rickets v. State of Delaware, 32, 45
Riggio, R. E., 73, 87
Romanczyk, A., 85, 87, 148, 165
Rosch, E., 13, 28
Rose, S. A., 153, 165
Ross, D. F., 1, 8, 65, 68, 71, 85, 87, 90, 107, 140, 145
Ross, M., 1, 8
Roth, D., 57, 61
Rudy, L., 91, 105, 107
Russell, J., 54, 61
Russow, L. M., 48, 51, 61

S

Saarni, C., 63, 68
Sachsenmaier, T., 2, 8, 42, 44, 102, 107
Saltzstein, H. D., 18, 28
Saywitz, K. J., 101, 108, 154, 166
Schetky, D. H., 35, 44
Schwartz-Kenney, B., 2, 8, 42, 44, 102, 107
Sears, R. R., 143, 146
Seeto, D., 12, 13, 28, 33, 45, 93–95, 108, 114, 126
Seyfarth, R. M., 48, 61
Sharpe, S., 54, 61
Shaver, P., 73, 86

Shepard, B., 66, 68
Siegler, F. A., 49, 61
Smith, E. E., 13, 27
Snow, A. L., 128, 132, 135, 136, 138, 140, 142, 143
Sodian, B., 54, 55, 62, 70, 74, 87, 98, 108, 118, 126
Sperber, D., 59, 62
Stafford, C. F., 158, 166
Stanger, C., 54, 61, 63–65, 70, 74, 75, 87, 97–99, 103, 108, 115, 126, 128, 136, 138, 146
State of Arizona v. Roberts, 31, 45
State of Arizona v. Superior Court, 32, 45
State of Kansas v. Colwell, 157, 167
State of Louisiana v. Edwards, 149, 167
State of Maine v. Hussey, 32, 45
State of Montana v. Eiler, 32, 45
State of New Jersey v. DR, 32, 45
State of New Jersey v. Interest of R., 158, 167
State of New Jersey v. Zamorsky, 152, 153, 167
State of North Carolina v. Barber, 158, 167
State of North Carolina v. Hicks, 153, 155, 167
State of Utah v. Bullock, 149, 167
State of Washington v. Hunsaker, 157, 167
State of Wisconsin v. Sorenson, 149, 167
Stephenson, G. M., 154, 165
Stern, C., 74, 87
Stern, W., 74, 87
Stone, J. I., 127, 146
Stone, M., 163, 166
Stouthamer-Loeber, M., 67, 68, 93, 97–99, 103, 108, 135, 146, 155, 166
Strichartz, A. F., 15, 17, 23, 28, 30, 34, 45, 96, 108, 114, 116, 129, 131, 135, 138, 147
Sullivan, M. W., 54, 61, 64, 65, 68, 70, 74, 75, 87, 97–99, 103, 108, 115, 126, 128, 136, 138, 146
Surber, C. F., 18, 28

T

Tate, C. S., 5, 8, 41, 45, 73, 87, 119, 120, 128, 132–141, 146, 148, 150

Taylor, C., 54, 62
Tepley, L., 158, 166
Tesman, J. R., 66, 68
Texas Family Code Annotated §51.03 [c] [Vernon,1986], 148, 167
Thomas, S., 2, 8, 42, 44, 102, 107
Thompson, W., 152
Throckmorton, B., 73, 87
Tidswell, T., 54, 61
Toglia, M. P., 1, 8, 65, 68, 71, 72, 74, 85–87, 90, 107, 134, 136, 139, 140, 145
Tucker, J., 73, 87
Tudor-Hart, B. E., 69, 87

U

Underwager, R., 69, 87
Uniform Juvenile Court Act §2[2] [12987], 148, 167
United States v. Perez, 32, 45

V

Vasek, M. F., 69, 85, 87, 148, 166
Veno, A., 163, 165

W

Wakefield, H., 69, 87
Walsh, R. P., 67, 68
Walters, P. S., 95, 108
Warren, A. R., 119, 120, 128, 132–140, 148, 150
Warren-Leubecker, A., 5, 8, 41, 45, 73, 87, 136, 140, 141, 146
Washington Statutes 9A.72.40, 147, 167
Weinstein, J. B., 31, 45, 109, 151, 157, 166
Weiss, M., 64, 68
Wellman, H. M., 119, 120, 126
Western Industries v. Newcor Canada Ltd., 31, 45
Wheeler v. United States, 29, 45, 89, 109, 157, 167
White, J., 100, 107

Whiten, A., 48, 61
Wigmore, J. H., 69, 87, 158, 161, 163, 166
Wilkening, F., 18, 28
Williams, F. E., 152, 166
Wilson, D., 59, 62
Wimmer, H., 12 13, 17, 28, 34, 45, 53, 56,
    59, 61, 62, 70, 75, 86, 87, 93, 98, 99,
    108, 109, 114, 126, 154, 166
Winner, E., 59, 62

Y

Yuille, J. C., 148, 166

Z

Zilinmon v. State of Georgia, 158, 167
Zuckerman, M., 127, 146

Subject Index

A

Age, 16, 73, 78, 80, 84, 104, 106, 115, 139–141, 143–144
  infants, 66, 69
  preschool, 1–4, 7, 13, 15–17, 22, 30, 32, 34–38, 41–42, 53–58, 60, 63 67, 70 71, 75, 93–100, 102–103, 105–106, 114, 119–120, 122, 133, 135–138, 142, 148, 155, 157, 159–160, 162, 164
  school-aged, 1, 11–13, 15–18, 22–23, 32–38, 41–42, 53, 55, 57, 59, 73–75, 93–100, 104, 114, 120, 134–137, 149, 154, 162
  adolescents, 18, 22, 32, 71, 74, 116, 148–149, 155, 157
  adults, 1, 12–18, 22, 34–38, 63, 70, 74, 106, 114–115, 127, 138, 143
Attorneys, 89, 148, 158, 160
Attribution, 49, 59, 115
  attributing beliefs, 54–60
  attributing intentions, 59
  attributing behavior, 54
Autism, 54, 57

B

Beliefs (see also attributing beliefs; false beliefs; lies), 54, 57–58, 120

understanding, 56–60
judging, 58

C

Cheating, 19, 41, 67
Child abuse (see also sexual abuse), 29–30, 35–36, 43, 69, 71–72, 75, 90–91, 94, 100, 131, 138, 141
Child-rearing styles, 18–19, 21–23
Coaching, 72–73, 75–76, 80, 84–85, 102, 132–133, 141, 148–150, 161
Competence (see also testimony; voir dire), 8, 29–33, 40, 42–43, 89–91, 104, 122, 150, 156, 160
  criteria for, 31–33, 89, 104, 122, 156
  hearings, 8, 24, 31–32, 43, 89, 156–158
Concealing the truth (eg. lies of omission) (see also truth; lies), 49, 52, 72, 74, 116, 130–131
Credibility (see also witnesses; testimony), 30–32, 40–41, 161, 163
Cross examination, 150, 160–165
Custody hearings, 35, 72, 141

D

Deception, 47–48, 54, 58, 60, 73, 92, 98–100, 102–103, 106, 118, 127, 143, 164

Deception (*cont.*)
non-verbal deception skills (see verbal
skills), 99–100
Divorce, 35
Due process, 160

E

Ecological validity, 40–44, 72, 85, 91, 94,
122, 131, 137, 144, 164, 154
Emotions (see also facial expressions), 66
expressing, 66
hiding, 99–100
Epistemic issues, 111–117, 121–125
Erroneous statements (see also lies; memories;
motives; mistakes)
social factors, 1–2, 35, 40
cognitive factors, 1–2
Errors of commission, 72–74
Ethical issues in research, 40, 42, 44, 85, 137
Expert witness, 31
Eyewitness testimony, 2, 29, 89, 91–92, 100,
138, 163–164

F

Facial expressions (see also leakage), 63, 66,
99–100, 138
False allegations (see also sexual abuse; custody hearings), 71–75, 84–85, 150
False beliefs, 17, 49, 52–53, 55–58, 67, 70,
72–73, 98–99, 112, 118–120
first order, 53–54
second order, 53, 59
Fantasy, 90–92, 120, 161
Federal Rules of Evidence, 157
"Full inquiry" rule, 158–160

G

Generalizability of research to legal context
(see also ecological validity), 42, 44, 71,
85, 104–106, 124, 131, 145

H

Honesty (see also truth; lies; cheating;
motives), 40–43, 90, 112, 123–125

I

Inferences, 24
Intention to deceive (see lies)
Interrogation (see also questioning; interview-
ing), 3–4, 138
Interviewing (see also questioning; interroga-
tion), 8, 37, 150
IQ, 37, 19–20, 38–39

J

Judges, 31–32, 43, 89–90, 92, 141, 151, 160
Juries, 8, 31, 36, 90–92, 141

L

Language ability (see verbal skills)
Leading questions, 8, 42, 91
Leakage, 99–100, 103, 106
Lies (see coaching, motives, questioning, sex
differences, truth, verbal skills), 2, 7, 15,
19, 21, 30, 36–37, 89, 91, 94, 97–105,
111, 114–117, 122–123, 125, 127–128,
139–143, 145, 156
accountability, 121
as prototypes, 13–14, 17, 19–20, 22–25,
34, 49, 113–117, 131
belief systems and, 13–14, 16–17, 20, 23–
24, 34–35, 40, 47–48, 70
definitions of, 47–48, 50, 112–121, 128–
132
detection of, 7, 47
development and, 7, 11–12, 15–17, 20,
22–23, 33–35, 47, 51–55, 59–60, 69–
70, 72–73, 75–80, 84, 92–97, 112, 114,
119, 133, 164
factuality (see also mistakes), 12–14, 16–
18, 20, 22–24, 33–35, 40, 49, 73, 114–
117, 131
familiarity, 77, 84, 132
goals of (see motives), 48, 49–50, 51, 53
intentions and, 11–14, 16–17, 20, 23–24,
33–35, 39–40, 48–53, 56, 58–60, 67–
70, 73, 92–95, 98–99, 111, 114–121,
128–129
judging, 11, 16, 18–19, 24, 31–35, 37–40,
43, 57–58, 93–97, 115, 143
learning about, 18, 19, 21–23, 34, 47, 51–
54, 99–100, 112

levels of, 48, 51–53, 59–60

lying, 19, 21, 36–37, 54–55, 57–58, 60, 64–65, 67, 69–70, 72, 76–80, 120, 133–134, 138, 144, 164

manipulation of behavior, 48–49, 51–55, 58, 60, 112

manipulation of beliefs, 49–60, 114–119

parents and (see also motives), 35–43

personality and, 120, 138

presence of others and, 140–142

strategies, 52, 54–56, 59–60

successful lying, 47, 50–53, 74–75, 78, 80, 84, 97, 99, 117, 119–120, 138

time intervals and, 138, 161

types of, 12, 24, 35, 47, 59, 74, 95–96, 113–114, 116–117, 123–124, 129–134, 136, 139

understanding of, 2, 11–13, 15–17, 33 40, 51–53, 58, 69–70, 84, 92–97, 104–105, 112–117, 125

M

Memory, 1–2, 7, 31–32, 37, 38–40, 72, 90–91, 131, 138, 149

alteration of trace, 1, 7, 30, 131, 150

suggestibility, 1, 6–8, 30, 38–40, 90–91, 149, 150, 161–162

trace, 1–2, 38–39, 161–162

Mental representation, 120

Mistakes, 11–13, 30, 34–35, 129

Modeling, 23

Motives for lying, 2, 5, 7, 24, 31, 48, 52, 60, 72–73, 80, 84–85, 92, 98, 101–105, 117, 127–129, 131–132, 134–145, 165

avoid embarrassment, 2, 4–6, 64–65, 72, 101, 134

avoid punishment, 2, 34, 52, 54, 65, 67, 72, 74, 84–85, 93–95, 101–103, 105, 117, 134–140, 148–150, 155

conforming to a stereotype, 2, 4–5, 134, 136

demand characteristics, 2, 4–5, 43–44, 101, 154

inducements (eg. rewards), 2–5, 48, 52, 72, 84, 101–103, 134, 136–139

protecting a loved one, 2–6, 35–37, 39–40, 42–43, 72, 84, 101–102, 115, 124, 134, 136, 140–141, 150

request of an adult (see coaching), 2, 35, 35–43, 43, 72, 101–102, 111, 121–125

social approval, 64–65, 72, 85, 101, 134–135, 139–140

sustaining a game, 2–5, 41–42, 54, 76, 101–102, 134, 136

Moral behavior, 69–70, 100–101, 103, 116, 124–125

Moral concepts, 19, 23, 96–97, 111, 114, 125

Moral development, 18–19, 21–23

Moral judgments, 57

Moral realism, 33

Moral reasoning, 69, 70–71, 100–101, 111, 158

Multiple abuse cases, 72, 89, 150

N

Network theory, 116

O

Oath administration, 150–153, 156, 160

"Oath understanding" test, 158–160

P

Parents (see child-rearing styles, motives, lies)

Peers, 23–24

Perjury (see also lies, motives), 129, 147, 162, 164

definition of, 147

children and, 148–151, 161 164

instruction about, 152–156

screening, 161

Perspective taking (see also recursive awareness, false beliefs, theory of mind), 2, 6–7, 47, 49–50, 52–56, 72, 117–121, 135

Physical abuse (see child abuse, sexual abuse)

Physical evidence, 29, 89

Prototypes (see also lies, truth)

elements, 14–15

cognitive development and, 17

complexity, 17

Q

Questioning (see also interrogation, interview), 42, 36, 138

facial expression of questioner, 63–67

R

Reality based responses, 57–58
Recursive awareness, 1–2, 6–7
Reliability screening, 161

S

Secrets, 2–4, 42
Self-sanctions, 103–104
Self-serving bias, 115, 121
Sex differences, 63–67
Sexual abuse (see also child abuse), 4–6, 29,
    32, 35, 69, 71–73, 85, 89, 91, 101–102,
    105, 131, 141, 149–150
  allegations of (see also false allegations),
    29, 69, 71, 89, 148, 150
  competence to testify about, 32, 73
  physical evidence, 29, 89
Social-cognitive theory, 92, 94, 100, 103
Stealing, 19, 21
Suggestibility (see memory)

T

Testimony (see also competence; credibility;
    eyewitness testimony), 7, 29–30, 35, 89,
    94, 101, 104–105, 151, 160, 164

conveying the importance of truth, 152–156
  trauma of providing, 29, 40–41, 101, 105,
    140, 149, 163
Theory of mind, 53, 70–71, 111, 117–121,
    125
Trier of fact, 31, 40
Truth (see also honesty, lies), 14, 29–30, 58,
    89, 91, 94, 97–105, 106, 123, 127, 150,
    164
  credibility and, 32
  judging, 16, 19–20, 29, 31–32, 35–40, 43,
    94–97
  parents and, 35–40
  prototype, 14, 17, 20, 22, 24
  tendency to tell, 30–31
  understanding of, 15–17, 22–23, 30–33,
    90, 92–97, 104–105, 164

V

Verbal skills, 76–80, 84, 98–99
Voir dire, 89–90, 104, 156, 158–164

W

Witnesses (see eyewitnesses)